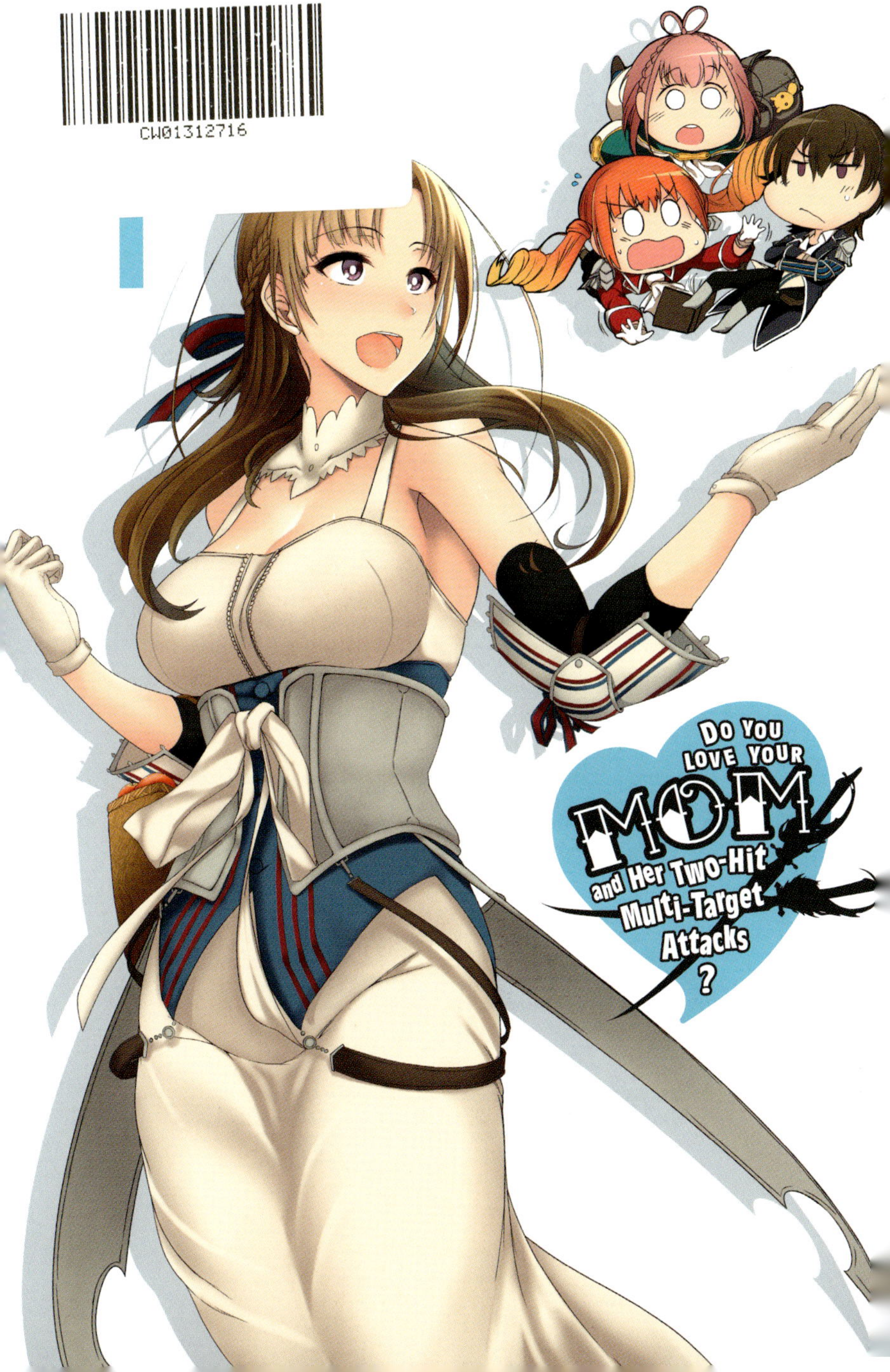
DO YOU LOVE YOUR
MOM
and Her Two-Hit Multi-Target Attacks
?

Do You Love Your Mom and Her Two-Hit Multi-Target Attacks?

CONTENTS

Chapter 1
The Boy Thought He Was Embarking on a Great Adventure... But, Uh, What's Going on Here? ①
003

Chapter 1
The Boy Thought He Was Embarking on a Great Adventure... But, Uh, What's Going on Here? ②
023

Chapter 1
The Boy Thought He Was Embarking on a Great Adventure... But, Uh, What's Going on Here? ③
045

Chapter 2
It's Just a Coincidence They're All Girls. Got That? Wipe That Smirk Off Your Face. ①
061

Chapter 2
It's Just a Coincidence They're All Girls. Got That? Wipe That Smirk Off Your Face. ②
081

Chapter 2
It's Just a Coincidence They're All Girls. Got That? Wipe That Smirk Off Your Face. ③
097

Chapter 2
It's Just a Coincidence They're All Girls. Got That? Wipe That Smirk Off Your Face. ④
123

Chapter 0
Episode: 0
159

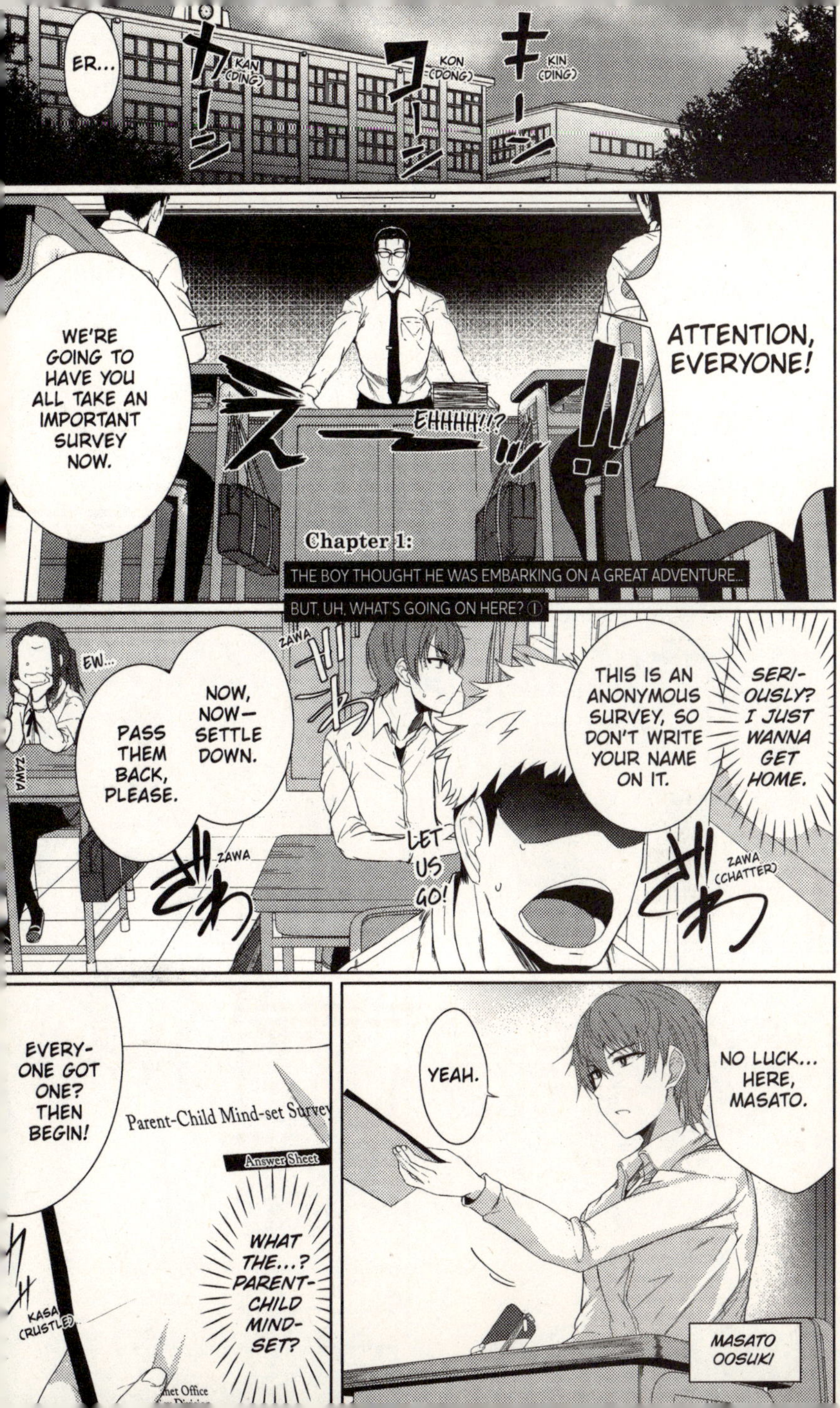
KIN (DING)
KON (DONG)
KAN (DING)
ER...
ATTENTION, EVERYONE!
WE'RE GOING TO HAVE YOU ALL TAKE AN IMPORTANT SURVEY NOW.
EHHHH!!?
Chapter 1:
THE BOY THOUGHT HE WAS EMBARKING ON A GREAT ADVENTURE...
BUT, UH, WHAT'S GOING ON HERE? ①
SERI-OUSLY? I JUST WANNA GET HOME.
ZAWA (CHATTER)
THIS IS AN ANONYMOUS SURVEY, SO DON'T WRITE YOUR NAME ON IT.
LET US GO!
ZAWA
NOW, NOW— SETTLE DOWN.
PASS THEM BACK, PLEASE.
ZAWA
EW...
ZAWA
NO LUCK... HERE, MASATO.
YEAH.
MASATO OOSUKI
EVERY-ONE GOT ONE? THEN BEGIN!
Parent-Child Mind-set Survey
Answer Sheet
WHAT THE...? PARENT-CHILD MIND-SET?
KASA (RUSTLE)

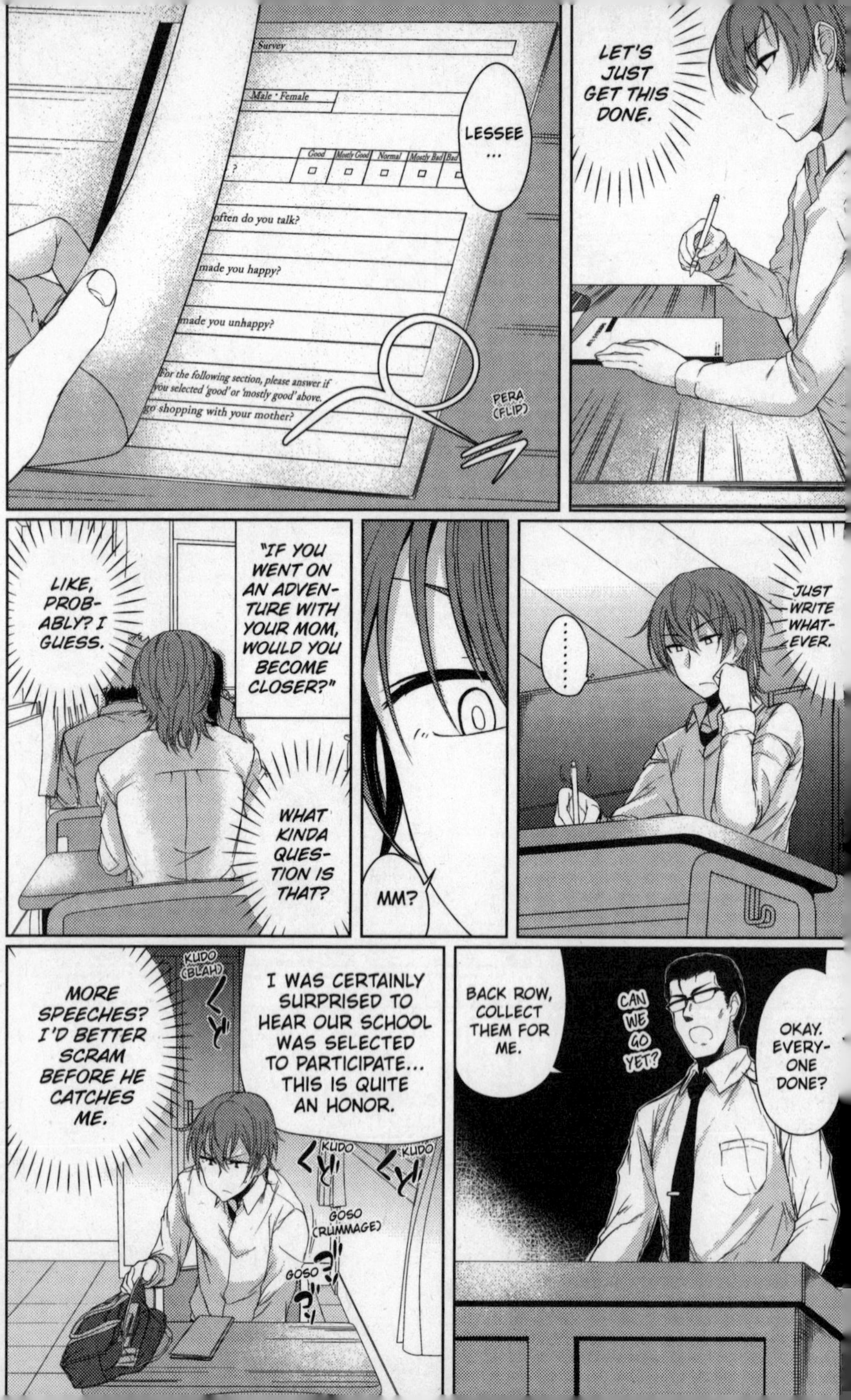
LET'S JUST GET THIS DONE.
Survey
Male・Female
Good Mostly Good Normal Mostly Bad Bad
often do you talk?
made you happy?
made you unhappy?
For the following section, please answer if you selected 'good' or 'mostly good' above.
go shopping with your mother?
LESSEE ...
PERA (FLIP)
JUST WRITE WHAT-EVER.
......
MM?
"IF YOU WENT ON AN ADVEN-TURE WITH YOUR MOM, WOULD YOU BECOME CLOSER?"
LIKE, PROB-ABLY? I GUESS.
WHAT KINDA QUES-TION IS THAT?
OKAY. EVERY-ONE DONE?
CAN WE GO YET?
BACK ROW, COLLECT THEM FOR ME.
I WAS CERTAINLY SURPRISED TO HEAR OUR SCHOOL WAS SELECTED TO PARTICIPATE... THIS IS QUITE AN HONOR.
KUDO (BLAH)
MORE SPEECHES? I'D BETTER SCRAM BEFORE HE CATCHES ME.
KUDO
KUDO
GOSO (RUMMAGE)
GOSO

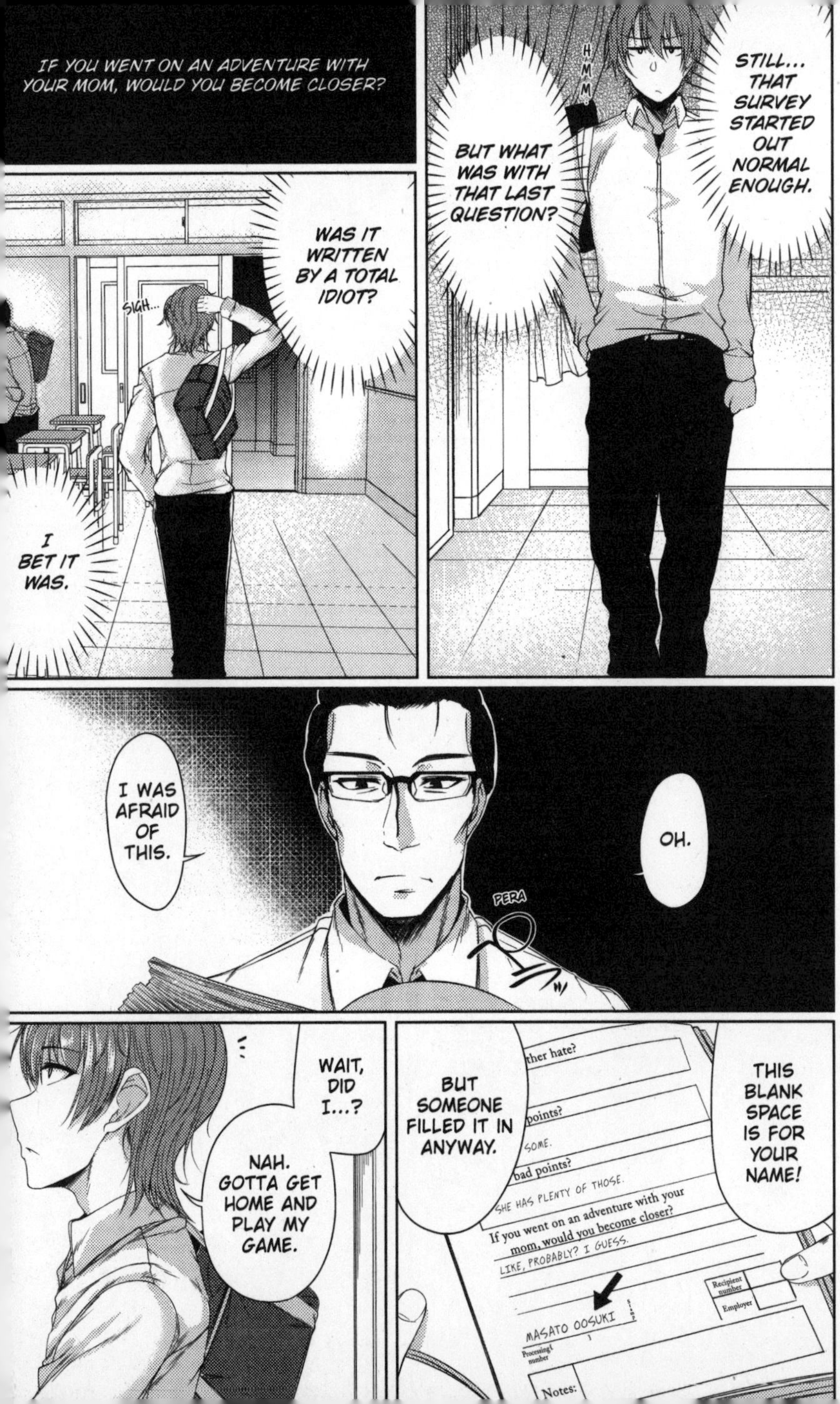
HMMM
STILL... THAT SURVEY STARTED OUT NORMAL ENOUGH.
BUT WHAT WAS WITH THAT LAST QUESTION?
IF YOU WENT ON AN ADVENTURE WITH YOUR MOM, WOULD YOU BECOME CLOSER?
WAS IT WRITTEN BY A TOTAL IDIOT?
SIGH...
I BET IT WAS.
OH.
PERA
I WAS AFRAID OF THIS.
THIS BLANK SPACE IS FOR YOUR NAME!
BUT SOMEONE FILLED IT IN ANYWAY.
bad points?
SOME.
SHE HAS PLENTY OF THOSE.
If you went on an adventure with your mom, would you become closer?
LIKE, PROBABLY? I GUESS.
MASATO OOSUKI
Recipient number
Employer
Notes:
WAIT, DID I...?
NAH. GOTTA GET HOME AND PLAY MY GAME.

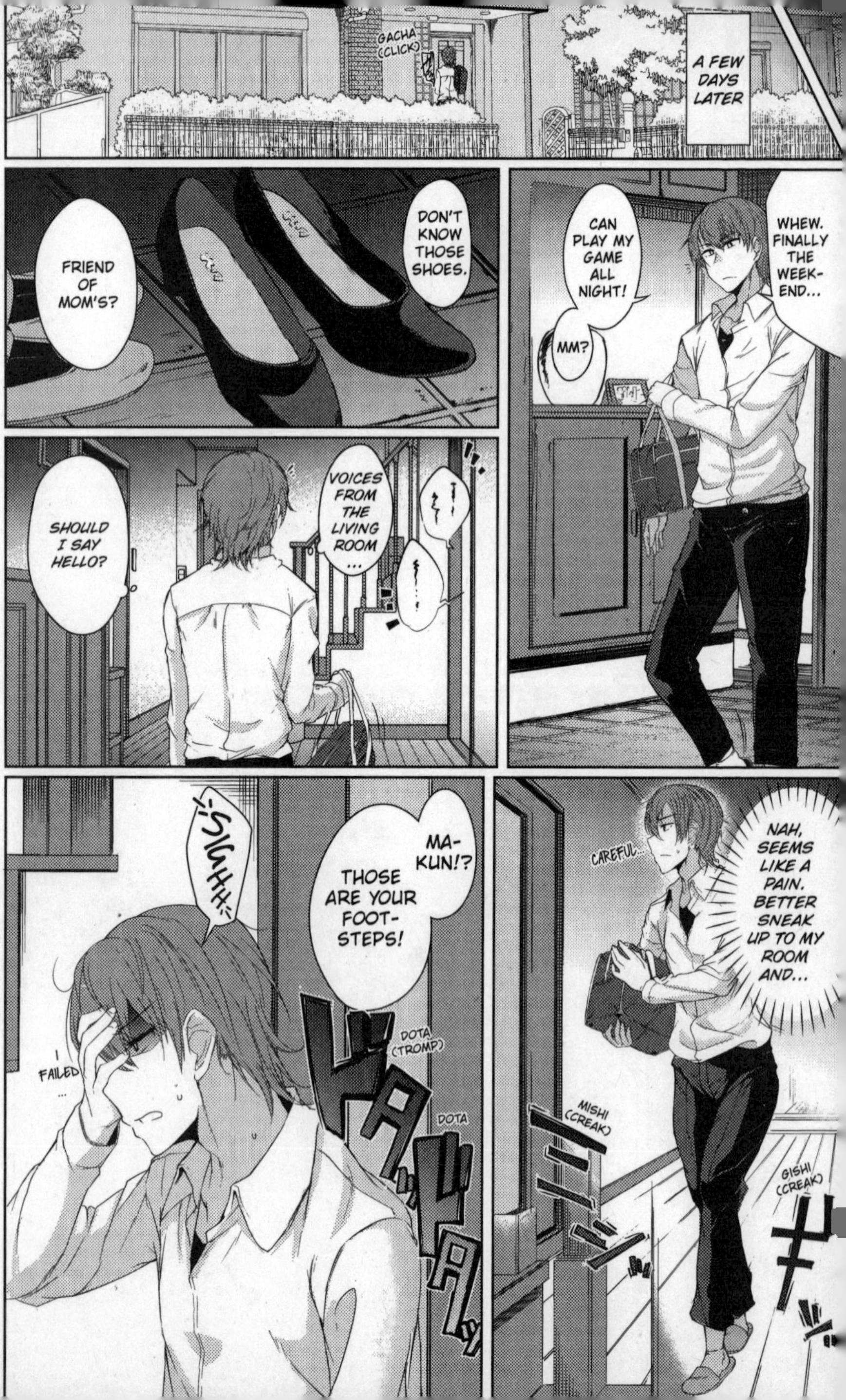
A FEW DAYS LATER
GACHA (CLICK)
WHEW. FINALLY THE WEEK-END...
CAN PLAY MY GAME ALL NIGHT!
MM?
DON'T KNOW THOSE SHOES.
FRIEND OF MOM'S?
VOICES FROM THE LIVING ROOM...
SHOULD I SAY HELLO?
NAH, SEEMS LIKE A PAIN. BETTER SNEAK UP TO MY ROOM AND...
CAREFUL...
GISHI (CREAK)
MISHI (CREAK)
MA-KUN!?
THOSE ARE YOUR FOOT-STEPS!
DOTA (TROMP)
DOTA
SIGHHH...!
I FAILED...

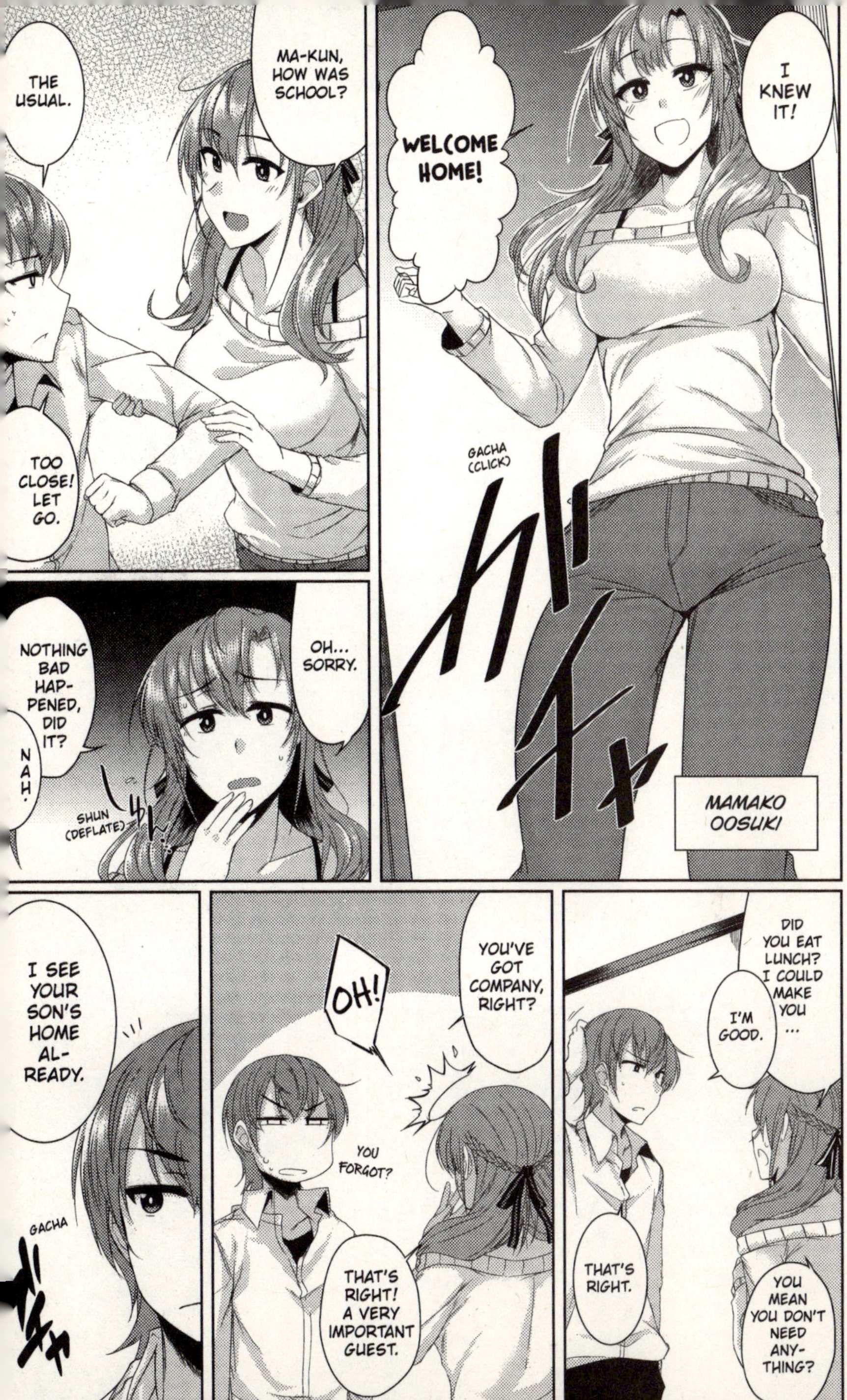
I KNEW IT!
WELCOME HOME!
GACHA (CLICK)
MAMAKO OOSUKI
MA-KUN, HOW WAS SCHOOL?
THE USUAL.
TOO CLOSE! LET GO.
OH... SORRY.
NOTHING BAD HAP-PENED, DID IT?
NAH.
SHUN (DEFLATE)
DID YOU EAT LUNCH? I COULD MAKE YOU ...
I'M GOOD.
YOU MEAN YOU DON'T NEED ANY-THING?
THAT'S RIGHT.
YOU'VE GOT COMPANY, RIGHT?
OH!
YOU FORGOT?
THAT'S RIGHT! A VERY IMPORTANT GUEST.
I SEE YOUR SON'S HOME AL-READY.
GACHA

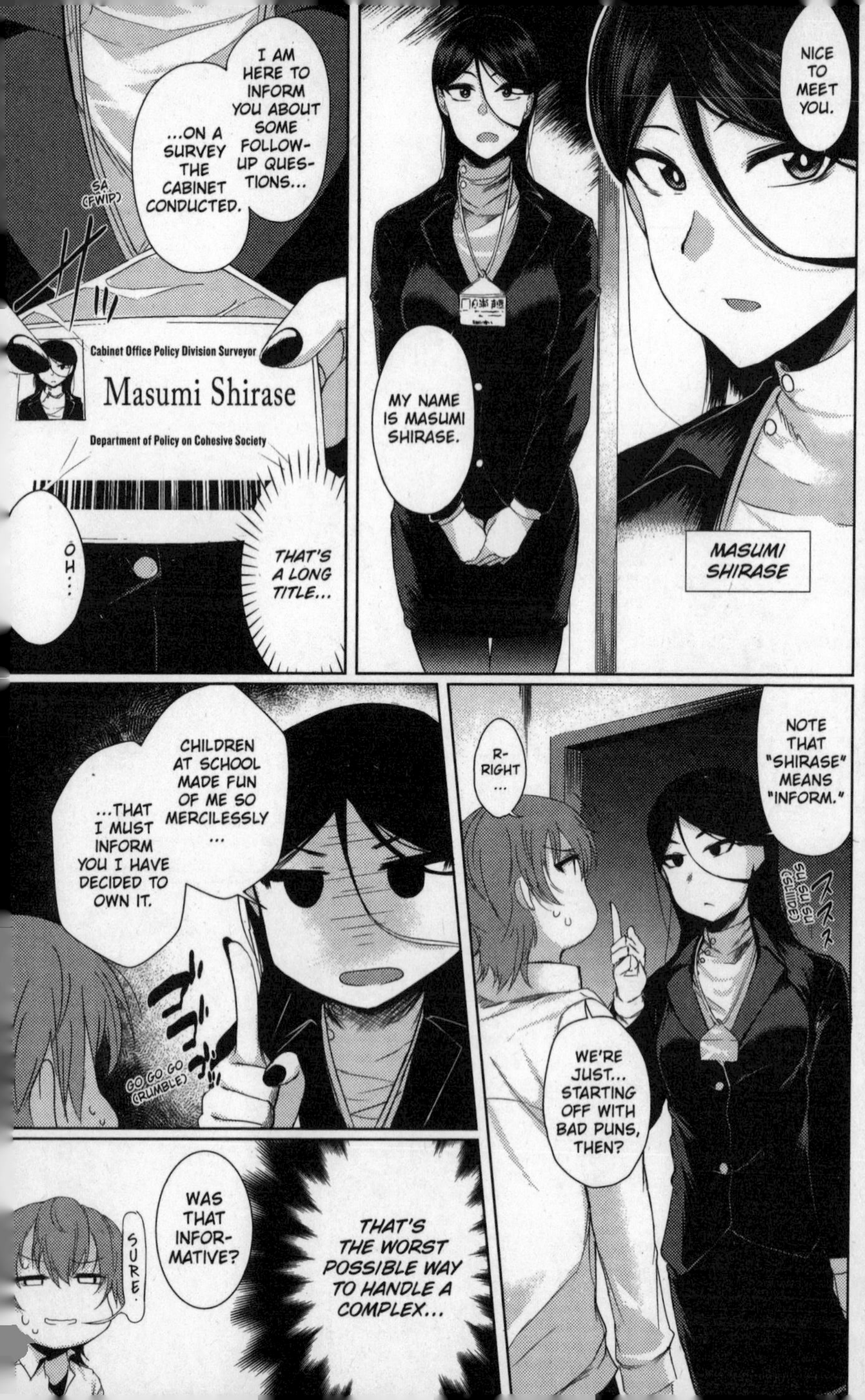
NICE TO MEET YOU.
MASUMI SHIRASE
MY NAME IS MASUMI SHIRASE.
I AM HERE TO INFORM YOU ABOUT SOME FOLLOW-UP QUESTIONS...
...ON A SURVEY THE CABINET CONDUCTED.
SA (FWIP)
Cabinet Office Policy Division Surveyor
Masumi Shirase
Department of Policy on Cohesive Society
THAT'S A LONG TITLE...
OH...
NOTE THAT "SHIRASE" MEANS "INFORM."
R-RIGHT...
SU SU SU (SLIIIDE)
WE'RE JUST... STARTING OFF WITH BAD PUNS, THEN?
CHILDREN AT SCHOOL MADE FUN OF ME SO MERCILESSLY...
...THAT I MUST INFORM YOU I HAVE DECIDED TO OWN IT.
GO GO GO (RUMBLE)
THAT'S THE WORST POSSIBLE WAY TO HANDLE A COMPLEX...
WAS THAT INFORMATIVE?
SURE.

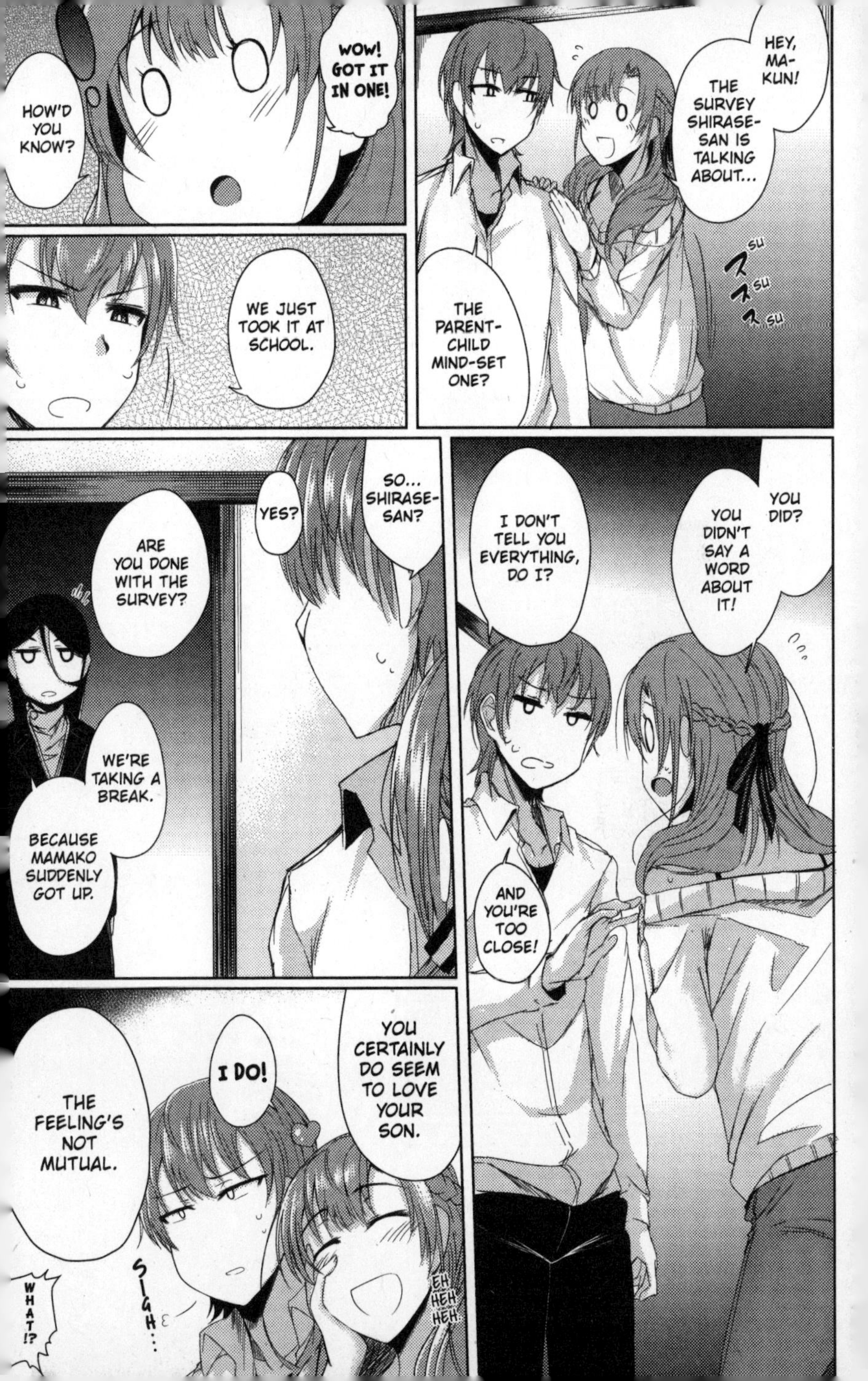
HEY, MA-KUN! THE SURVEY SHIRASE-SAN IS TALKING ABOUT...
SU SU SU
THE PARENT-CHILD MIND-SET ONE?
WOW! GOT IT IN ONE!
HOW'D YOU KNOW?
WE JUST TOOK IT AT SCHOOL.
YOU DID?
YOU DIDN'T SAY A WORD ABOUT IT!
I DON'T TELL YOU EVERYTHING, DO I?
AND YOU'RE TOO CLOSE!
SO... SHIRASE-SAN?
YES?
ARE YOU DONE WITH THE SURVEY?
WE'RE TAKING A BREAK.
BECAUSE MAMAKO SUDDENLY GOT UP.
YOU CERTAINLY DO SEEM TO LOVE YOUR SON.
I DO!
EH HEH HEH.
THE FEELING'S NOT MUTUAL.
SIGH...
WHAT!?

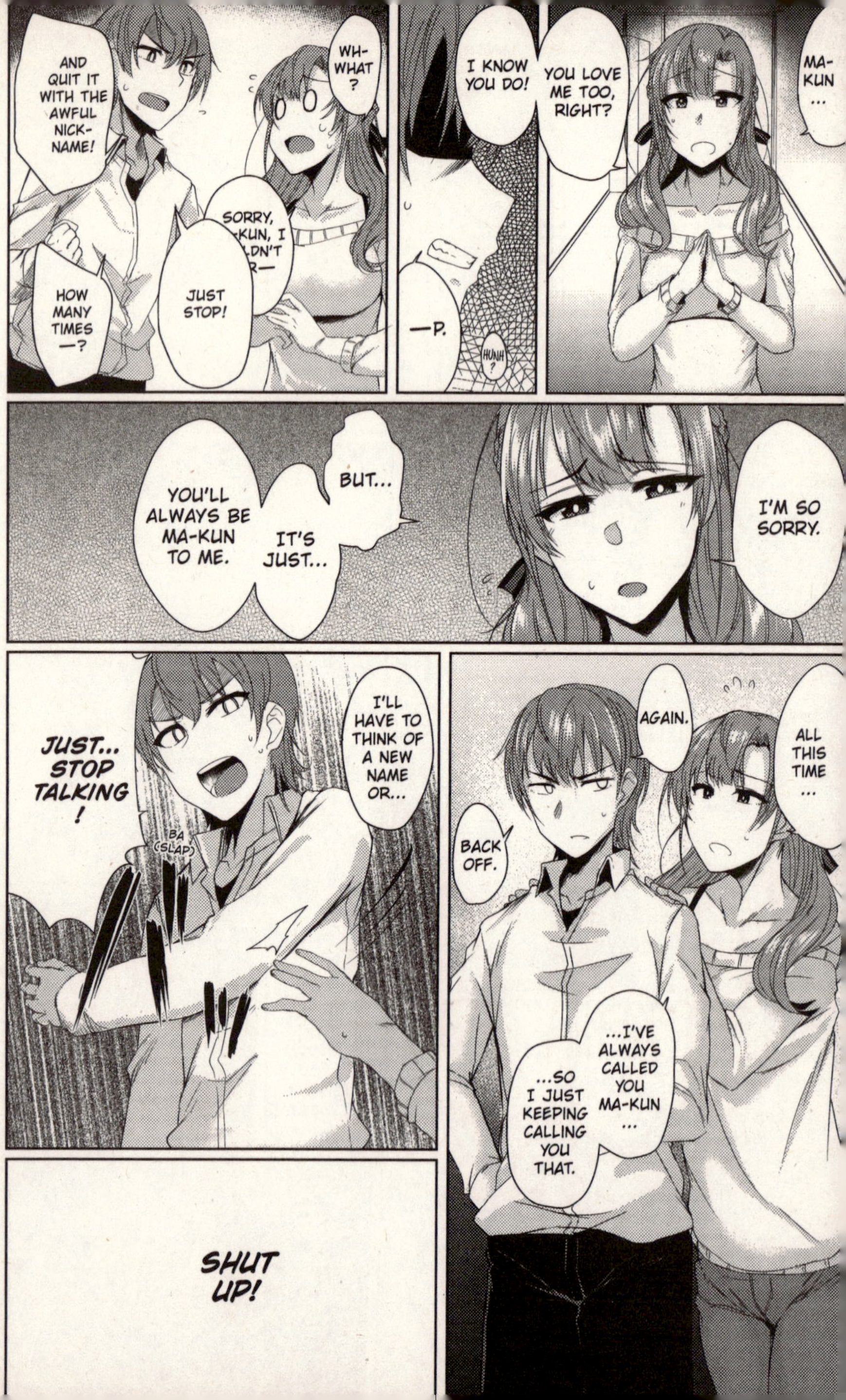
MA-KUN ...
YOU LOVE ME TOO, RIGHT?
I KNOW YOU DO!
—P.
HUNH?
WH-WHAT?
AND QUIT IT WITH THE AWFUL NICK-NAME!
SORRY, KUN, I LDN'T R—
JUST STOP!
HOW MANY TIMES —?
I'M SO SORRY.
BUT...
IT'S JUST...
YOU'LL ALWAYS BE MA-KUN TO ME.
ALL THIS TIME ...
AGAIN.
BACK OFF.
...I'VE ALWAYS CALLED YOU MA-KUN ...
...SO I JUST KEEPING CALLING YOU THAT.
I'LL HAVE TO THINK OF A NEW NAME OR...
JUST... STOP TALKING!
BA (SLAP)
SHUT UP!

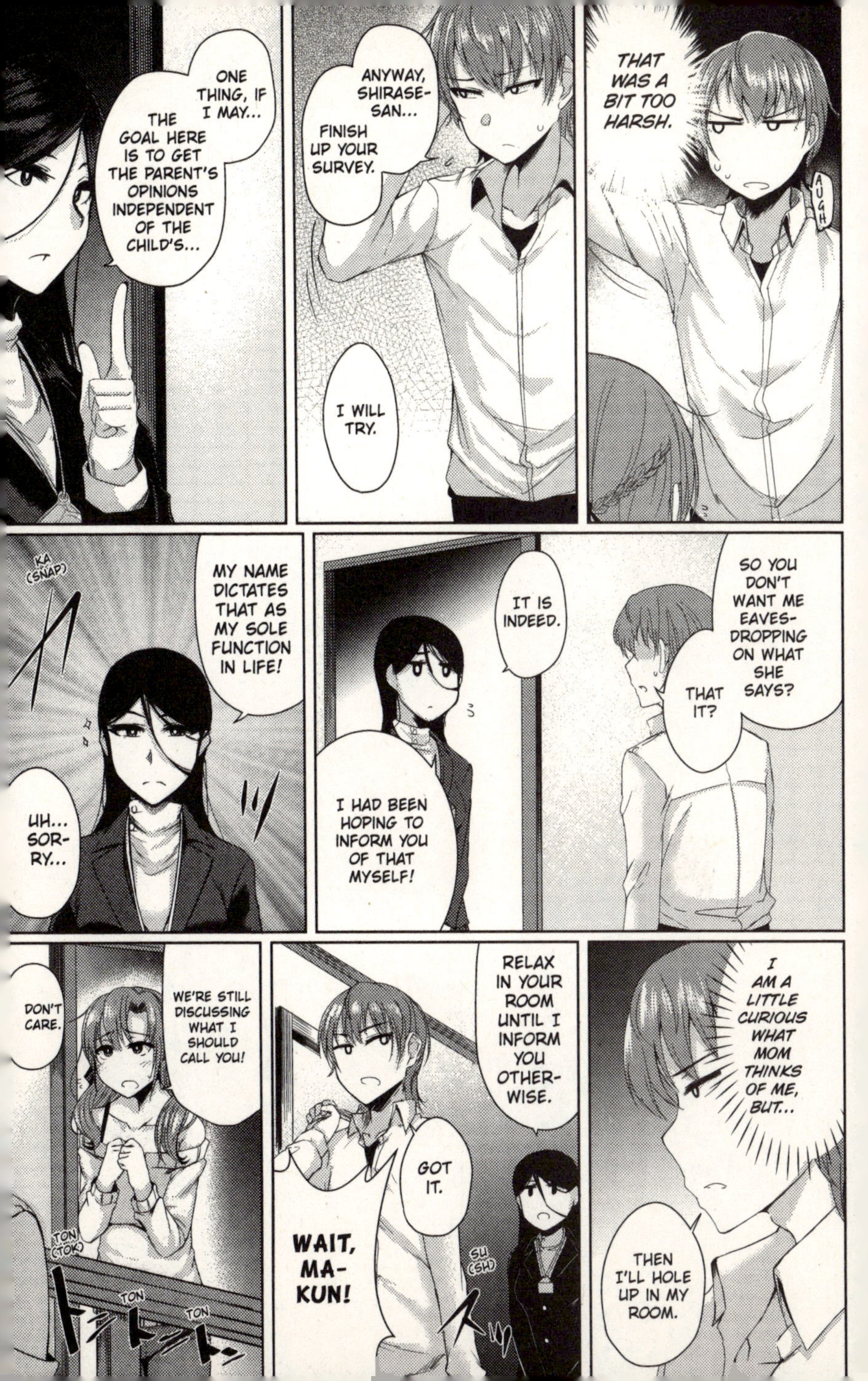
THAT WAS A BIT TOO HARSH.
AUGH
ANYWAY, SHIRASE-SAN... FINISH UP YOUR SURVEY.
I WILL TRY.
ONE THING, IF I MAY...
THE GOAL HERE IS TO GET THE PARENT'S OPINIONS INDEPENDENT OF THE CHILD'S...
SO YOU DON'T WANT ME EAVESDROPPING ON WHAT SHE SAYS?
THAT IT?
IT IS INDEED.
I HAD BEEN HOPING TO INFORM YOU OF THAT MYSELF!
KA (SNAP)
MY NAME DICTATES THAT AS MY SOLE FUNCTION IN LIFE!
UH... SORRY...
I AM A LITTLE CURIOUS WHAT MOM THINKS OF ME, BUT...
THEN I'LL HOLE UP IN MY ROOM.
RELAX IN YOUR ROOM UNTIL I INFORM YOU OTHERWISE.
GOT IT.
WAIT, MA-KUN!
SU (SH)
WE'RE STILL DISCUSSING WHAT I SHOULD CALL YOU!
DON'T CARE.
TON (TOK)
TON
TON

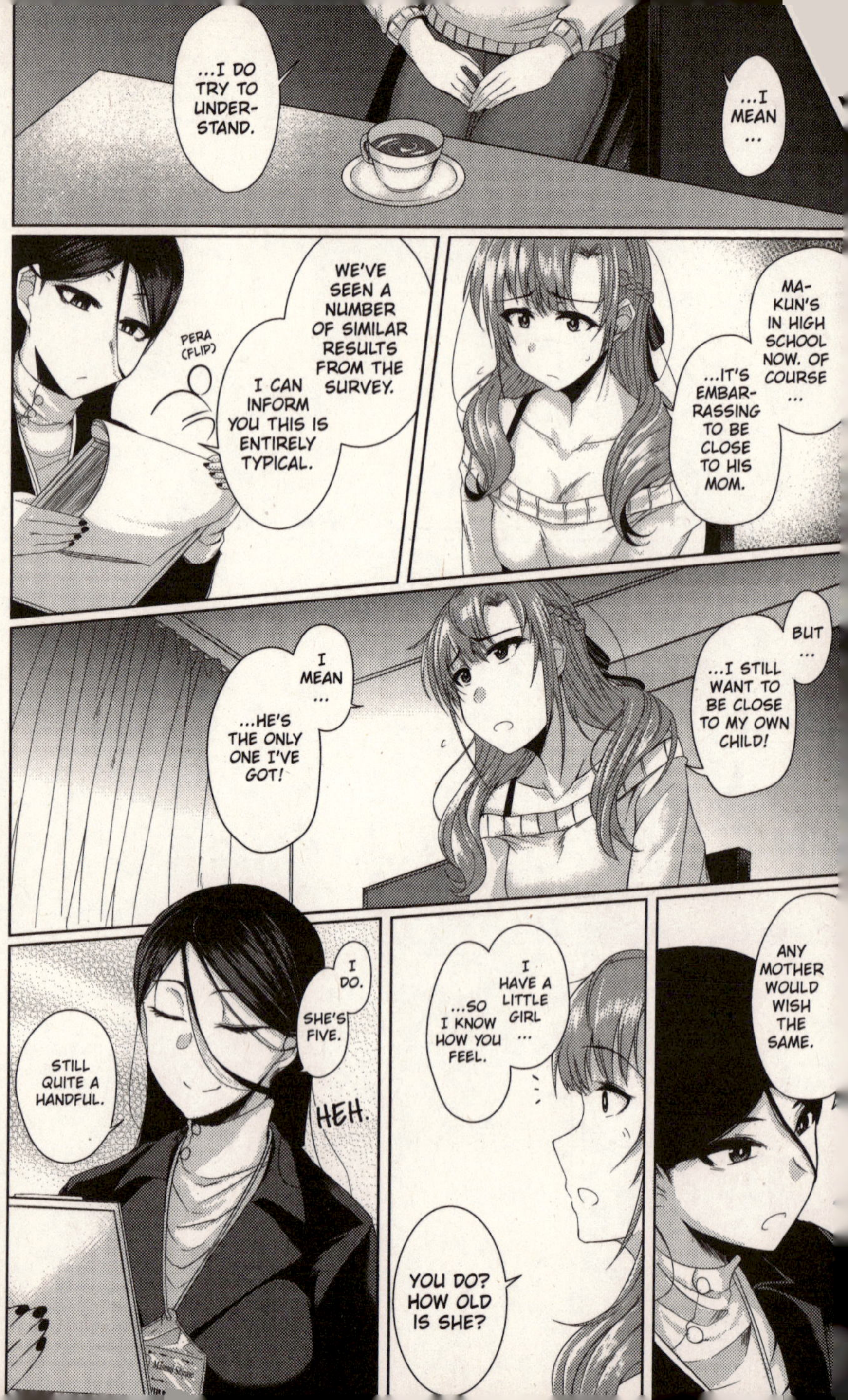
...I MEAN ...
...I DO TRY TO UNDER-STAND.
MA-KUN'S IN HIGH SCHOOL NOW. OF COURSE ...
...IT'S EMBAR-RASSING TO BE CLOSE TO HIS MOM.
WE'VE SEEN A NUMBER OF SIMILAR RESULTS FROM THE SURVEY.
PERA (FLIP)
I CAN INFORM YOU THIS IS ENTIRELY TYPICAL.
BUT ...
...I STILL WANT TO BE CLOSE TO MY OWN CHILD!
I MEAN ...
...HE'S THE ONLY ONE I'VE GOT!
ANY MOTHER WOULD WISH THE SAME.
I HAVE A LITTLE GIRL ...
...SO I KNOW HOW YOU FEEL.
YOU DO? HOW OLD IS SHE?
I DO.
SHE'S FIVE.
HEH.
STILL QUITE A HANDFUL.

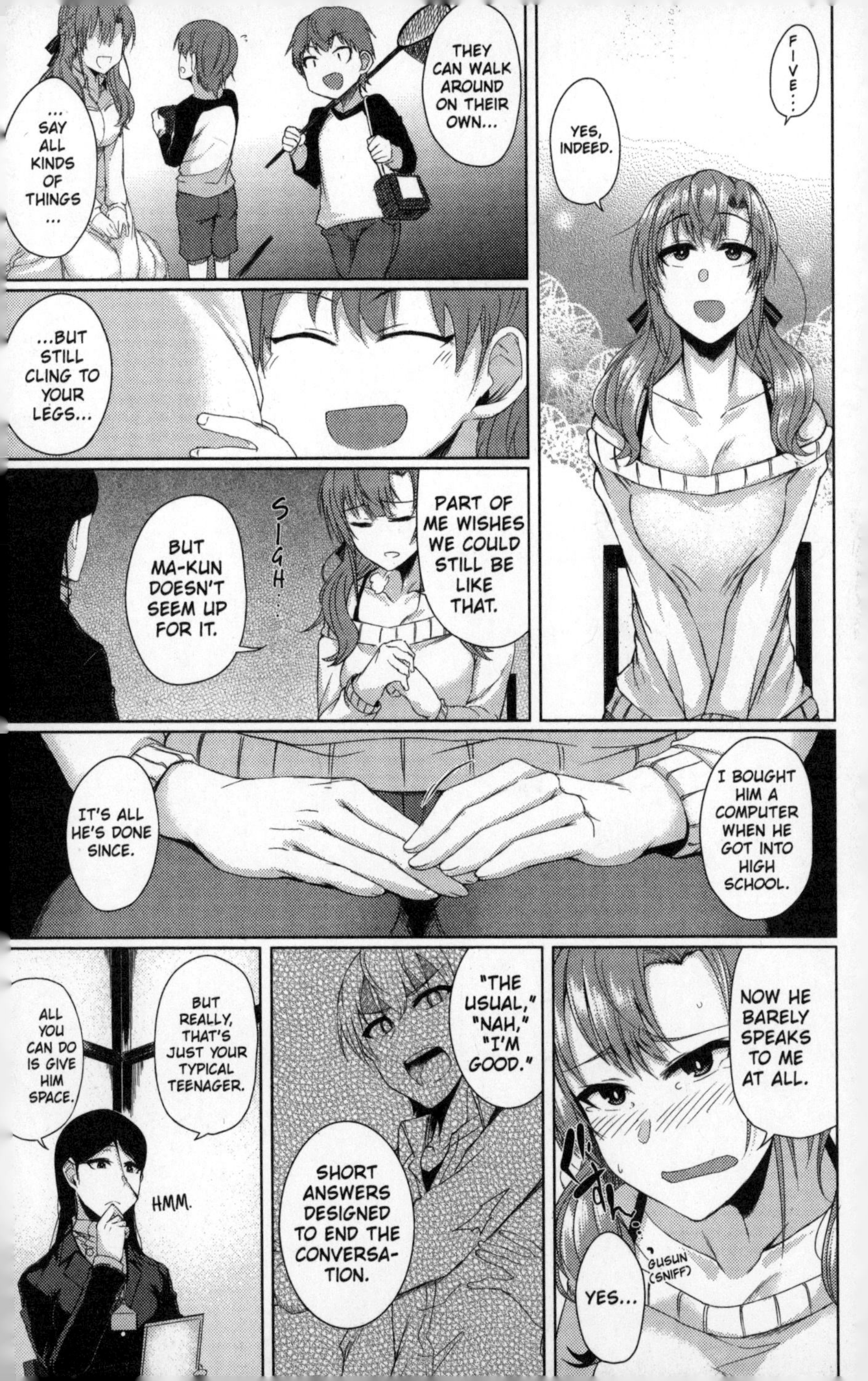
FIVE...
YES, INDEED.
THEY CAN WALK AROUND ON THEIR OWN...
...SAY ALL KINDS OF THINGS...
...BUT STILL CLING TO YOUR LEGS...
PART OF ME WISHES WE COULD STILL BE LIKE THAT.
SIGH...
BUT MA-KUN DOESN'T SEEM UP FOR IT.
I BOUGHT HIM A COMPUTER WHEN HE GOT INTO HIGH SCHOOL.
IT'S ALL HE'S DONE SINCE.
NOW HE BARELY SPEAKS TO ME AT ALL.
GUSUN (SNIFF)
YES...
"THE USUAL," "NAH," "I'M GOOD."
SHORT ANSWERS DESIGNED TO END THE CONVERSA-TION.
BUT REALLY, THAT'S JUST YOUR TYPICAL TEENAGER.
ALL YOU CAN DO IS GIVE HIM SPACE.
HMM.

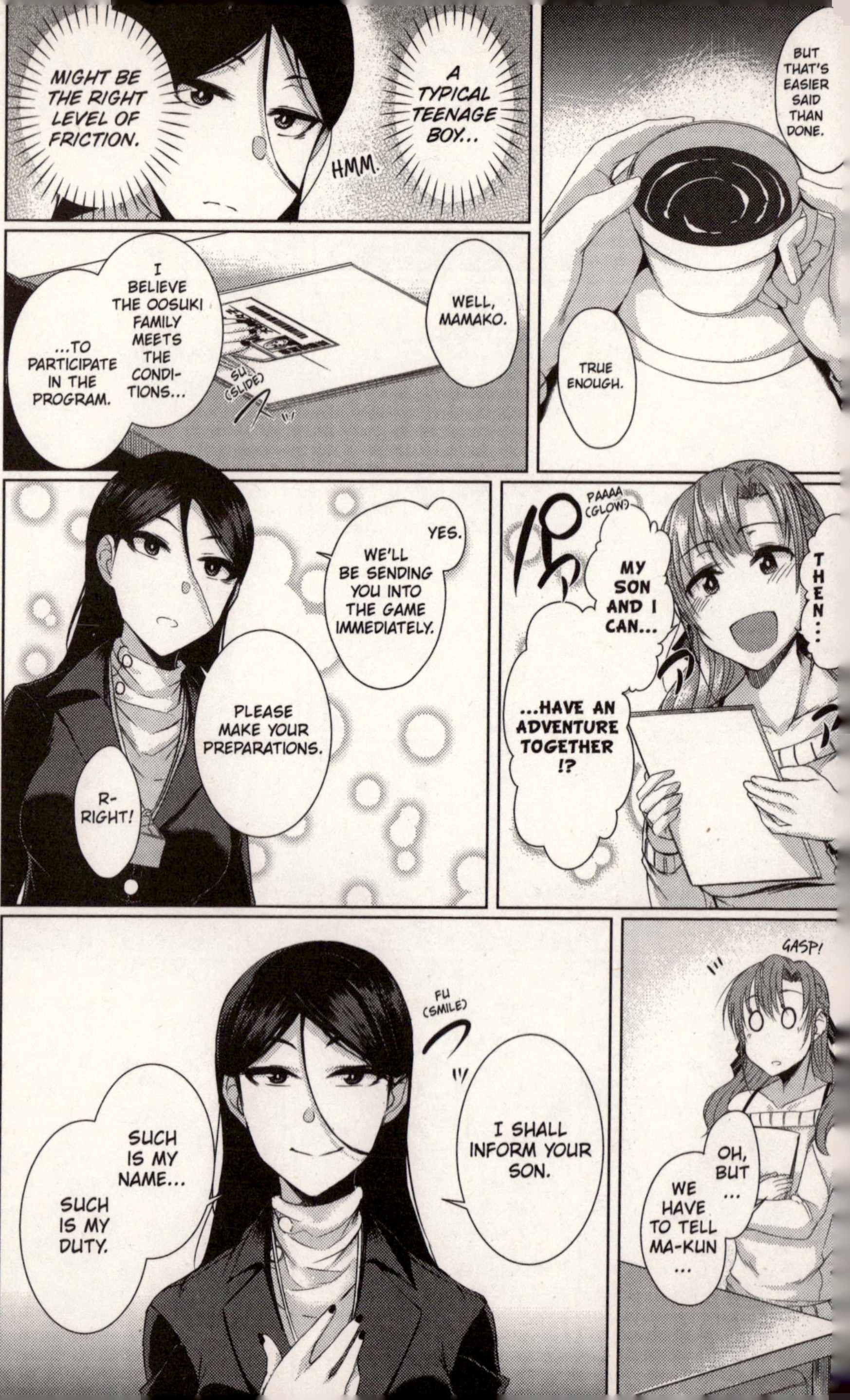
A TYPICAL TEENAGE BOY...
MIGHT BE THE RIGHT LEVEL OF FRICTION.
HMM.
BUT THAT'S EASIER SAID THAN DONE.
TRUE ENOUGH.
WELL, MAMAKO.
I BELIEVE THE OOSUKI FAMILY MEETS THE CONDITIONS...
SU (SLIDE)
...TO PARTICIPATE IN THE PROGRAM.
THEN...
PAAAA (GLOW)
MY SON AND I CAN...
...HAVE AN ADVENTURE TOGETHER!?
YES. WE'LL BE SENDING YOU INTO THE GAME IMMEDIATELY.
PLEASE MAKE YOUR PREPARATIONS.
R-RIGHT!
GASP!
OH, BUT...
WE HAVE TO TELL MA-KUN...
FU (SMILE)
I SHALL INFORM YOUR SON.
SUCH IS MY NAME...
SUCH IS MY DUTY.

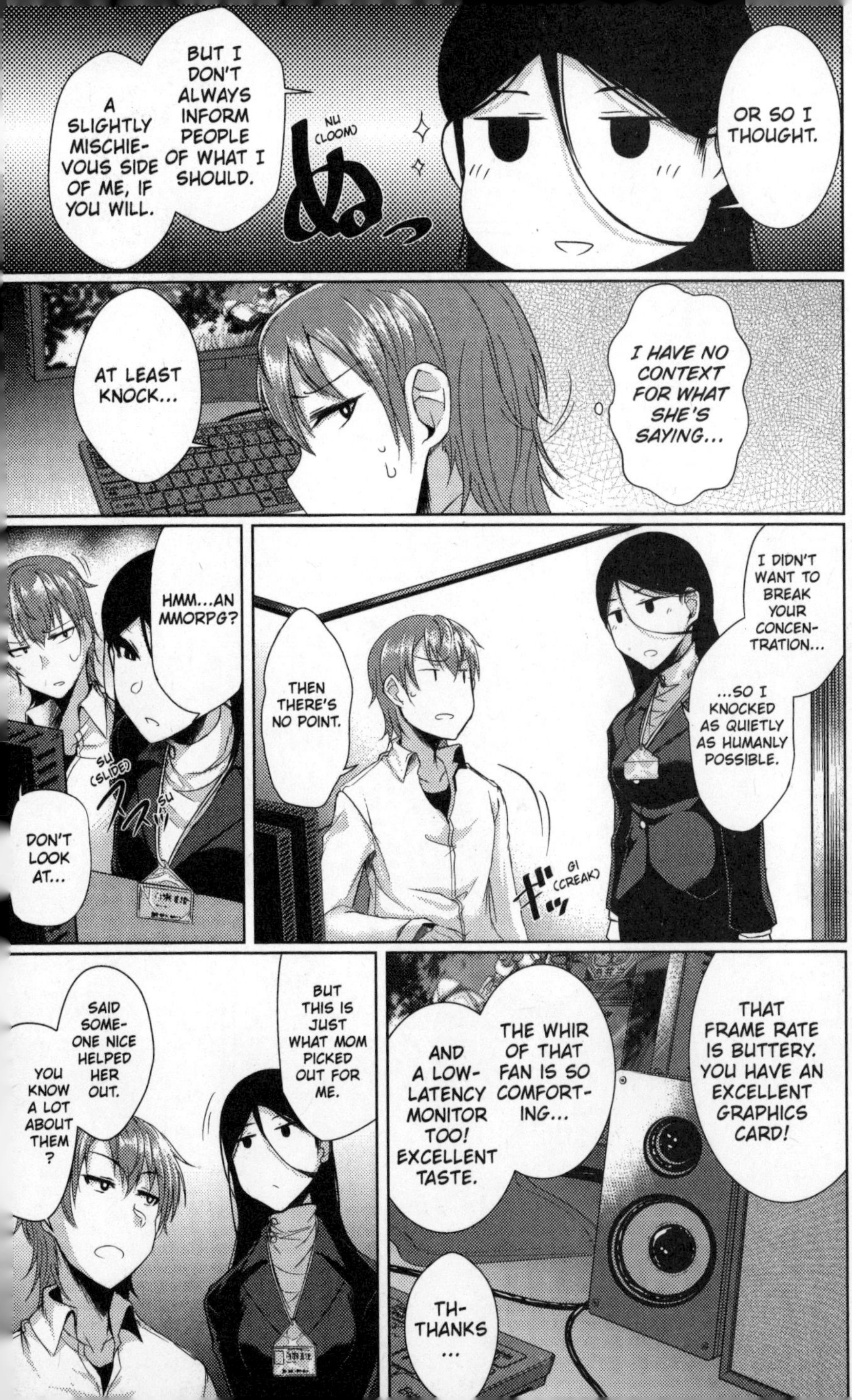
OR SO I THOUGHT.
BUT I DON'T ALWAYS INFORM PEOPLE OF WHAT I SHOULD.
A SLIGHTLY MISCHIE-VOUS SIDE OF ME, IF YOU WILL.
NU (LOOM)
I HAVE NO CONTEXT FOR WHAT SHE'S SAYING...
AT LEAST KNOCK...
I DIDN'T WANT TO BREAK YOUR CONCEN-TRATION...
...SO I KNOCKED AS QUIETLY AS HUMANLY POSSIBLE.
GI (CREAK)
THEN THERE'S NO POINT.
HMM...AN MMORPG?
SU (SLIDE)
SU
DON'T LOOK AT...
THAT FRAME RATE IS BUTTERY. YOU HAVE AN EXCELLENT GRAPHICS CARD!
THE WHIR OF THAT FAN IS SO COMFORT-ING...
AND A LOW-LATENCY MONITOR TOO! EXCELLENT TASTE.
TH-THANKS...
BUT THIS IS JUST WHAT MOM PICKED OUT FOR ME.
SAID SOME-ONE NICE HELPED HER OUT.
YOU KNOW A LOT ABOUT THEM?

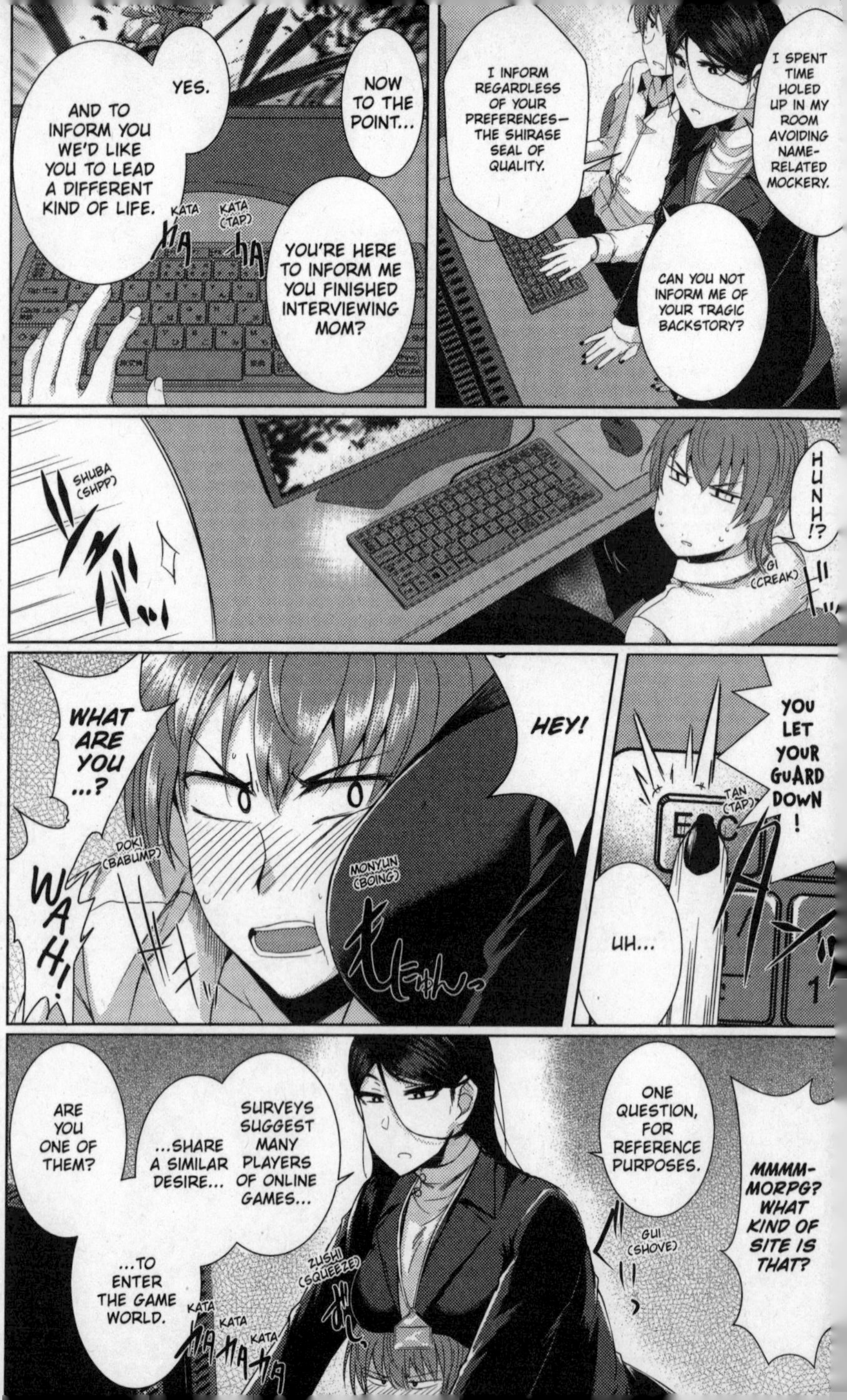
I SPENT TIME HOLED UP IN MY ROOM AVOIDING NAME-RELATED MOCKERY.
CAN YOU NOT INFORM ME OF YOUR TRAGIC BACKSTORY?
I INFORM REGARDLESS OF YOUR PREFERENCES—THE SHIRASE SEAL OF QUALITY.
NOW TO THE POINT...
YOU'RE HERE TO INFORM ME YOU FINISHED INTERVIEWING MOM?
KATA (TAP)
KATA
YES.
AND TO INFORM YOU WE'D LIKE YOU TO LEAD A DIFFERENT KIND OF LIFE.
HUNH!?
GI (CREAK)
SHUBA (SHPP)
YOU LET YOUR GUARD DOWN!
TAN (TAP)
UH...
HEY!
MONYUN (BOING)
WHAT ARE YOU...?
DOKI (BABUMP)
WAH!
MMMM-MORPG? WHAT KIND OF SITE IS THAT?
GUI (SHOVE)
ONE QUESTION, FOR REFERENCE PURPOSES.
SURVEYS SUGGEST MANY PLAYERS OF ONLINE GAMES...
...SHARE A SIMILAR DESIRE...
ARE YOU ONE OF THEM?
...TO ENTER THE GAME WORLD.
ZUSHI (SQUEEZE)
KATA
KATA
KATA

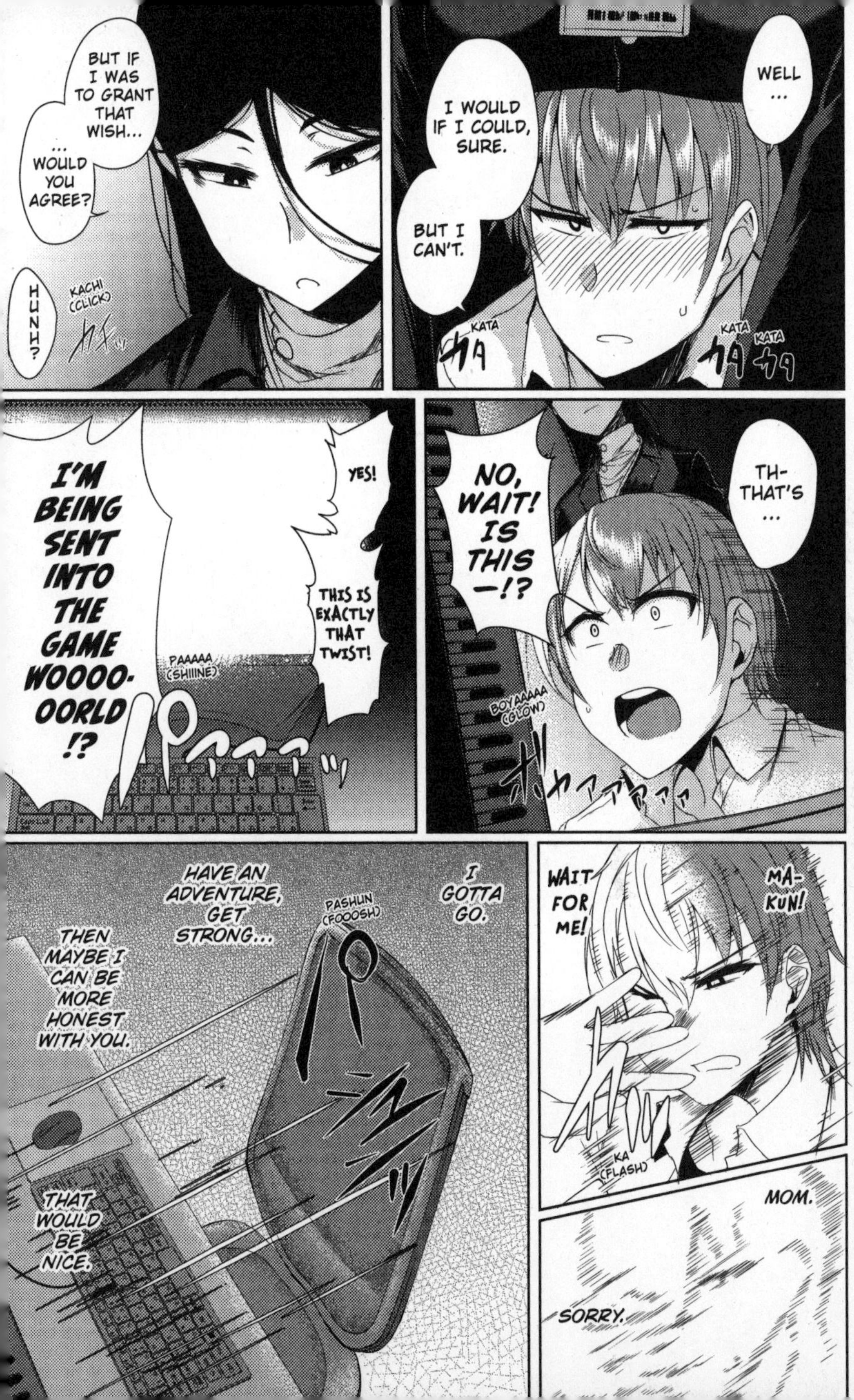
WELL ...
I WOULD IF I COULD, SURE.
BUT I CAN'T.
KATA
KATA
KATA
BUT IF I WAS TO GRANT THAT WISH...
... WOULD YOU AGREE?
KACHI (CLICK)
HUNH?
TH- THAT'S ...
NO, WAIT! IS THIS —!?
BOYAAAAA (GLOW)
YES!
THIS IS EXACTLY THAT TWIST!
I'M BEING SENT INTO THE GAME WOOOO-OORLD!?
PAAAAA (SHIIINE)
MA-KUN!
WAIT FOR ME!
KA (FLASH)
MOM.
SORRY.
I GOTTA GO.
HAVE AN ADVENTURE, GET STRONG...
PASHUN (FOOOSH)
THEN MAYBE I CAN BE MORE HONEST WITH YOU.
THAT WOULD BE NICE.

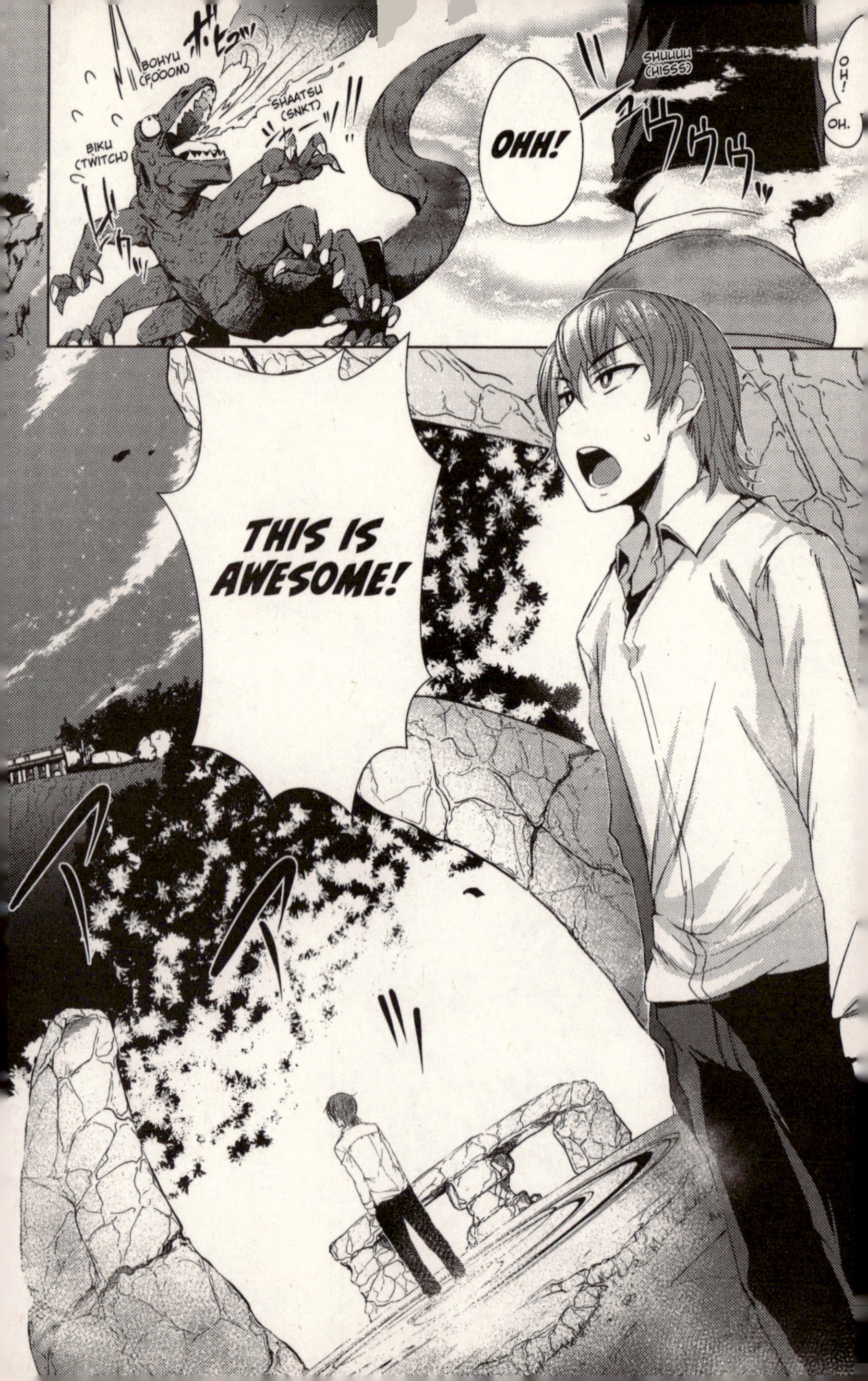

OH! OH.
SHULLLU (HISSS)
OHH!
BOHYU (FOOOM)
SHAATSU (SNKT)
BIKU (TWITCH)
THIS IS AWESOME!

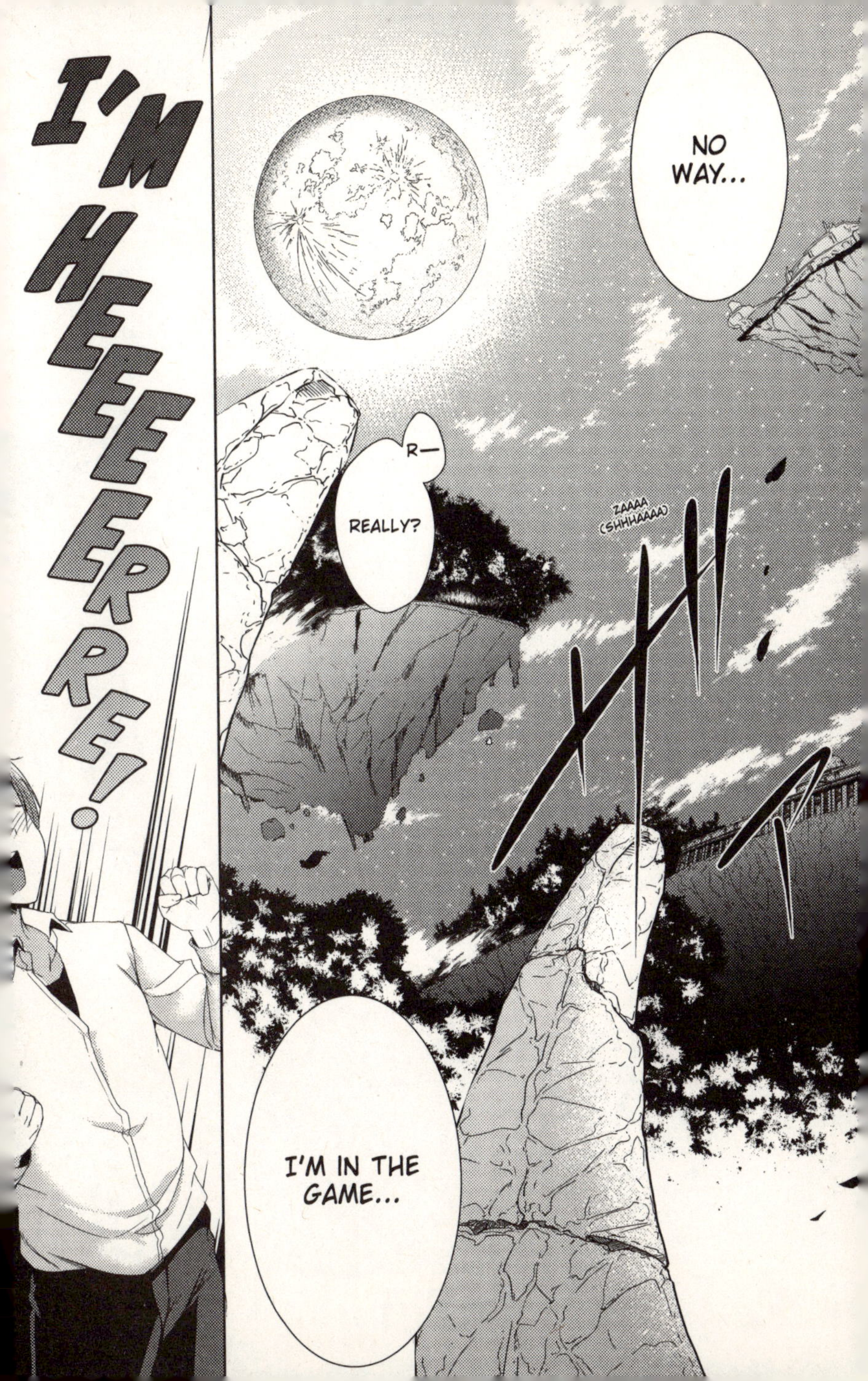
NO WAY...
R—
REALLY?
ZAAAA (SHHHAAAA)
I'M IN THE GAME...
I'M HEEEERRRE!

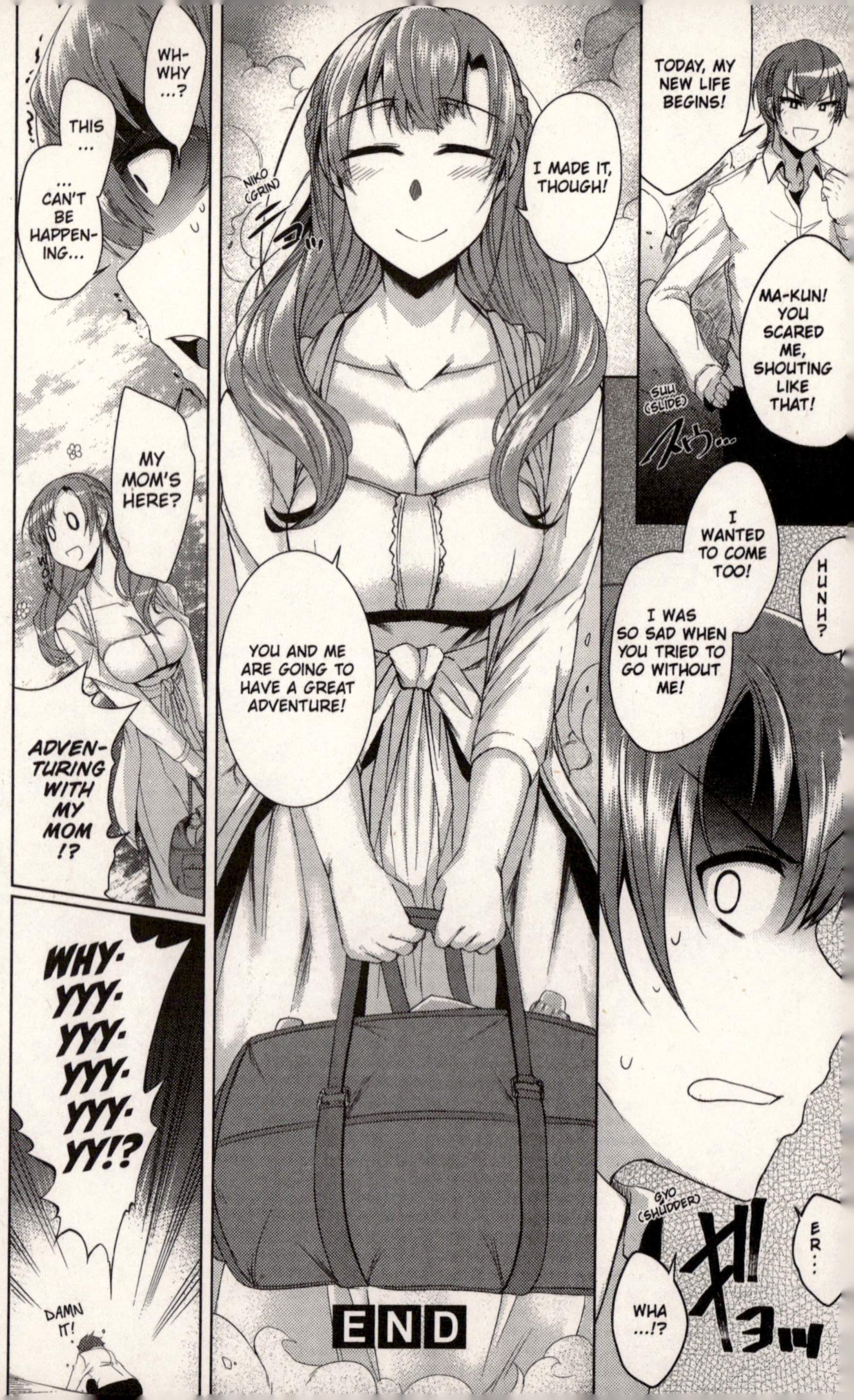
TODAY, MY NEW LIFE BEGINS!
MA-KUN! YOU SCARED ME, SHOUTING LIKE THAT!
SUU (SLIDE)
HUNH?
I WANTED TO COME TOO!
I WAS SO SAD WHEN YOU TRIED TO GO WITHOUT ME!
ER...
GYO (SHUDDER)
WHA ...!?
I MADE IT, THOUGH!
NIKO (GRIN)
YOU AND ME ARE GOING TO HAVE A GREAT ADVENTURE!
END
WH-WHY ...?
THIS ...
... CAN'T BE HAPPENING...
MY MOM'S HERE?
ADVENTURING WITH MY MOM !?
WHY-YYY-YYY-YYY-YYY-YY!?
DAMN IT!

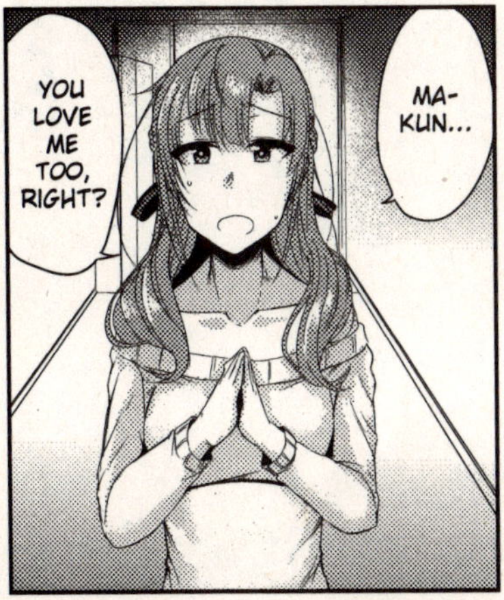
MA-KUN...
YOU LOVE ME TOO, RIGHT?

DO YOU LOVE YOUR MOM AND HER TWO-HIT MULTI-TARGET ATTACKS?

COMIC: MEICHA
STORY: DACHIMA INAKA, ILLUST: IIDA POCHI.
VOLUME 1

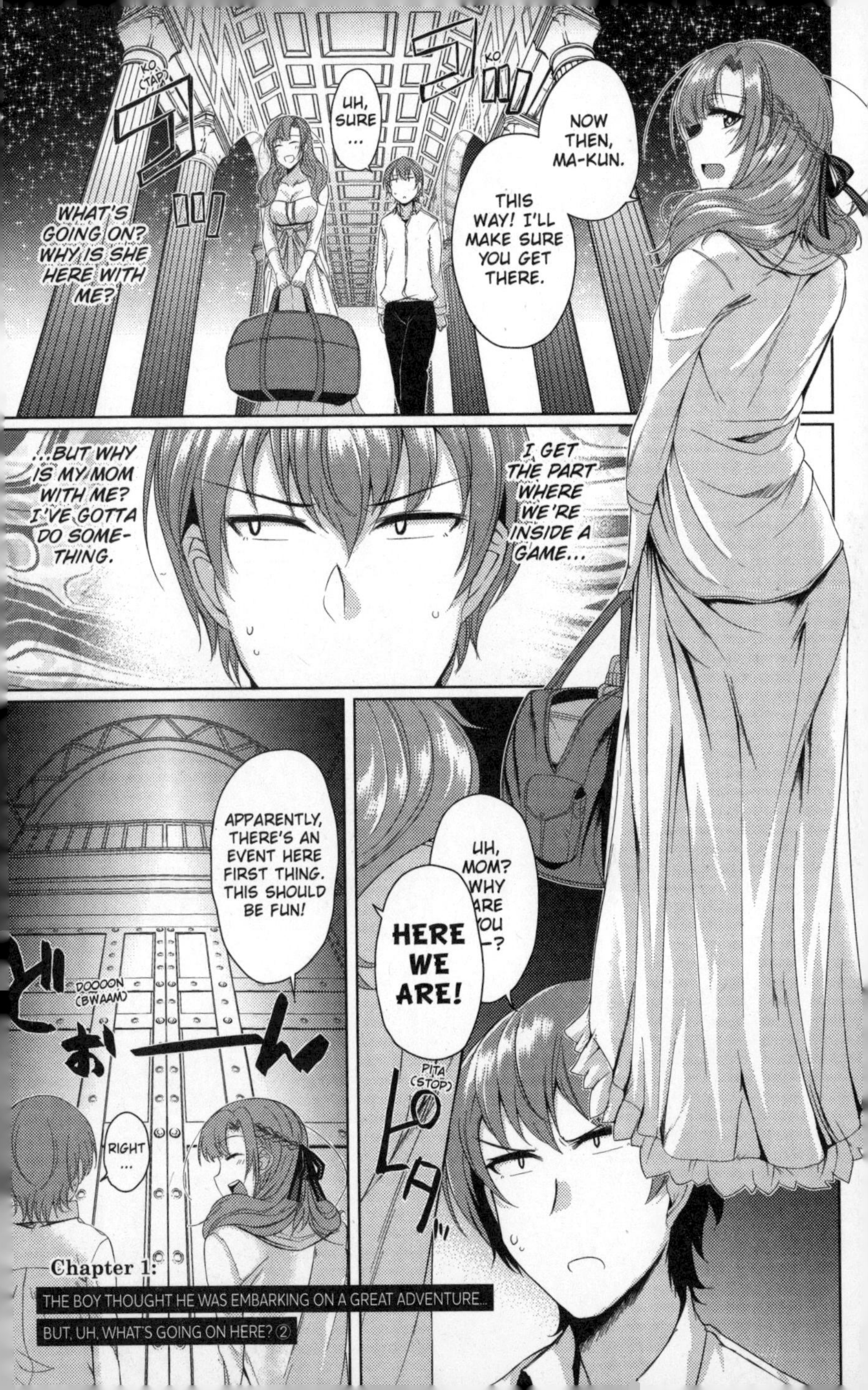
KO
NOW THEN, MA-KUN.
THIS WAY! I'LL MAKE SURE YOU GET THERE.
UH, SURE ...
KO (TAP)
WHAT'S GOING ON? WHY IS SHE HERE WITH ME?
I GET THE PART WHERE WE'RE INSIDE A GAME...
...BUT WHY IS MY MOM WITH ME? I'VE GOTTA DO SOME-THING.
UH, MOM? WHY ARE YOU —?
HERE WE ARE!
PITA (STOP)
APPARENTLY, THERE'S AN EVENT HERE FIRST THING. THIS SHOULD BE FUN!
DOOOON (BWAAM)
RIGHT ...
Chapter 1:
THE BOY THOUGHT HE WAS EMBARKING ON A GREAT ADVENTURE...
BUT, UH, WHAT'S GOING ON HERE? ②

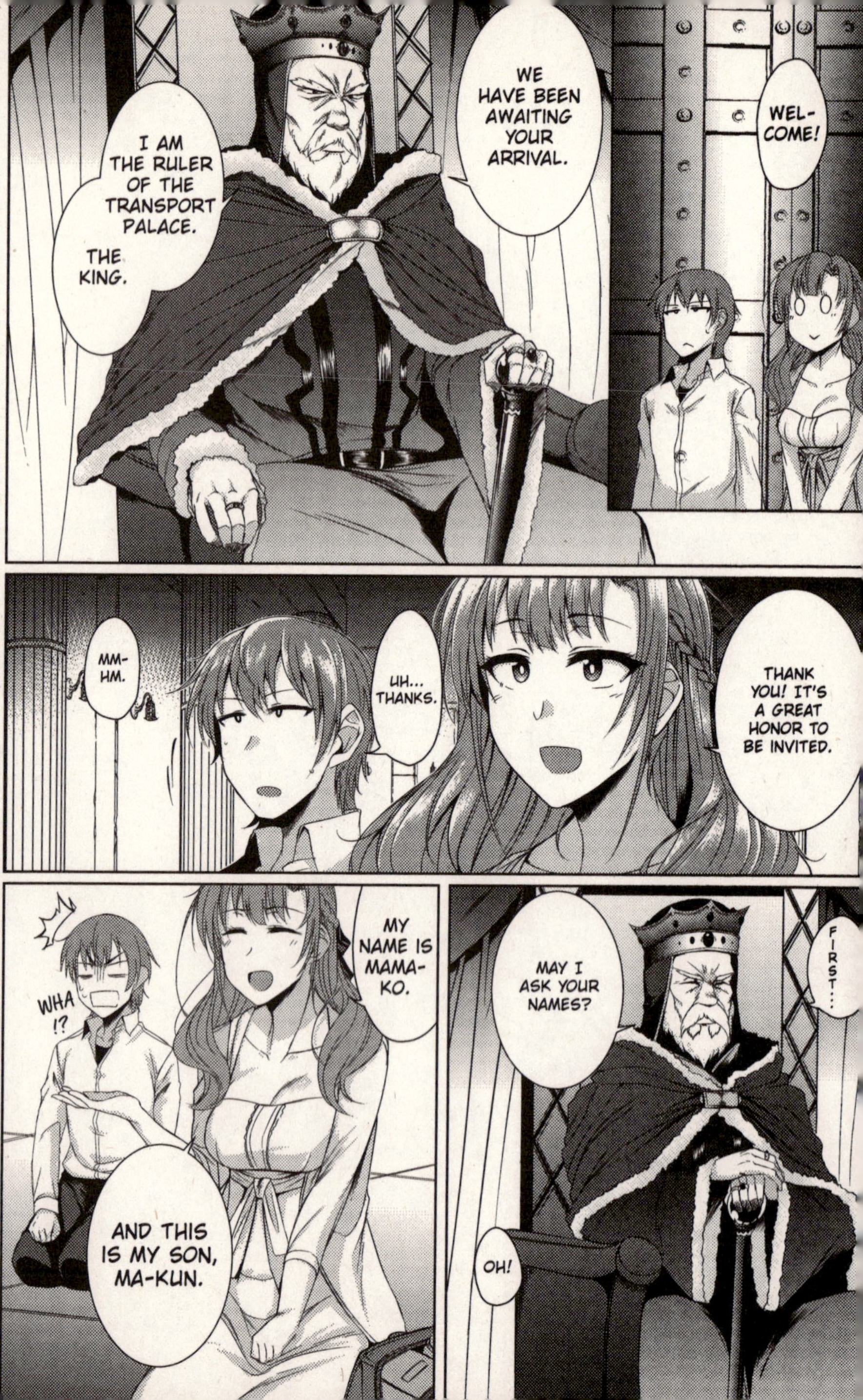
WEL-COME!
WE HAVE BEEN AWAITING YOUR ARRIVAL.
I AM THE RULER OF THE TRANSPORT PALACE.
THE KING.
THANK YOU! IT'S A GREAT HONOR TO BE INVITED.
UH... THANKS.
MM-HM.
FIRST...
MAY I ASK YOUR NAMES?
OH!
MY NAME IS MAMA-KO.
WHA!?
AND THIS IS MY SON, MA-KUN.

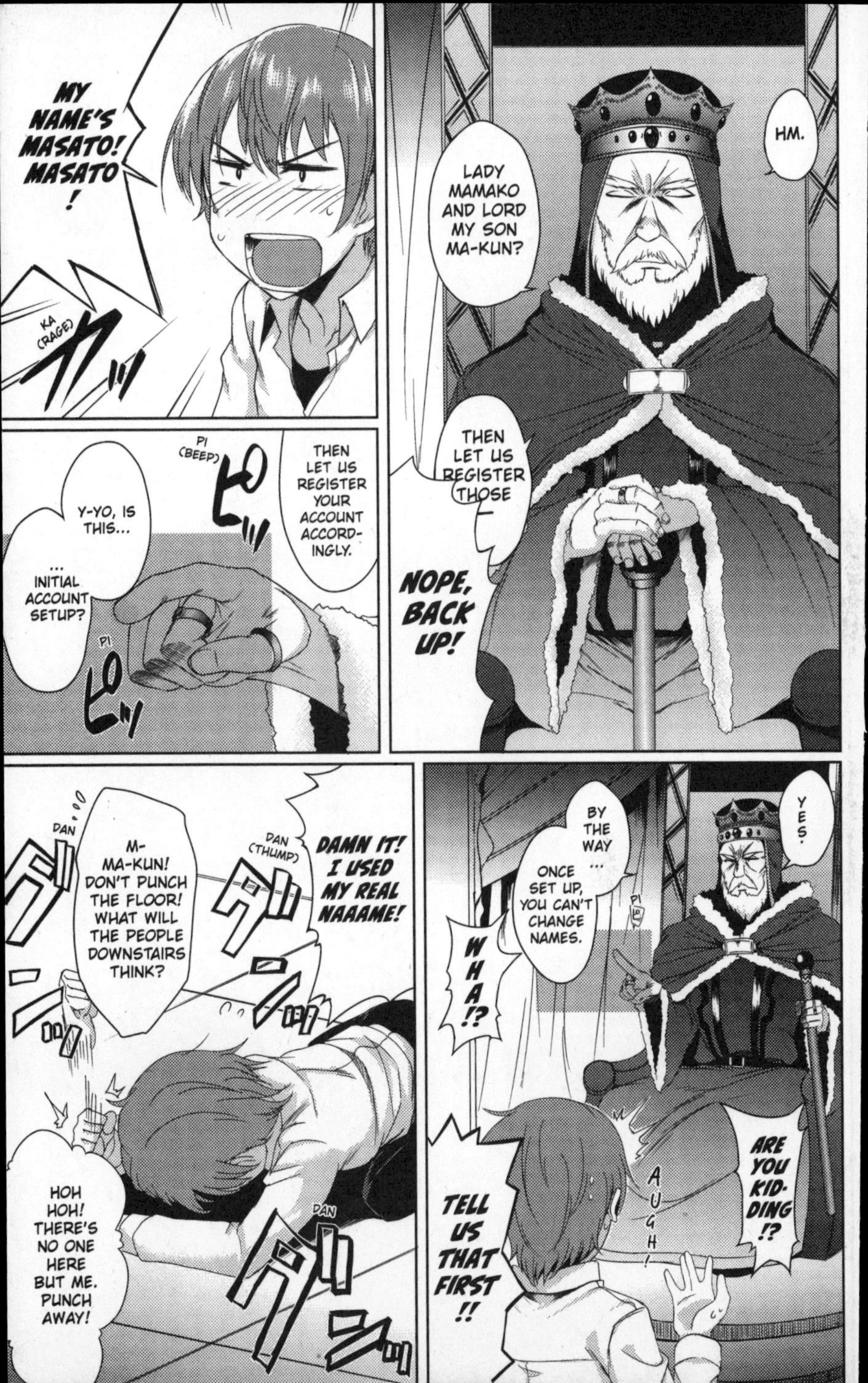
HM.
LADY MAMAKO AND LORD MY SON MA-KUN?
THEN LET US REGISTER THOSE
NOPE, BACK UP!
MY NAME'S MASATO! MASATO!
KA (RAGE)
THEN LET US REGISTER YOUR ACCOUNT ACCORDINGLY.
PI (BEEP)
Y-YO, IS THIS...
...INITIAL ACCOUNT SETUP?
PI
YES.
BY THE WAY...
ONCE SET UP, YOU CAN'T CHANGE NAMES.
PI
WHA!?
ARE YOU KIDDING!?
AUGH!
TELL US THAT FIRST!!
DAMN IT! I USED MY REAL NAAAME!
DAN (THUMP)
M-MA-KUN! DON'T PUNCH THE FLOOR! WHAT WILL THE PEOPLE DOWNSTAIRS THINK?
DAN
HOH HOH! THERE'S NO ONE HERE BUT ME. PUNCH AWAY!
DAN

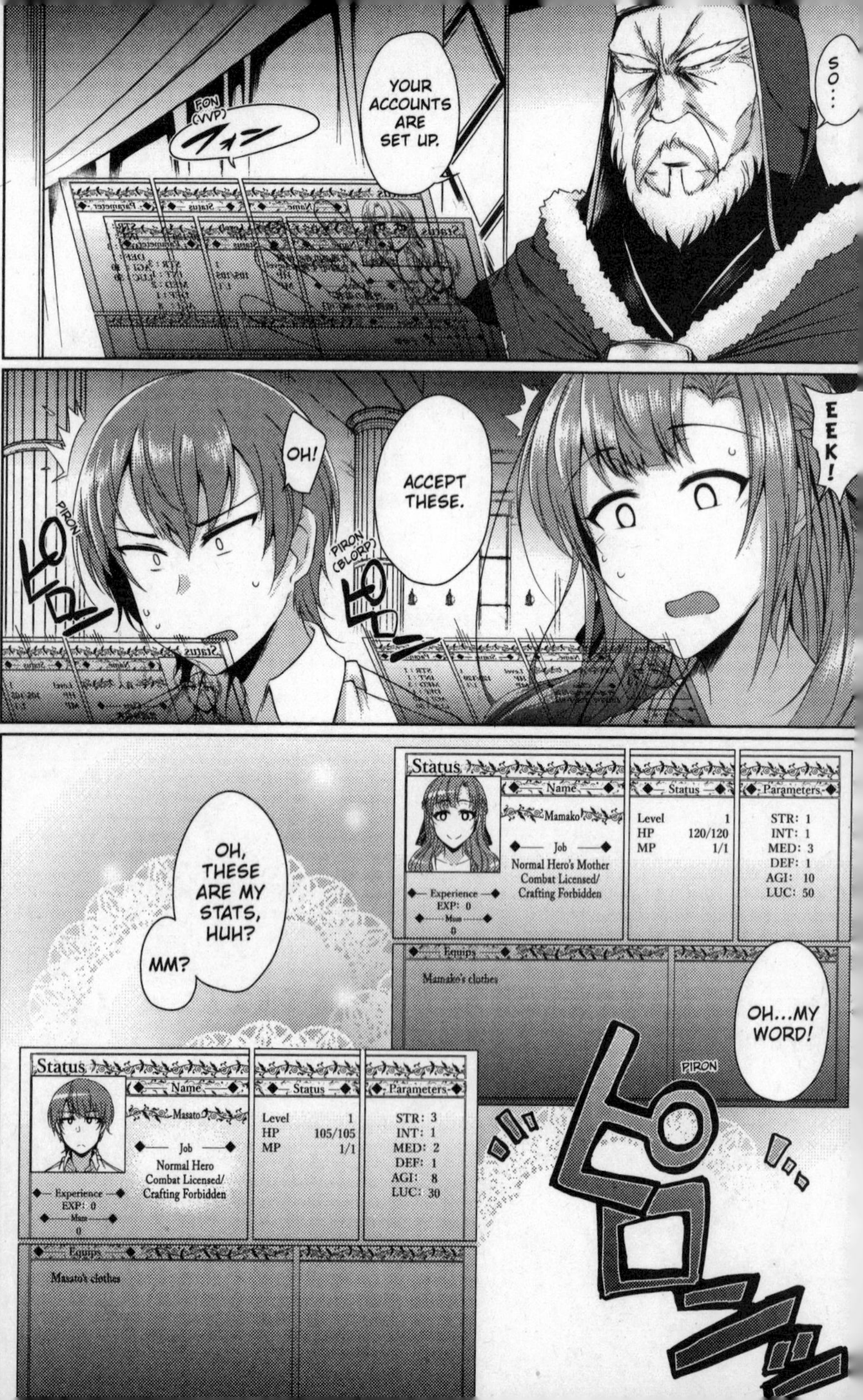
SO...
YOUR ACCOUNTS ARE SET UP.
FON (VVP)
EEK!
ACCEPT THESE.
PIRON (BLORP)
OH!
PIRON
Status
Name
Mamako
Job
Normal Hero's Mother
Combat Licensed/
Crafting Forbidden
Experience
EXP: 0
Mom
0
Status
Level 1
HP 120/120
MP 1/1
Parameters
STR: 1
INT: 1
MED: 3
DEF: 1
AGI: 10
LUC: 50
Equips
Mamako's clothes
OH...MY WORD!
PIRON
OH, THESE ARE MY STATS, HUH?
MM?
Status
Name
Masato
Job
Normal Hero
Combat Licensed/
Crafting Forbidden
Experience
EXP: 0
Mom
0
Status
Level 1
HP 105/105
MP 1/1
Parameters
STR: 3
INT: 1
MED: 2
DEF: 1
AGI: 8
LUC: 30
Equips
Masato's clothes

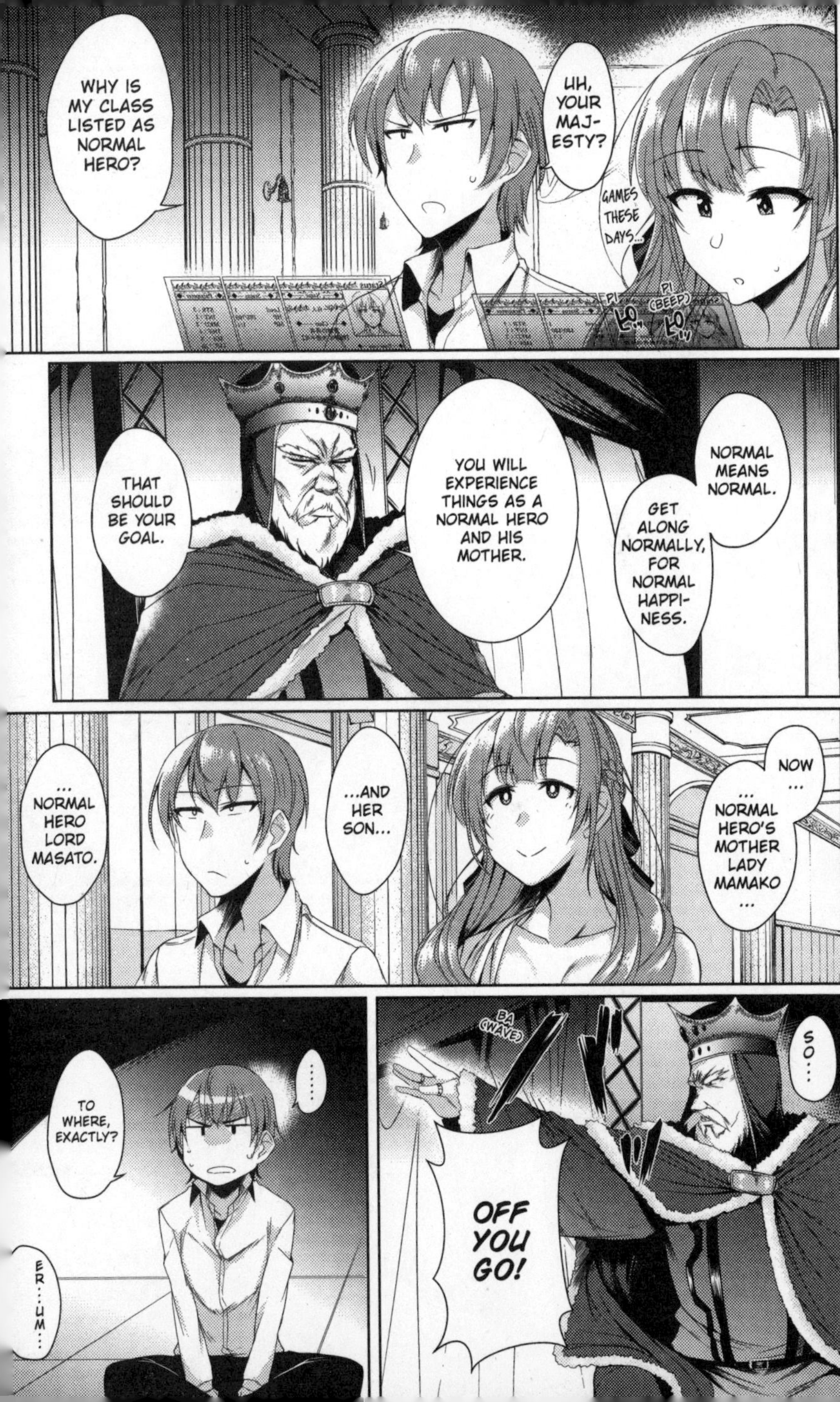
UH, YOUR MAJ-ESTY?
WHY IS MY CLASS LISTED AS NORMAL HERO?
GAMES THESE DAYS...
PI PI (BEEP)
NORMAL MEANS NORMAL.
GET ALONG NORMALLY, FOR NORMAL HAPPI-NESS.
YOU WILL EXPERIENCE THINGS AS A NORMAL HERO AND HIS MOTHER.
THAT SHOULD BE YOUR GOAL.
NOW... ...NORMAL HERO'S MOTHER LADY MAMAKO...
...AND HER SON...
...NORMAL HERO LORD MASATO.
SO...
BA (WAVE)
OFF YOU GO!
......
TO WHERE, EXACTLY?
ER...UM...

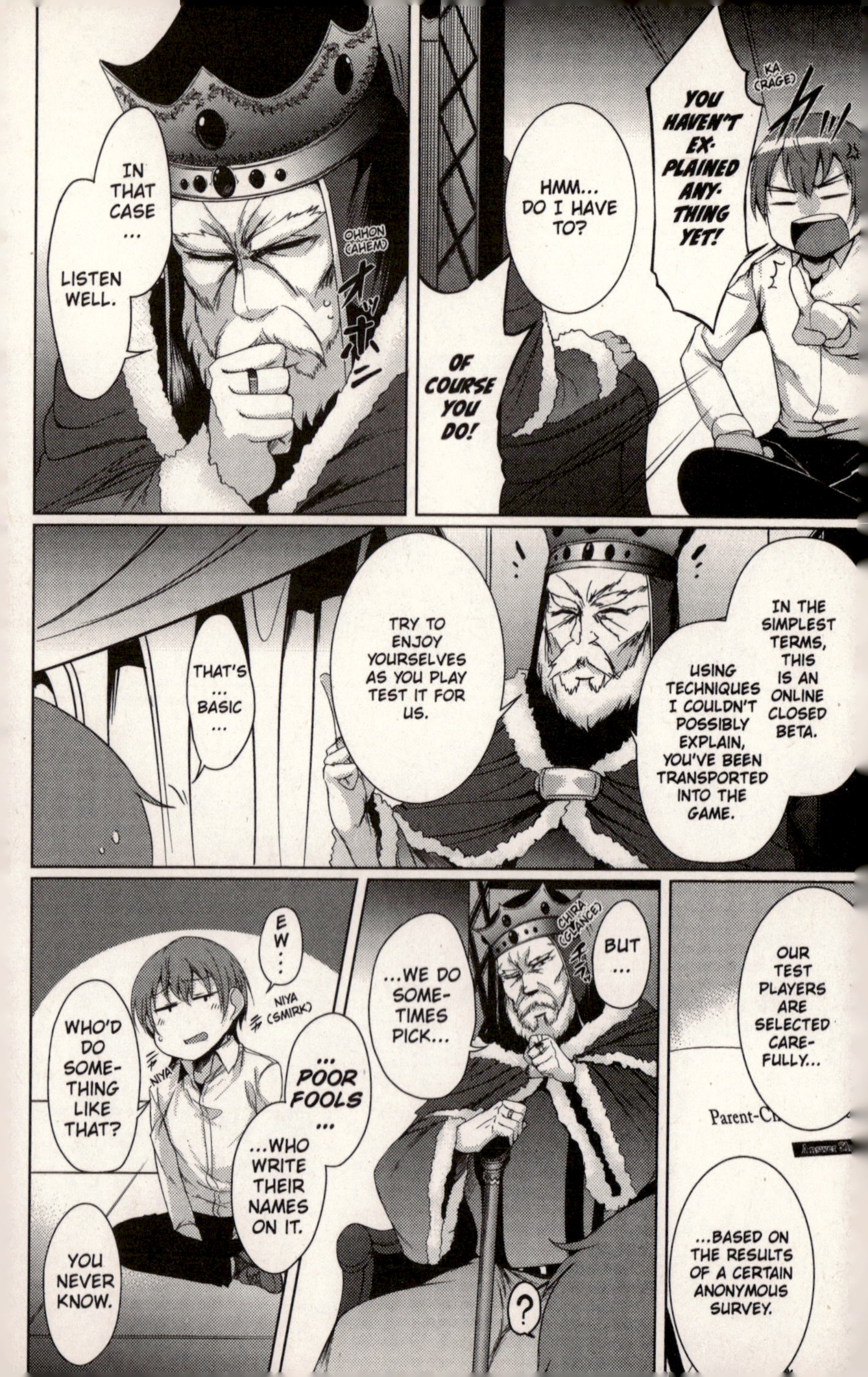
KA (RAGE)
YOU HAVEN'T EX-PLAINED ANY-THING YET!
HMM... DO I HAVE TO?
OF COURSE YOU DO!
OHHON (AHEM)
IN THAT CASE ...
LISTEN WELL.
IN THE SIMPLEST TERMS, THIS IS AN ONLINE CLOSED BETA.
USING TECHNIQUES I COULDN'T POSSIBLY EXPLAIN, YOU'VE BEEN TRANSPORTED INTO THE GAME.
TRY TO ENJOY YOURSELVES AS YOU PLAY TEST IT FOR US.
THAT'S ... BASIC ...
OUR TEST PLAYERS ARE SELECTED CARE-FULLY...
...BASED ON THE RESULTS OF A CERTAIN ANONYMOUS SURVEY.
CHIRA (GLANCE)
BUT ...
...WE DO SOME-TIMES PICK...
... POOR FOOLS ...
...WHO WRITE THEIR NAMES ON IT.
?
EW...
NIYA (SMIRK)
WHO'D DO SOME-THING LIKE THAT?
YOU NEVER KNOW.

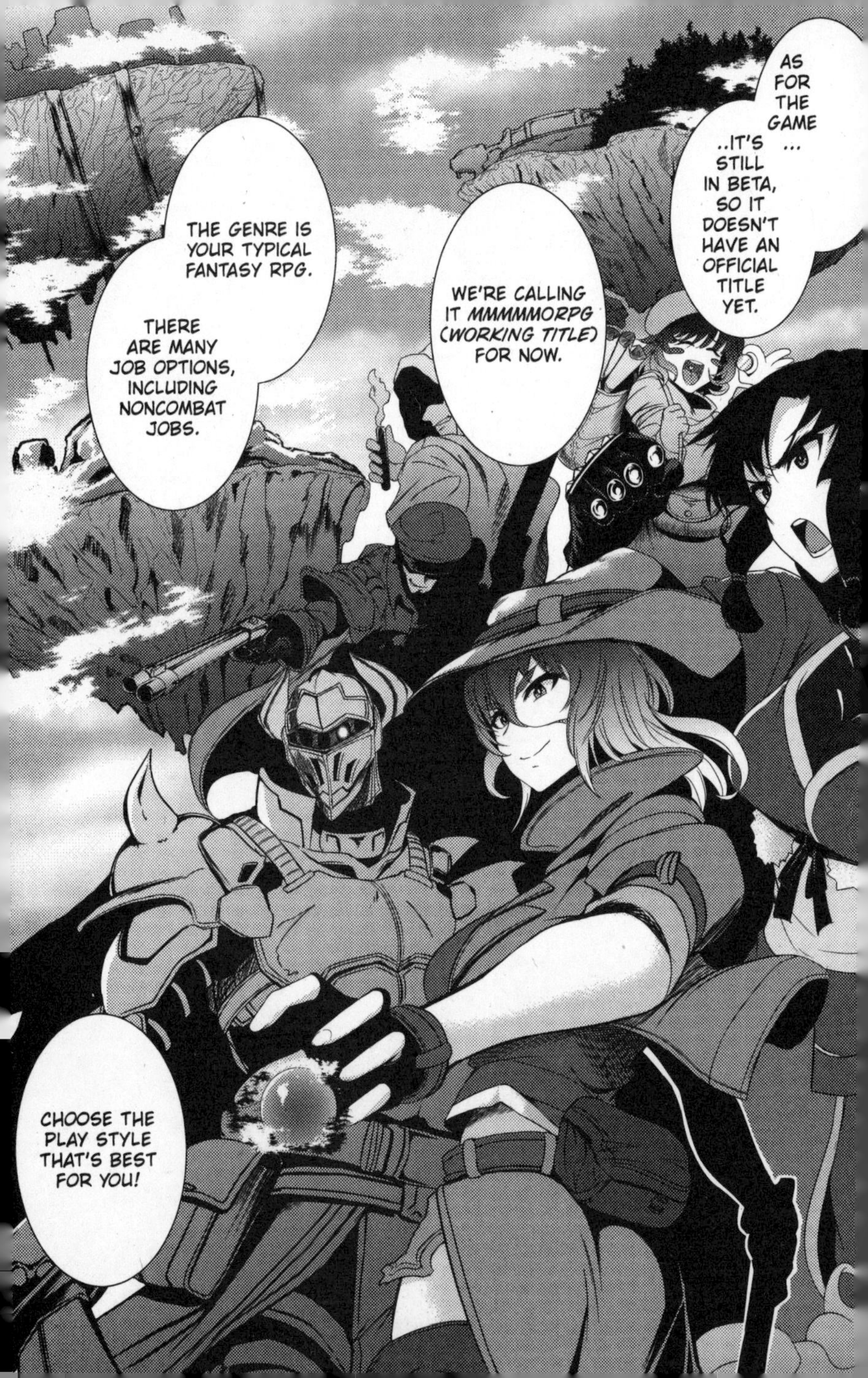
AS FOR THE GAME ...
..IT'S STILL IN BETA, SO IT DOESN'T HAVE AN OFFICIAL TITLE YET.
WE'RE CALLING IT *MMMMMORPG (WORKING TITLE)* FOR NOW.
THE GENRE IS YOUR TYPICAL FANTASY RPG.
THERE ARE MANY JOB OPTIONS, INCLUDING NONCOMBAT JOBS.
CHOOSE THE PLAY STYLE THAT'S BEST FOR YOU!

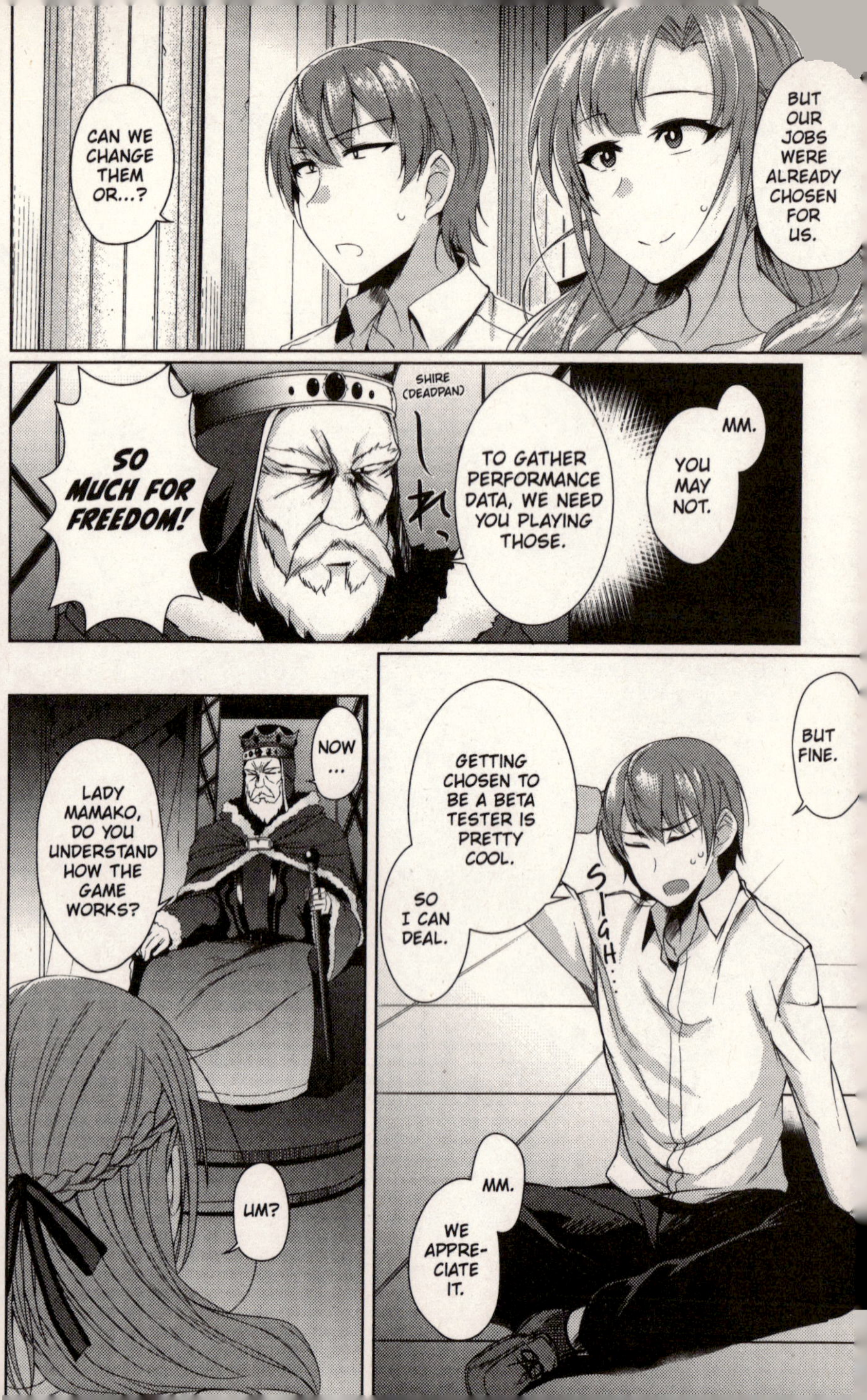
BUT OUR JOBS WERE ALREADY CHOSEN FOR US.
CAN WE CHANGE THEM OR...?
MM.
YOU MAY NOT.
TO GATHER PERFORMANCE DATA, WE NEED YOU PLAYING THOSE.
SHIRE (DEADPAN)
SO MUCH FOR FREEDOM!
BUT FINE.
GETTING CHOSEN TO BE A BETA TESTER IS PRETTY COOL.
SO I CAN DEAL.
SIGH...
MM.
WE APPRECIATE IT.
NOW...
LADY MAMAKO, DO YOU UNDERSTAND HOW THE GAME WORKS?
UM?

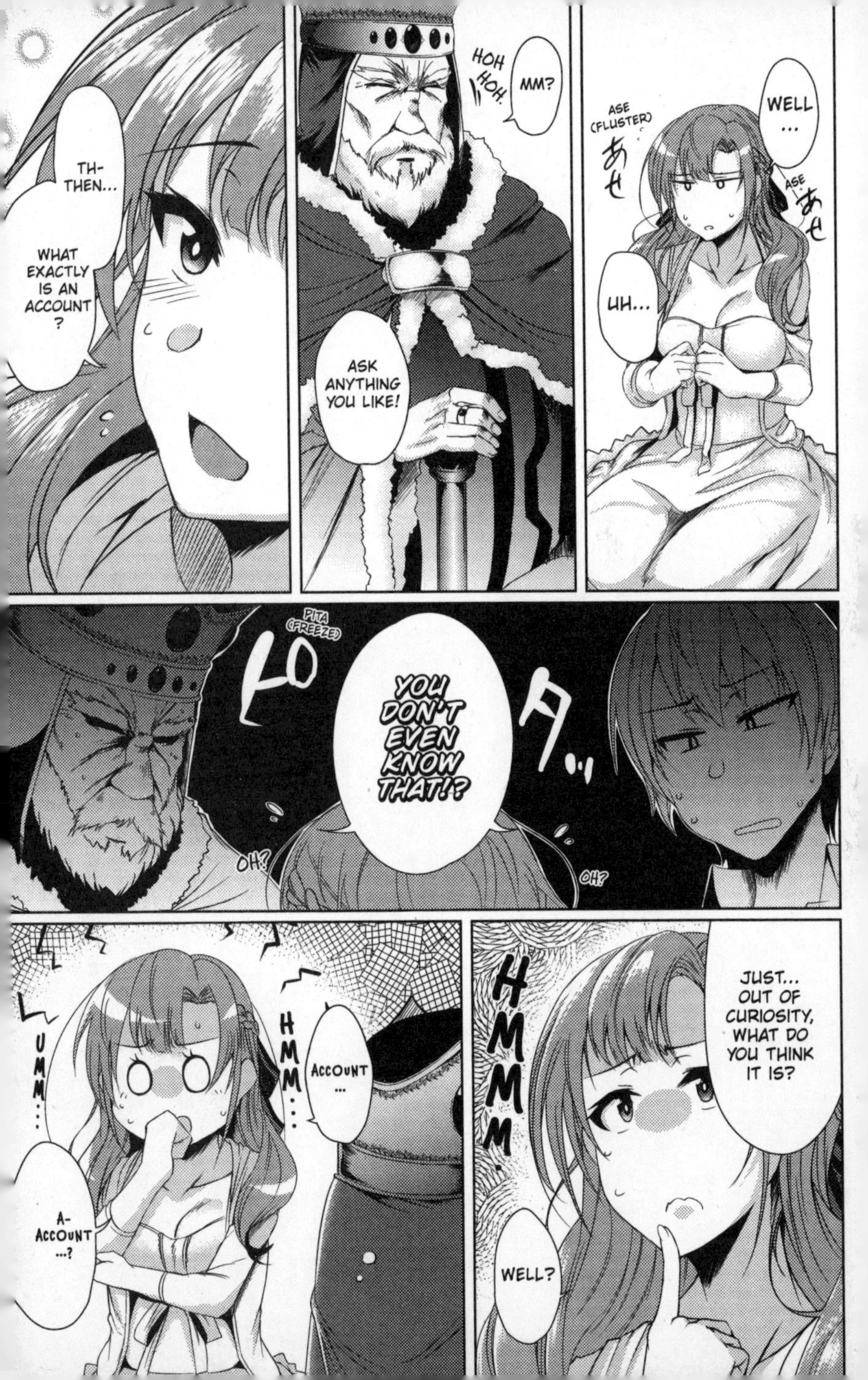
WELL...
ASE (FLUSTER)
あせ
ASE
あせ
UH...
MM?
HOH HOH
ASK ANYTHING YOU LIKE!
TH-THEN...
WHAT EXACTLY IS AN ACCOUNT?
PITA (FREEZE)
ピ
タッ
YOU DON'T EVEN KNOW THAT!?
OH?
OH?
JUST... OUT OF CURIOSITY, WHAT DO YOU THINK IT IS?
HMMM
WELL?
HMM...
ACCOUNT...
UMM...
A-ACCOUNT...?

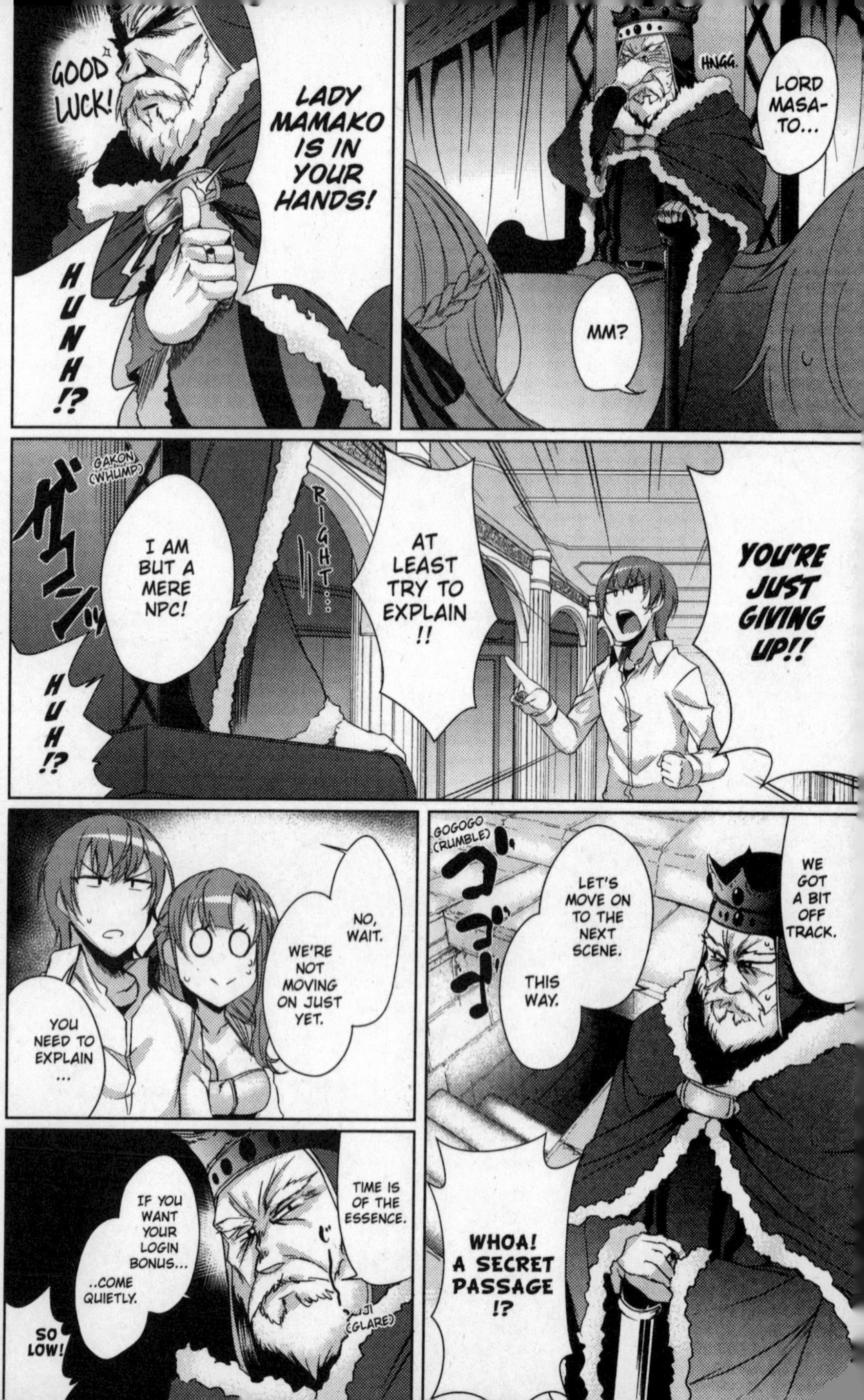
HNGG.
LORD MASA-TO...
MM?
GOOD LUCK!
LADY MAMAKO IS IN YOUR HANDS!
HUNH!?
YOU'RE JUST GIVING UP!!
AT LEAST TRY TO EXPLAIN!!
RIGHT...
GAKON (WHUMP)
I AM BUT A MERE NPC!
HUH!?
WE GOT A BIT OFF TRACK.
LET'S MOVE ON TO THE NEXT SCENE.
THIS WAY.
GOGOGO (RUMBLE)
WHOA! A SECRET PASSAGE!?
NO, WAIT.
WE'RE NOT MOVING ON JUST YET.
YOU NEED TO EXPLAIN...
TIME IS OF THE ESSENCE.
IF YOU WANT YOUR LOGIN BONUS...
..COME QUIETLY.
JI (GLARE)
SO LOW!

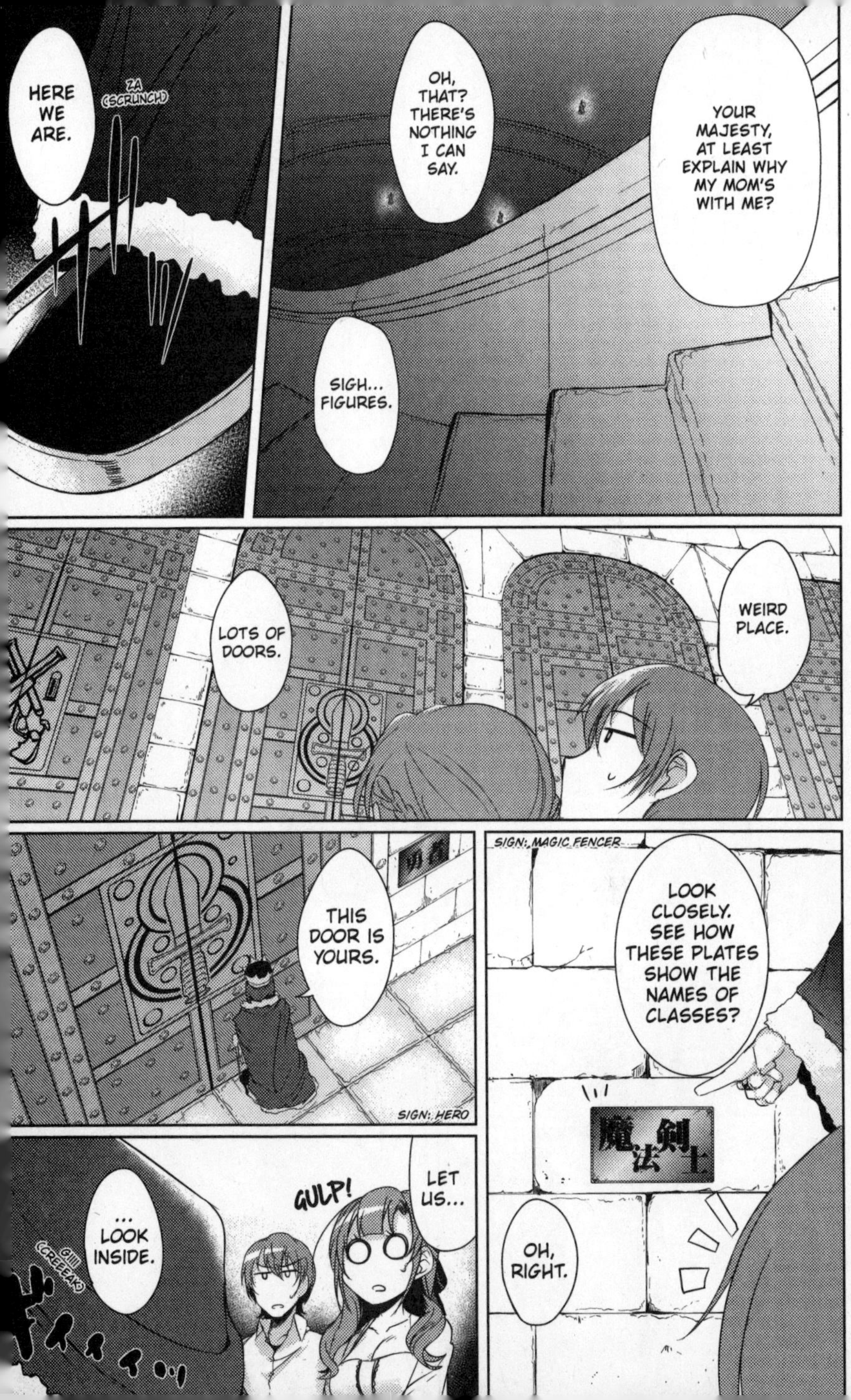
YOUR MAJESTY, AT LEAST EXPLAIN WHY MY MOM'S WITH ME?
OH, THAT? THERE'S NOTHING I CAN SAY.
SIGH... FIGURES.
ZA (SCRUNCH)
HERE WE ARE.
WEIRD PLACE.
LOTS OF DOORS.
SIGN: MAGIC FENCER
LOOK CLOSELY. SEE HOW THESE PLATES SHOW THE NAMES OF CLASSES?
魔法剣士
OH, RIGHT.
THIS DOOR IS YOURS.
SIGN: HERO
LET US...
GULP!
... LOOK INSIDE.
GIIII (CREEEAK)

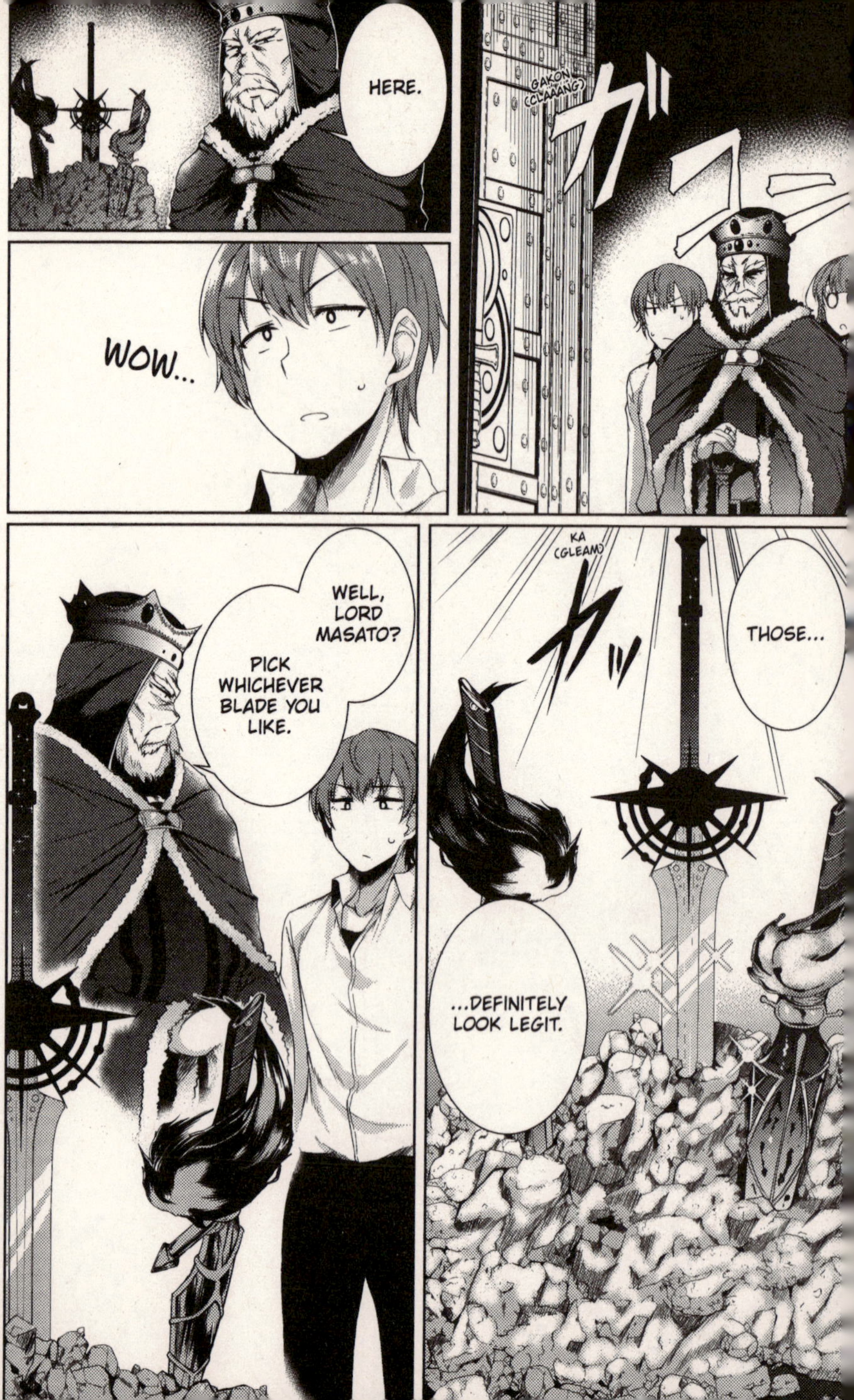
GAKON (CLAAANG)
HERE.
WOW...
KA (GLEAM)
THOSE...
...DEFINITELY LOOK LEGIT.
WELL, LORD MASATO?
PICK WHICHEVER BLADE YOU LIKE.

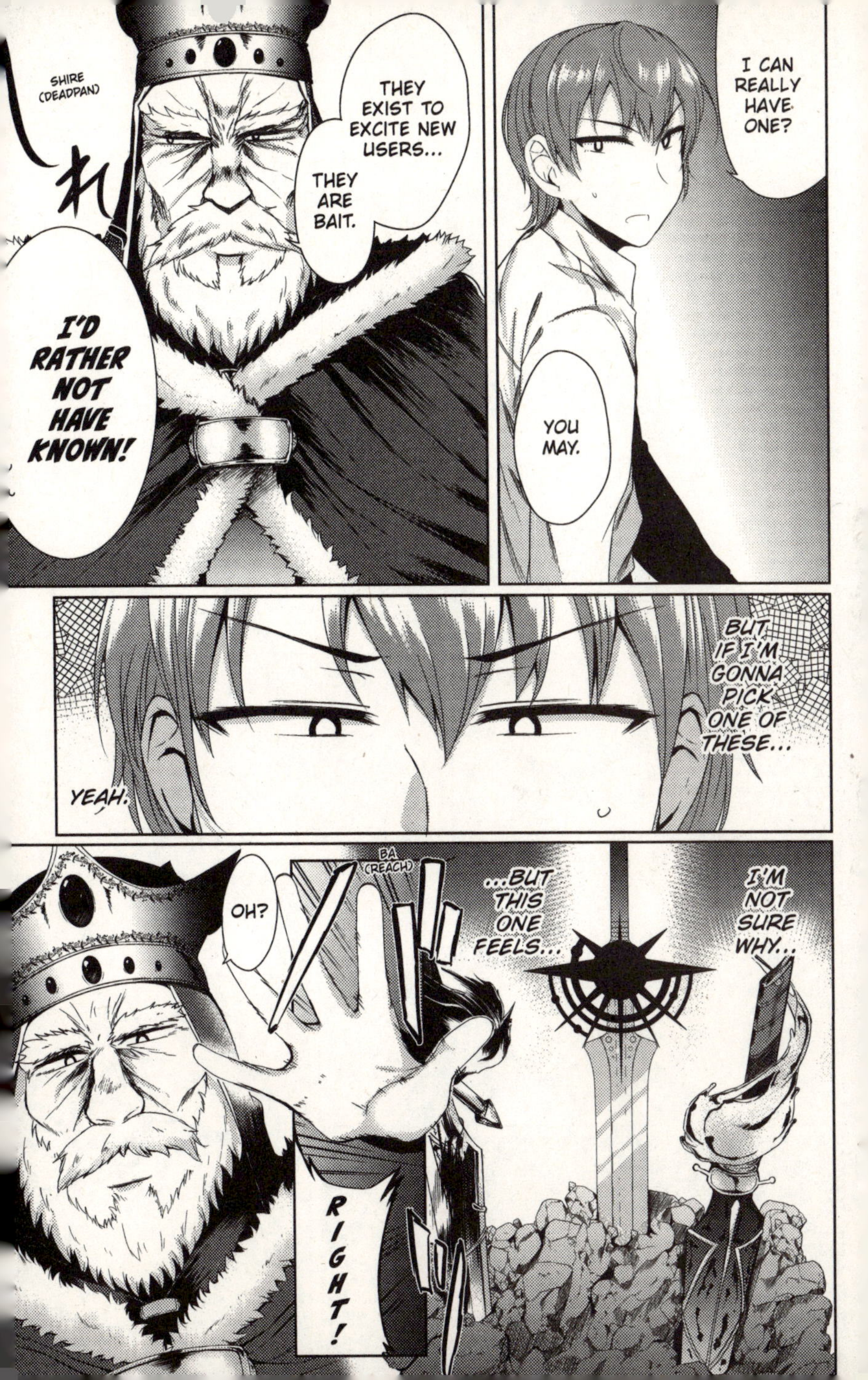
I CAN REALLY HAVE ONE?
YOU MAY.
THEY EXIST TO EXCITE NEW USERS...
THEY ARE BAIT.
SHIRE (DEADPAN)
I'D RATHER NOT HAVE KNOWN!
BUT IF I'M GONNA PICK ONE OF THESE...
YEAH.
I'M NOT SURE WHY...
...BUT THIS ONE FEELS...
RIGHT!
BA (REACH)
OH?

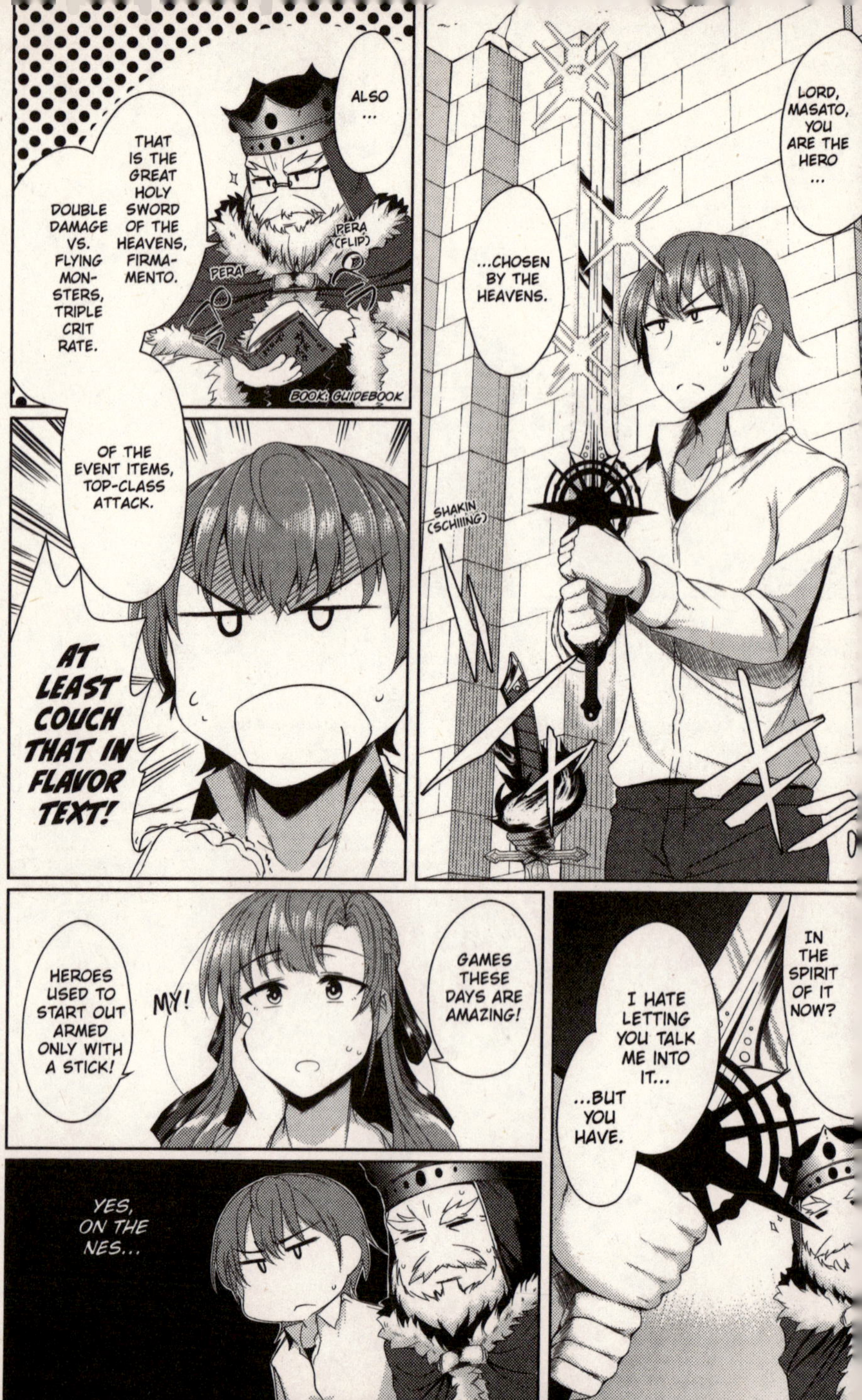
LORD, MASATO, YOU ARE THE HERO ...
...CHOSEN BY THE HEAVENS.
SHAKIN (SCHIIING)
ALSO ...
THAT IS THE GREAT HOLY SWORD OF THE HEAVENS, FIRMAMENTO.
PERA (FLIP)
PERA
DOUBLE DAMAGE VS. FLYING MONSTERS, TRIPLE CRIT RATE.
BOOK: GUIDEBOOK
OF THE EVENT ITEMS, TOP-CLASS ATTACK.
AT LEAST COUCH THAT IN FLAVOR TEXT!
IN THE SPIRIT OF IT NOW?
I HATE LETTING YOU TALK ME INTO IT...
...BUT YOU HAVE.
GAMES THESE DAYS ARE AMAZING!
MY!
HEROES USED TO START OUT ARMED ONLY WITH A STICK!
YES, ON THE NES...

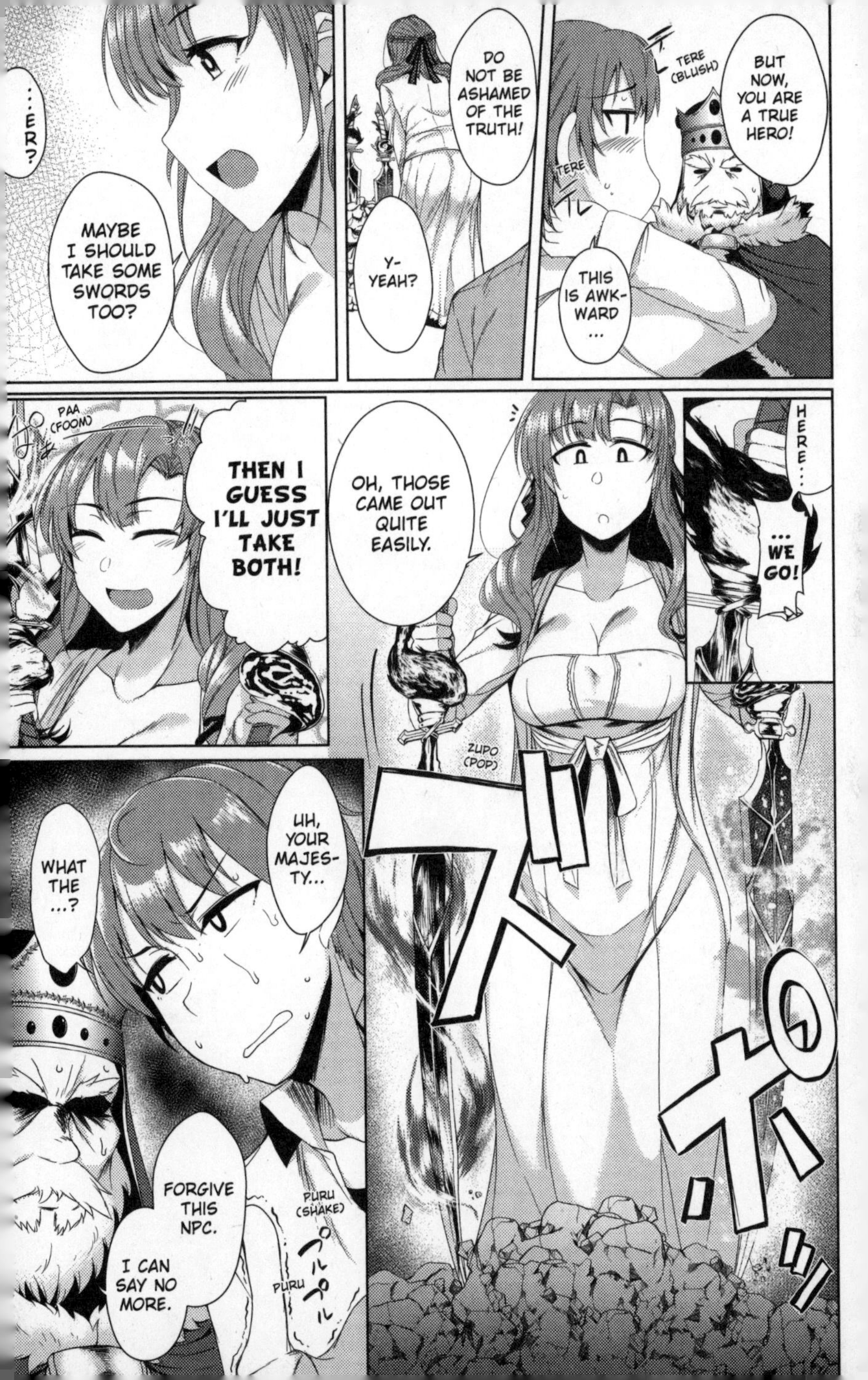
BUT NOW, YOU ARE A TRUE HERO!
TERE (BLUSH)
TERE
THIS IS AWK-WARD ...
DO NOT BE ASHAMED OF THE TRUTH!
Y-YEAH?
...ER?
MAYBE I SHOULD TAKE SOME SWORDS TOO?
HERE...
...WE GO!
OH, THOSE CAME OUT QUITE EASILY.
ZUPO (POP)
PAA (FOOM)
THEN I GUESS I'LL JUST TAKE BOTH!
UH, YOUR MAJESTY...
WHAT THE ...?
PURU (SHAKE)
PURU
FORGIVE THIS NPC.
I CAN SAY NO MORE.

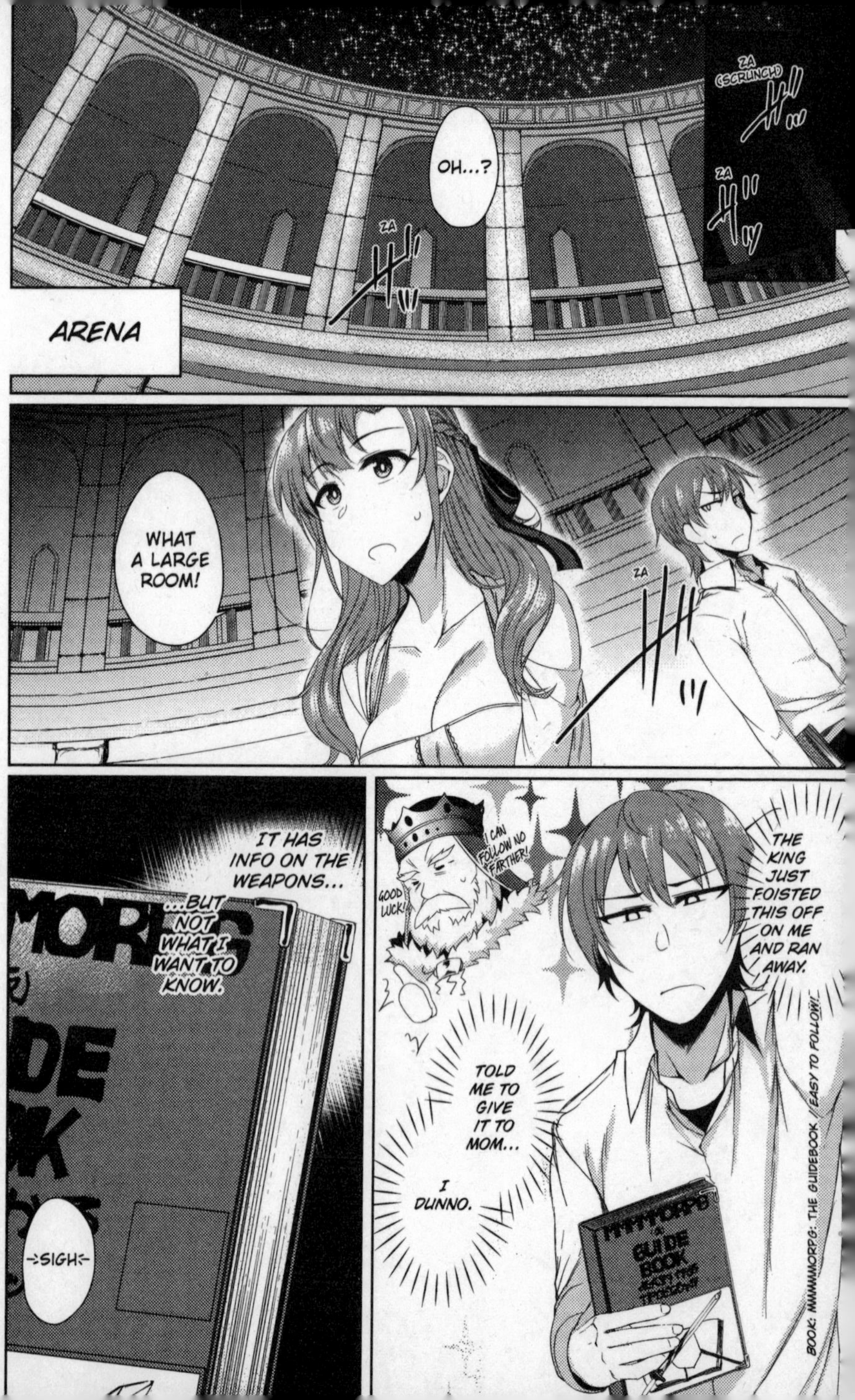
ZA (SCRUNCH)
ZA
OH...?
ZA
ARENA
ZA
WHAT A LARGE ROOM!
THE KING JUST FOISTED THIS OFF ON ME AND RAN AWAY.
I CAN FOLLOW NO FARTHER!
GOOD LUCK!
TOLD ME TO GIVE IT TO MOM...
I DUNNO.
BOOK: MMMMMORPG: THE GUIDEBOOK / EASY TO FOLLOW!
IT HAS INFO ON THE WEAPONS...
...BUT NOT WHAT I WANT TO KNOW.
-SIGH-

Welcome to the tutorial battle!
OH!?
BIKU (TWITCH)
Tutorial
Here you can try out your weapons.
FLOATING LETTERS!
MA-KUN!
WHEW!
DIDN'T EXPECT AN AN-NOUNCER...
Are you ready to begin!?
NO POINT THINKING ABOUT IT.
LET'S TRY THESE NEW WEAPONS OUT!
OF COURSE I AM!
Very well.
Then let's get started!
GOT A LOT TO GRIPE ABOUT...
SUCHA (SCHNK)
BUT FIRST, I GOTTA TRY THIS!
Bat-tle...
GRRRRRR!
BAAAN (WHOOM)
WHAT ARE THESE?
Start!
MA-KUN, LEAVE THIS TO MOMMY!
HYOI (SHOVE)
HUH?
WHOA?
WAIT, MOM!?

LET'S SEE WHAT MOMMY CAN DO!
JUST WATCH, MA-KUN!
HYAH!
BA (SHNK)
DO
HAH!
THE HOLY SWORD OF MOTHER OCEAN, ALTURA

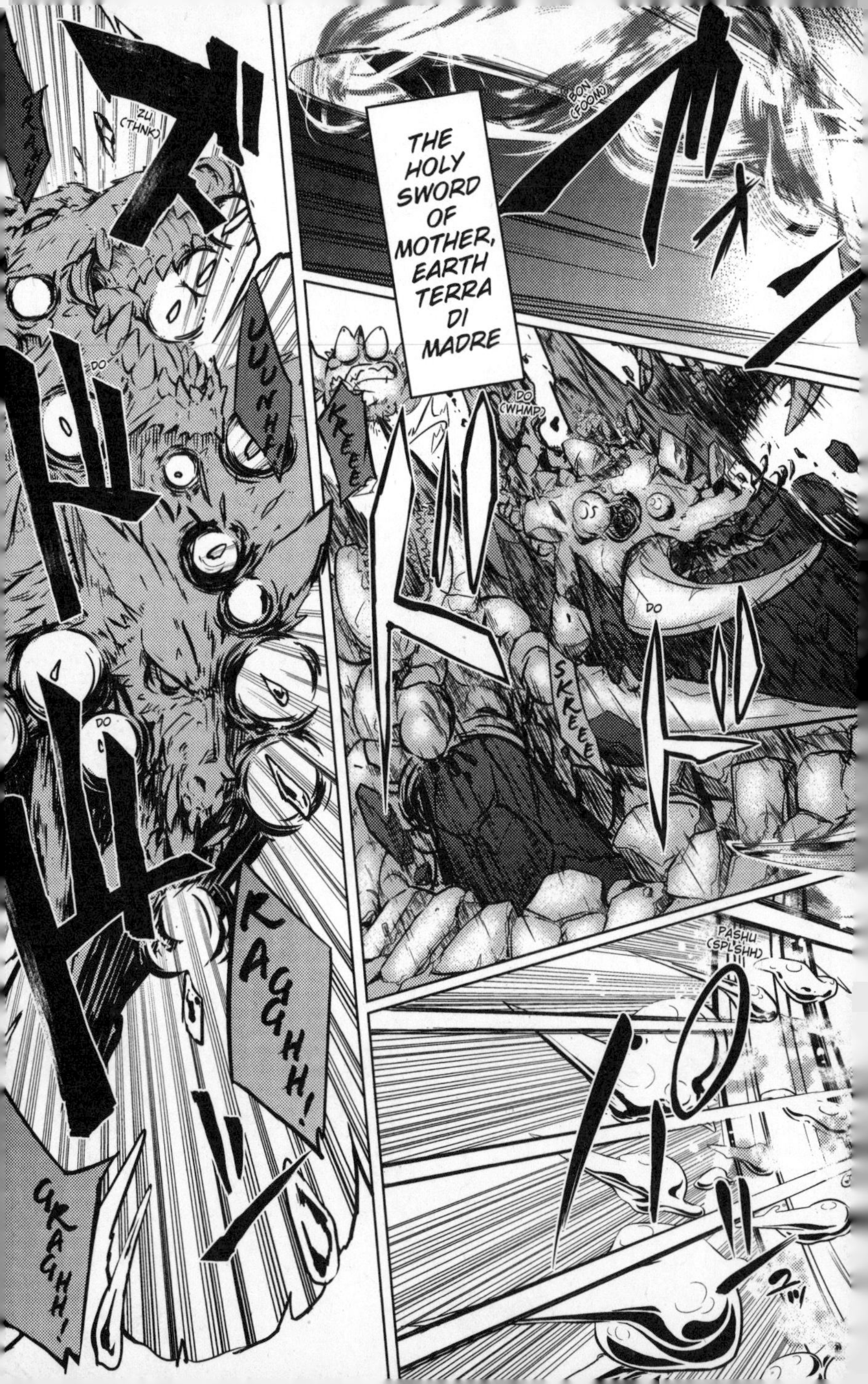
BON (FOOM)
THE HOLY SWORD OF MOTHER, EARTH TERRA DI MADRE
DO (WHMP)
KREEE
SKREEE
DO
PASHU (SPLSHH)
ZU (THNK)
UUUNH!
DO
DO
RAGGHH!
UGAGH!

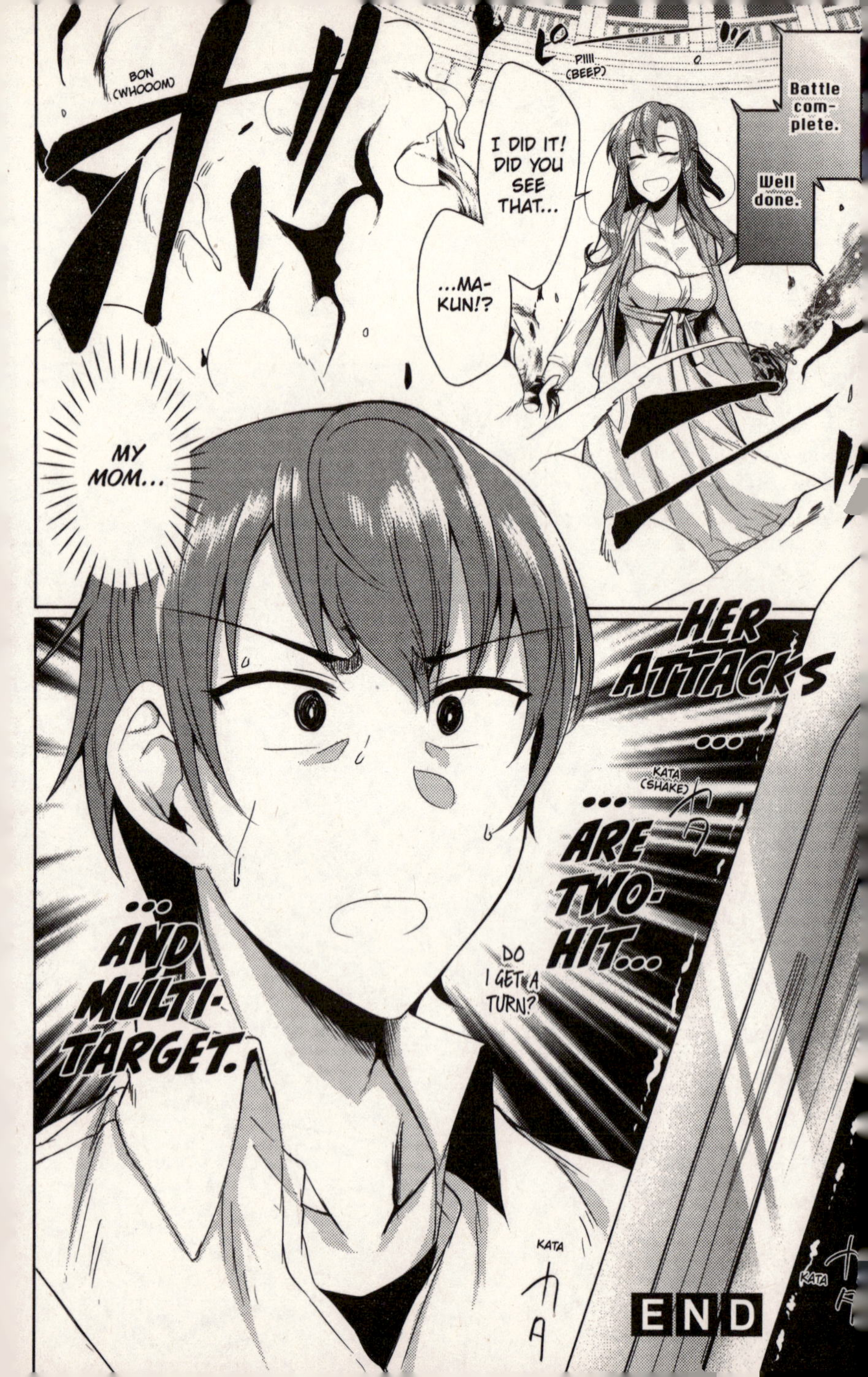
Battle complete.
Well done.
PIII (BEEP)
I DID IT! DID YOU SEE THAT...
...MA-KUN!?
BON (WHOOOM)
MY MOM...
HER ATTACKS...
KATA (SHAKE)
...ARE TWO-HIT...
DO I GET A TURN?
...AND MULTI-TARGET.
KATA
KATA
END

GAMES THESE DAYS ARE AMAZING!
MY!
HEROES USED TO START OUT ARMED ONLY WITH A STICK!

Do You Love Your Mom?

DO YOU LOVE YOUR MOM?

Chapter 1:
THE BOY THOUGHT HE WAS EMBARKING ON A GREAT ADVENTURE...
BUT, UH, WHAT'S GOING ON HERE? ③
WHY...?
KARAAAAN (CLAAANG)
ZUUN (THUD)
WHY IS THIS HAPPEN-ING!?
KU (NGH)
MA-KUN!?
WH-WHAT'S WRONG, MA-KUN!?
ARE YOU HURT?
NO.
THAT'S NOT IT.
THE PROBLEM HERE IS...
HNGG
...THOSE SWORDS.

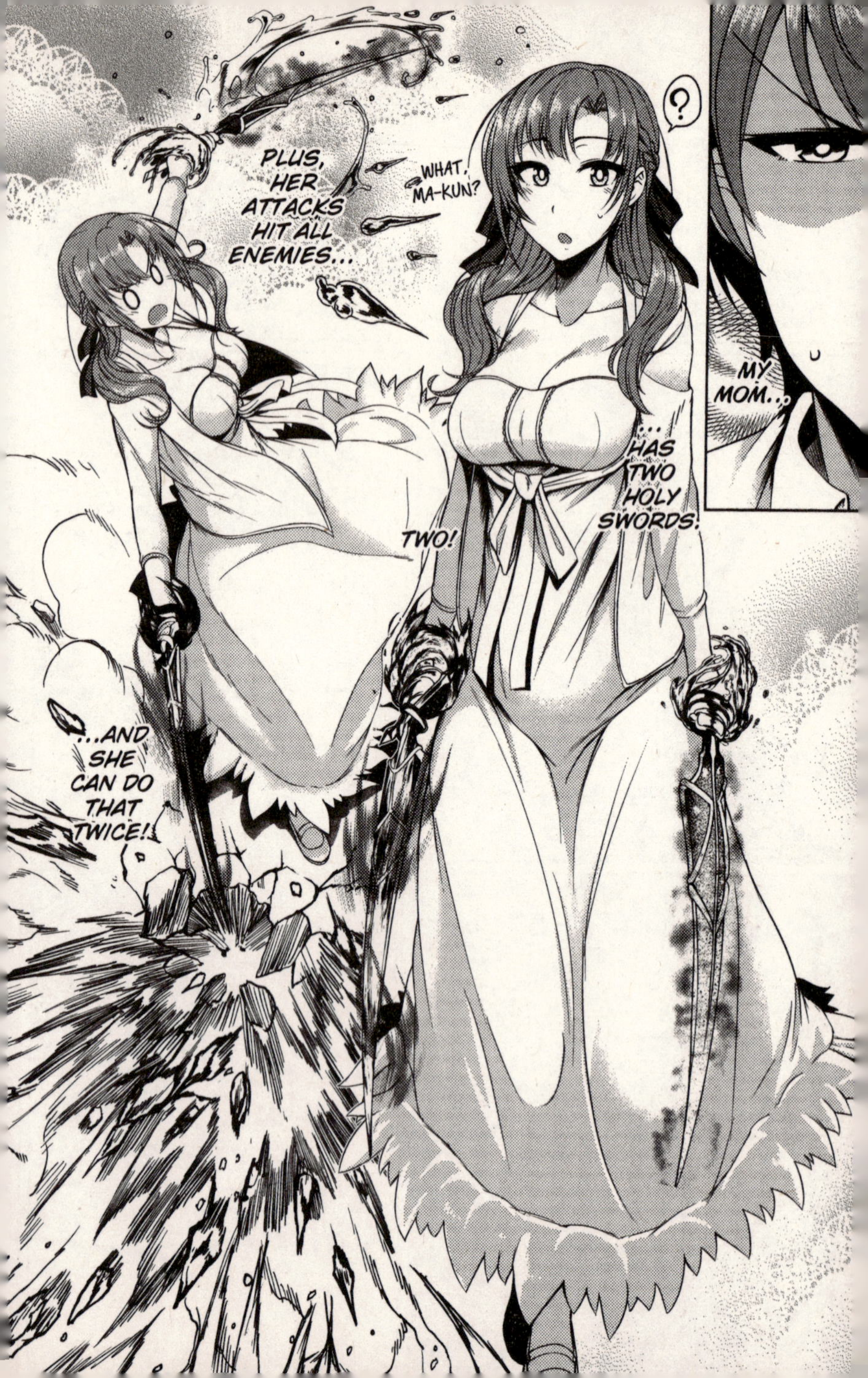
MY MOM...
...HAS TWO HOLY SWORDS!
?
WHAT, MA-KUN?
TWO!
PLUS, HER ATTACKS HIT ALL ENEMIES...
...AND SHE CAN DO THAT TWICE!

THE SWORD FIRES A HOMING BEAM, WHICH IS COOL!

I MANAGED TO BEAT ONE ENEMY DURING THAT BATTLE...

IT'S COOL, BUT...

WHILE MY SWORD...

KACHA (SHNK)

...I PALE BY COMPARISON!

HNGG.

IF SHE BEATS ALL THE ENEMIES BEFORE I GET AN ATTACK OFF...

MA-KUN! CHEER UP!

YOUR ATTACK WAS AMAZING!

THAT CLEAR THING WENT "WHOOSH," AND I WAS SO SUR-PRISED!

IT WAS VERY COOL!

BUN (SHAKE)

BUN (SHAKE)

PLEASE STOP TRYING TO CHEER ME UP.

HEH.

THIS IS JUST... SAD.

WHY NOT JUST LET MOM DO IT ALL BY HERSELF?

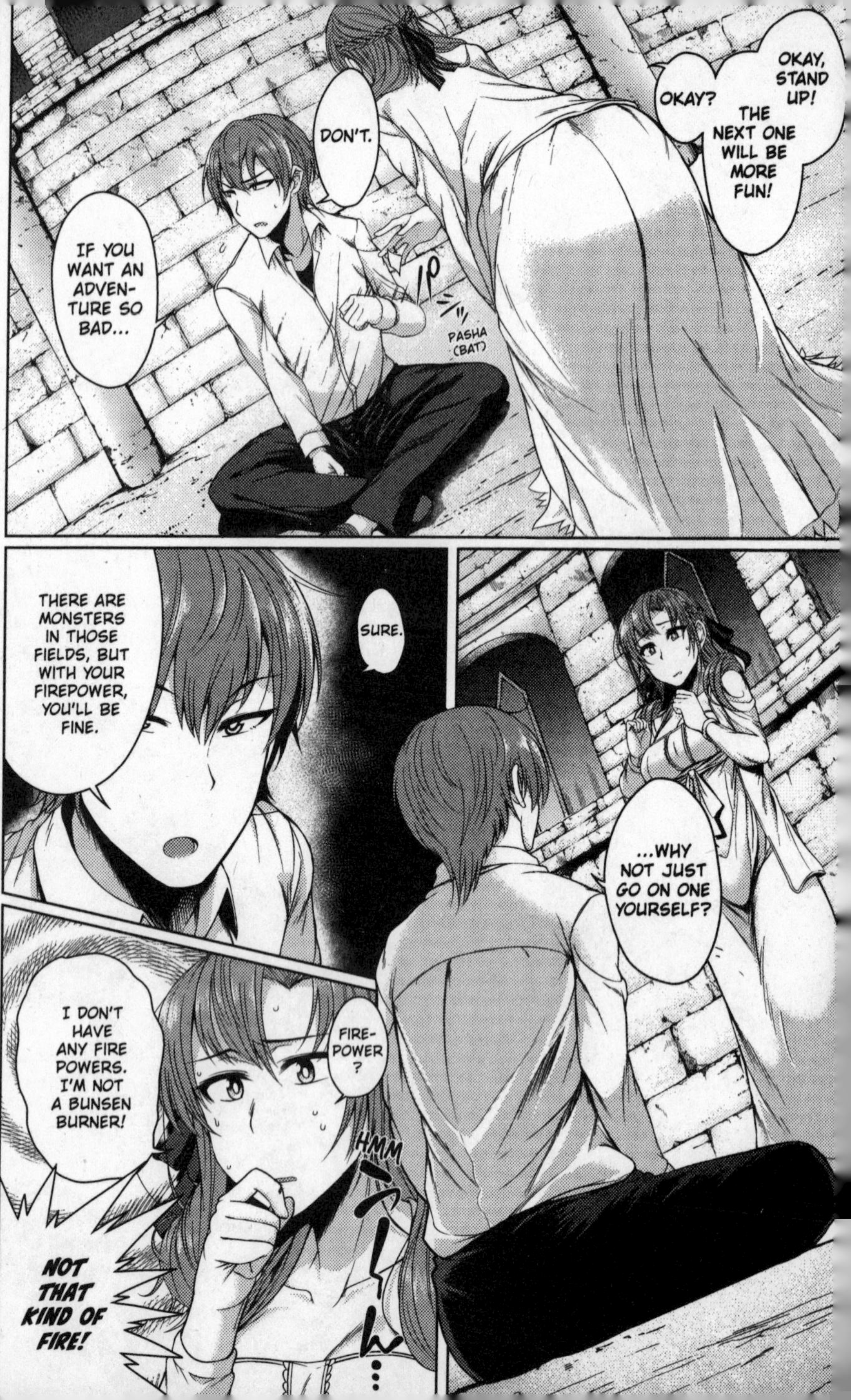
OKAY, STAND UP! THE NEXT ONE WILL BE MORE FUN!
OKAY?
DON'T.
PASHA (BAT)
IF YOU WANT AN ADVENTURE SO BAD...
...WHY NOT JUST GO ON ONE YOURSELF?
SURE.
THERE ARE MONSTERS IN THOSE FIELDS, BUT WITH YOUR FIREPOWER, YOU'LL BE FINE.
FIRE-POWER?
I DON'T HAVE ANY FIRE POWERS. I'M NOT A BUNSEN BURNER!
HMM
NOT THAT KIND OF FIRE!

YOU GO ON AHEAD.

I'LL COME ALONG LATER.

"FIRE-POWER" MEANS... OH, NEVER MIND.

I DON'T KNOW WHAT TO DO WHEN YOU'RE LIKE THIS.

AWAWA (PANIC)

HERO (FLUSTER) HERO

PETAN (FOOMP)

OH...?

GORON (FLOP)

JUST LEAVE ME ALONE.

MA-KUN!?

HERE IT IS!

WHAT TO DO WHEN YOUR HERO SON DOESN'T WANT TO ADVENTURE WITH YOU...

STRAT-EGY TIPS...

UM...

UM...

OH, THAT'S RIGHT!

PARA PARA PARA (FLIP)

REALLY!? WHAT KINDA GUIDE-BOOK IS THAT!?

GYO (SHOCK)

IT'S NOT GONNA BE THAT SPECIFIC!

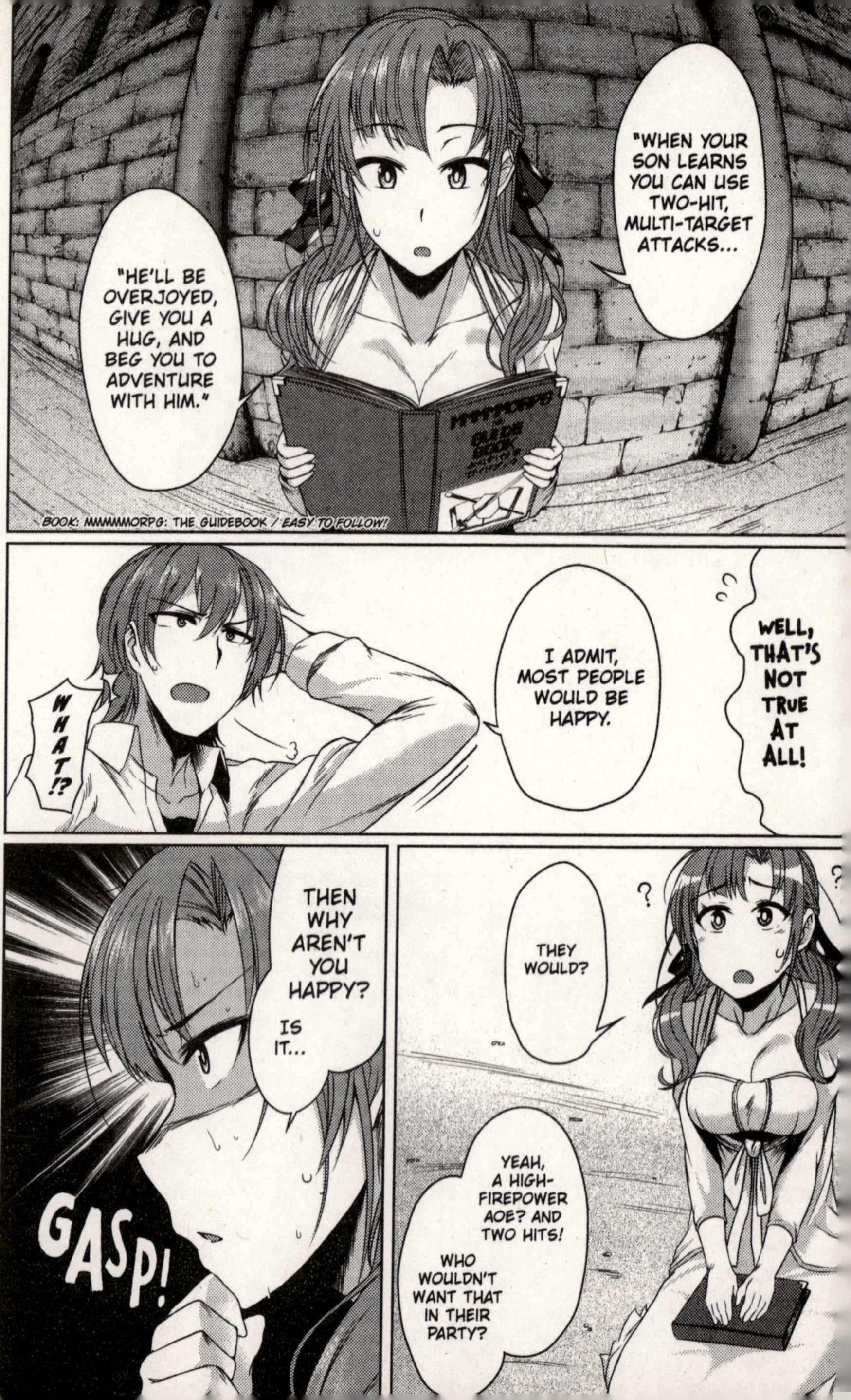
"WHEN YOUR SON LEARNS YOU CAN USE TWO-HIT, MULTI-TARGET ATTACKS...
"HE'LL BE OVERJOYED, GIVE YOU A HUG, AND BEG YOU TO ADVENTURE WITH HIM."
BOOK: MMMMMORPG: THE GUIDEBOOK / EASY TO FOLLOW!
WELL, THAT'S NOT TRUE AT ALL!
I ADMIT, MOST PEOPLE WOULD BE HAPPY.
WHAT!?
THEY WOULD?
YEAH, A HIGH-FIREPOWER AOE? AND TWO HITS!
WHO WOULDN'T WANT THAT IN THEIR PARTY?
THEN WHY AREN'T YOU HAPPY?
IS IT...
GASP!

IS IT BECAUSE...
GAAAN (DUN)
...I'M YOUR MOM!?
GAAAN
GAAAN
MM-HMM.
THAT IS EXACTLY MY BIGGEST PROBLEM.
CAN I ASK YOU SOMETHING?
CAN YOU EXPLAIN THIS?
E-EXPLAIN WHAT?
ALL OF THIS. WHAT'S GOING ON HERE?
THEY TOLD YOU EVERYTHING, RIGHT?
W-WELL...
UM...

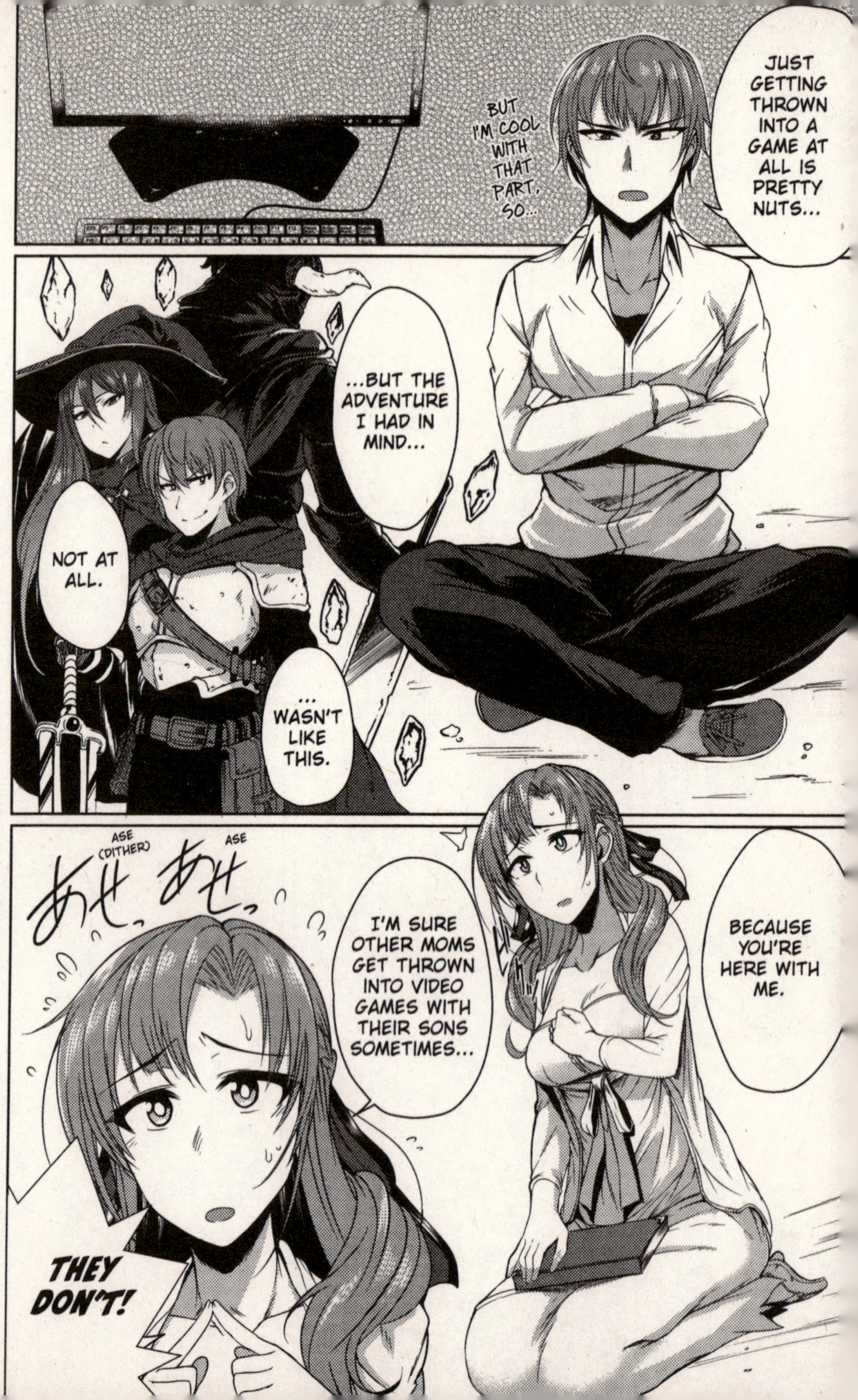
JUST GETTING THROWN INTO A GAME AT ALL IS PRETTY NUTS...
BUT I'M COOL WITH THAT PART, SO...
...BUT THE ADVENTURE I HAD IN MIND...
...WASN'T LIKE THIS.
NOT AT ALL.
BECAUSE YOU'RE HERE WITH ME.
I'M SURE OTHER MOMS GET THROWN INTO VIDEO GAMES WITH THEIR SONS SOMETIMES...
ASE (DITHER) ASE
あせっ あせっ
THEY DON'T!

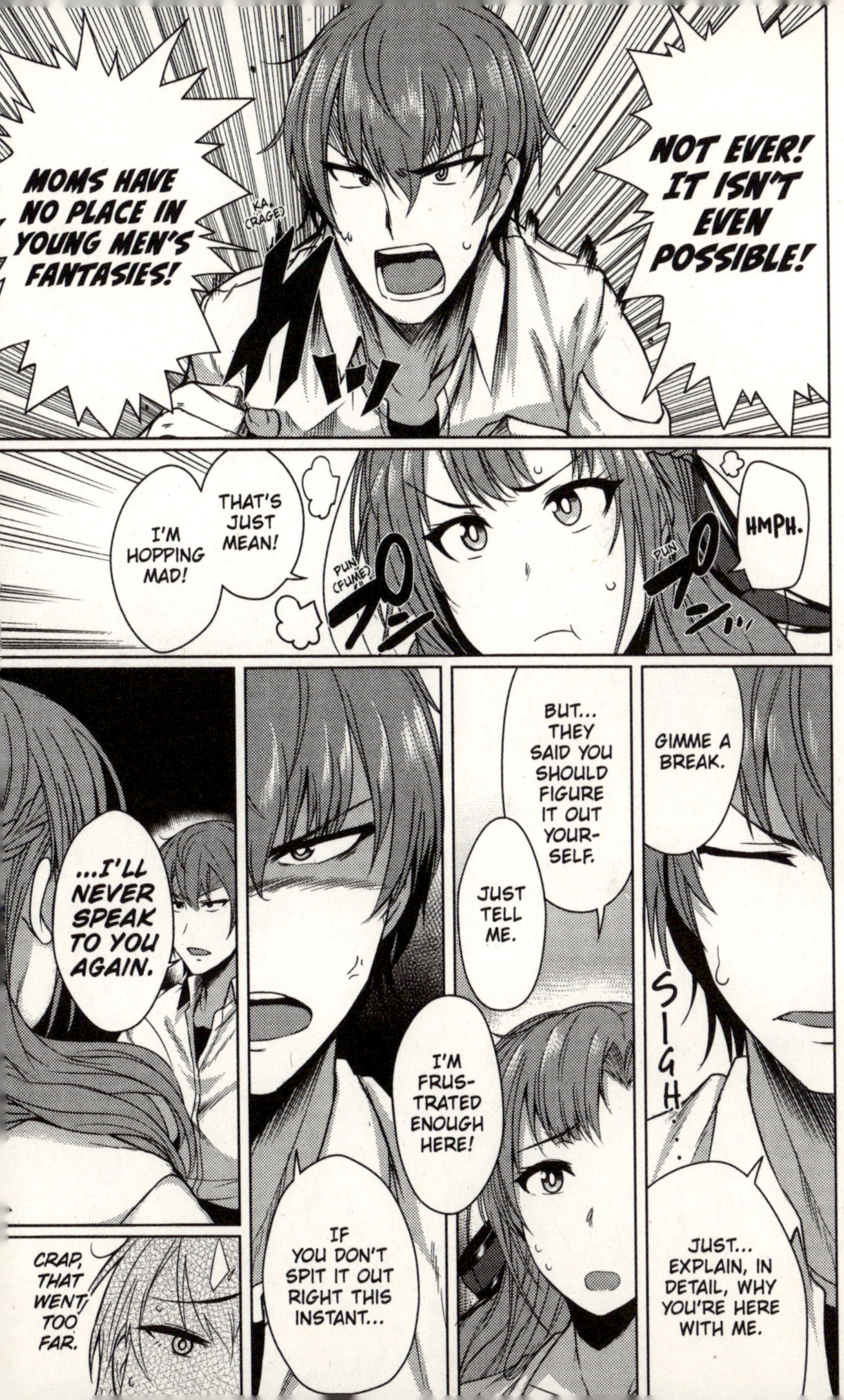
NOT EVER! IT ISN'T EVEN POSSIBLE!
KA (RAGE)
MOMS HAVE NO PLACE IN YOUNG MEN'S FANTASIES!
HMPH.
PUN
PUN (FUME)
THAT'S JUST MEAN!
I'M HOPPING MAD!
GIMME A BREAK.
SIGH
JUST... EXPLAIN, IN DETAIL, WHY YOU'RE HERE WITH ME.
BUT... THEY SAID YOU SHOULD FIGURE IT OUT YOUR-SELF.
JUST TELL ME.
I'M FRUS-TRATED ENOUGH HERE!
IF YOU DON'T SPIT IT OUT RIGHT THIS INSTANT...
...I'LL NEVER SPEAK TO YOU AGAIN.
CRAP, THAT WENT TOO FAR.

I'M SORRY.
ポタタ
POTATA (DRIP)
I JUST DON'T KNOW HOW OR WHAT TO EXPLAIN.
I'M SORRY, MA-KUN.
I DON'T KNOW HOW MUCH I CAN TELL YOU.

SHIRASE-SAN AND HER PEOPLE HAVE A LOT GOING ON AND...
O-OKAY!
PORO
PORO (DRIP)
AWAWA (FLUSTER)
I GET IT. IF YOU CAN'T SAY...
I JUST WANT TO GET ALONG WITH YOU, MA-KUN.
I WON'T EVER TRICK OR DO ANYTHING TO HURT YOU.
WILL YOU BELIEVE THAT, AT LEAST?
SO...
PLEASE JUST...
GYU (CLENCH)
NEVER SAY ANYTHING THAT AWFUL EVER AGAIN.
THAT WAS THE WORST THING ANYONE'S EVER SAID TO ME...
...IN MY WHOLE LIFE.
IT BROKE MY HEART.

GABA (BOW)

I'M REALLY SORRY.

SORRY.

IT JUST CAME OUT...

SU (SHF)

I NEVER MEANT TO SAY THAT!

PEKO (GROVEL)

I DIDN'T MEAN THAT!

PEKO

PEKO

MOMMY LOVES IT...

...WHEN YOU'RE BEING CONSIDERATE, MA-KUN.

HEH.

NADE (RUB)
NADE

MA-KUN, ENOUGH. HEAD UP!

I DIDN'T MEAN IT...AT ALL.

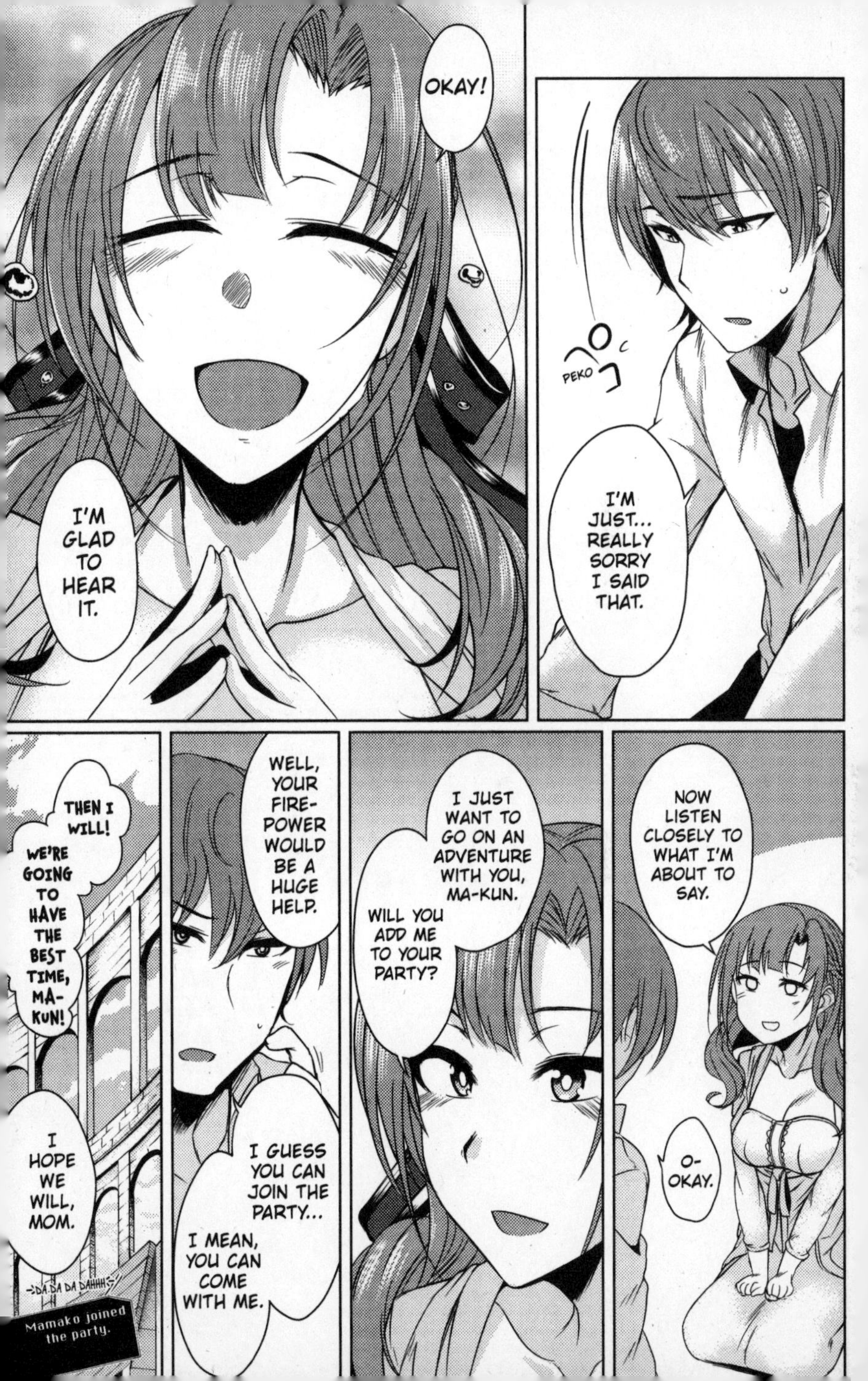
PEKO
I'M JUST... REALLY SORRY I SAID THAT.
OKAY!
I'M GLAD TO HEAR IT.
NOW LISTEN CLOSELY TO WHAT I'M ABOUT TO SAY.
O-OKAY.
I JUST WANT TO GO ON AN ADVENTURE WITH YOU, MA-KUN.
WILL YOU ADD ME TO YOUR PARTY?
WELL, YOUR FIRE-POWER WOULD BE A HUGE HELP.
I GUESS YOU CAN JOIN THE PARTY...
I MEAN, YOU CAN COME WITH ME.
THEN I WILL!
WE'RE GOING TO HAVE THE BEST TIME, MA-KUN!
I HOPE WE WILL, MOM.
DA DA DA DAHHH
Mamako joined the party.

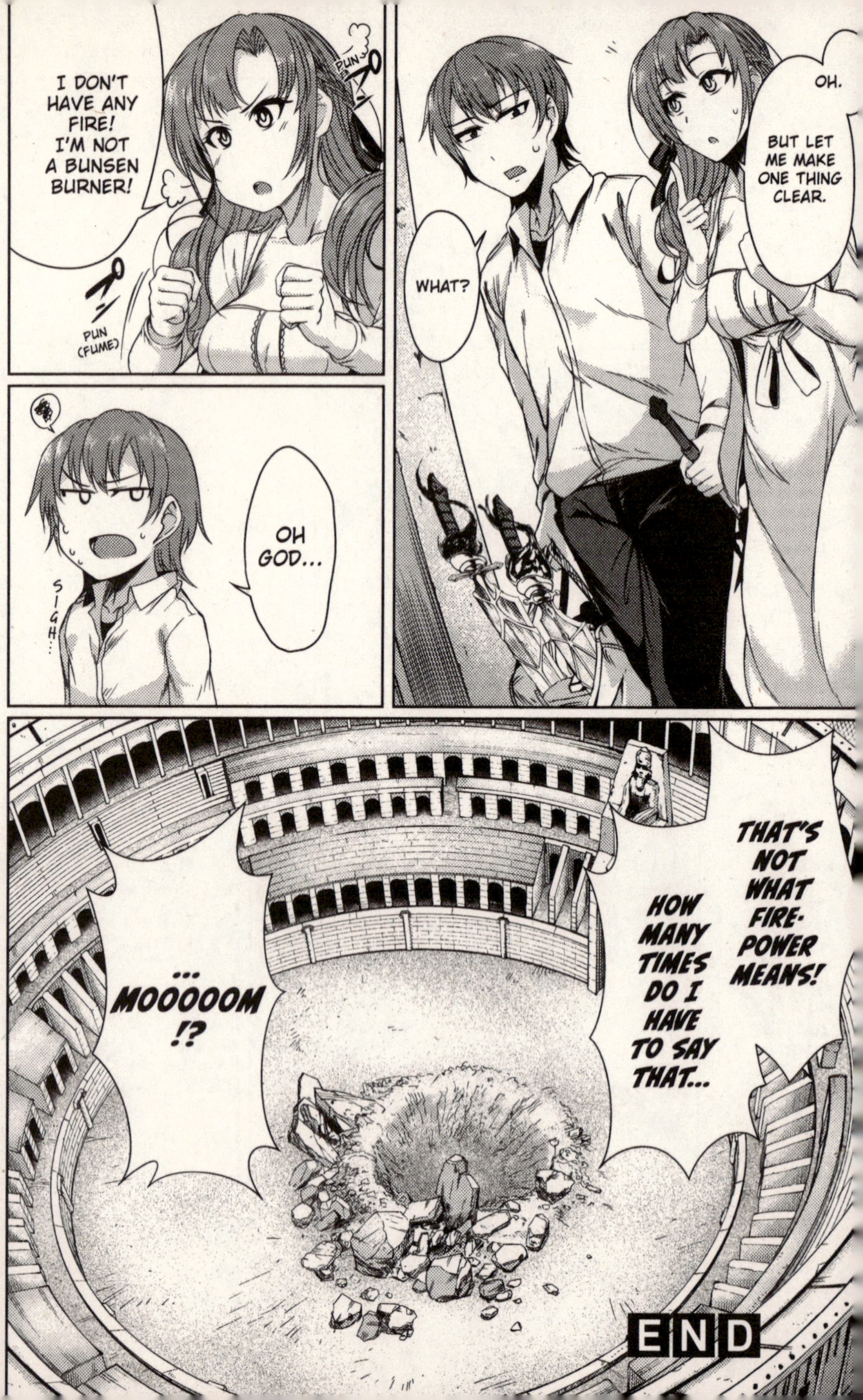
OH.
BUT LET ME MAKE ONE THING CLEAR.
WHAT?
I DON'T HAVE ANY FIRE! I'M NOT A BUNSEN BURNER!
PUN
PUN (FUME)
OH GOD...
SIGH...
THAT'S NOT WHAT FIRE-POWER MEANS!
HOW MANY TIMES DO I HAVE TO SAY THAT...
...MOOOOOM!?
END

ASE (OTHER) あせ、 ASE あせっ

I'M SURE OTHER MOMS GET THROWN INTO VIDEO GAMES WITH THEIR SONS SOMETIMES...

THEY DON'T!

DO YOU LOVE YOUR MOM AND
HER TWO-HIT, MULTI-TARGET ATTACKS?

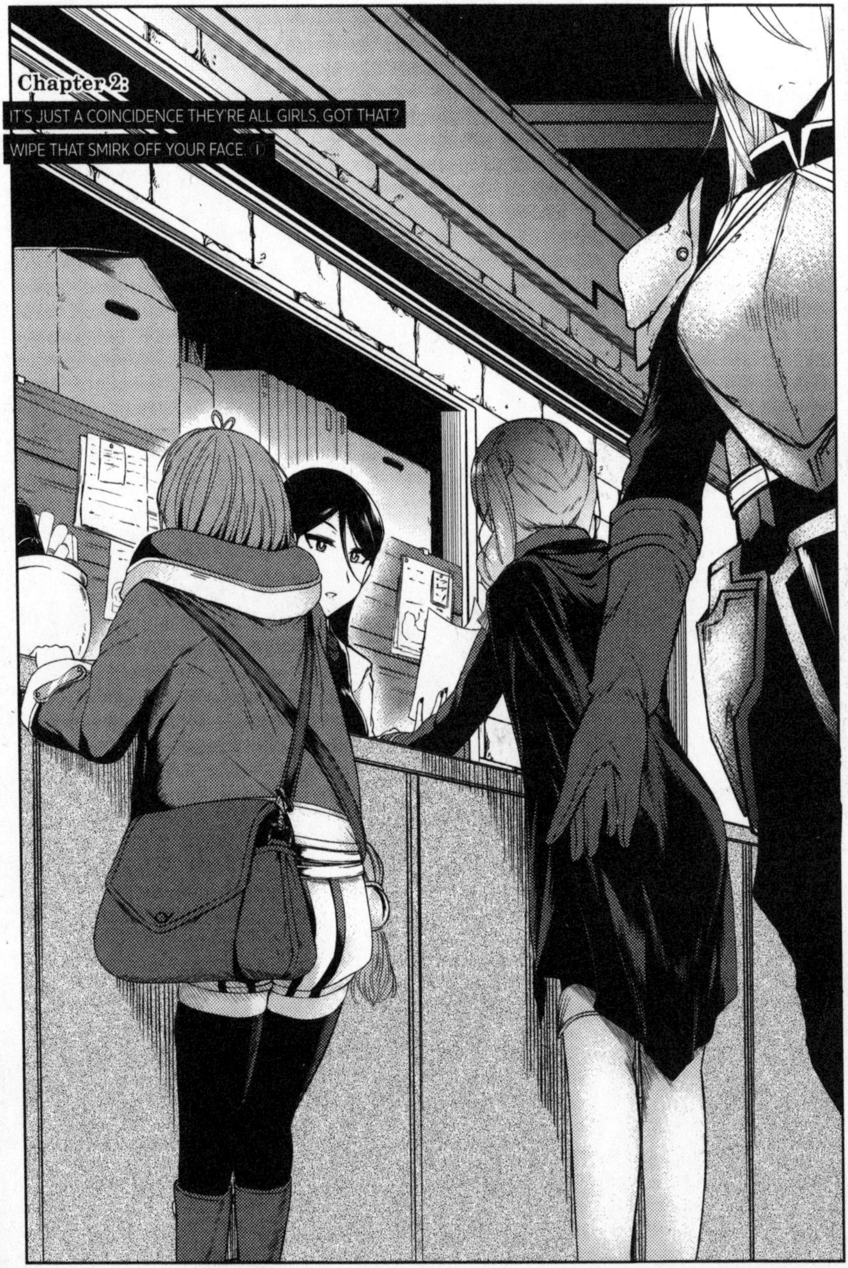
Chapter 2:
IT'S JUST A COINCIDENCE THEY'RE ALL GIRLS. GOT THAT?
WIPE THAT SMIRK OFF YOUR FACE. ①

OH, HEY, MA-KUN!
THIS BOOK SAYS TIME IN THE GAME AND THE REAL WORLD ARE THE SAME!
OH?
I SEE...
SO, MOM...
WE GOING THE RIGHT WAY?
YES, ACCORDING TO THE BOOK, AT LEAST.
OH?

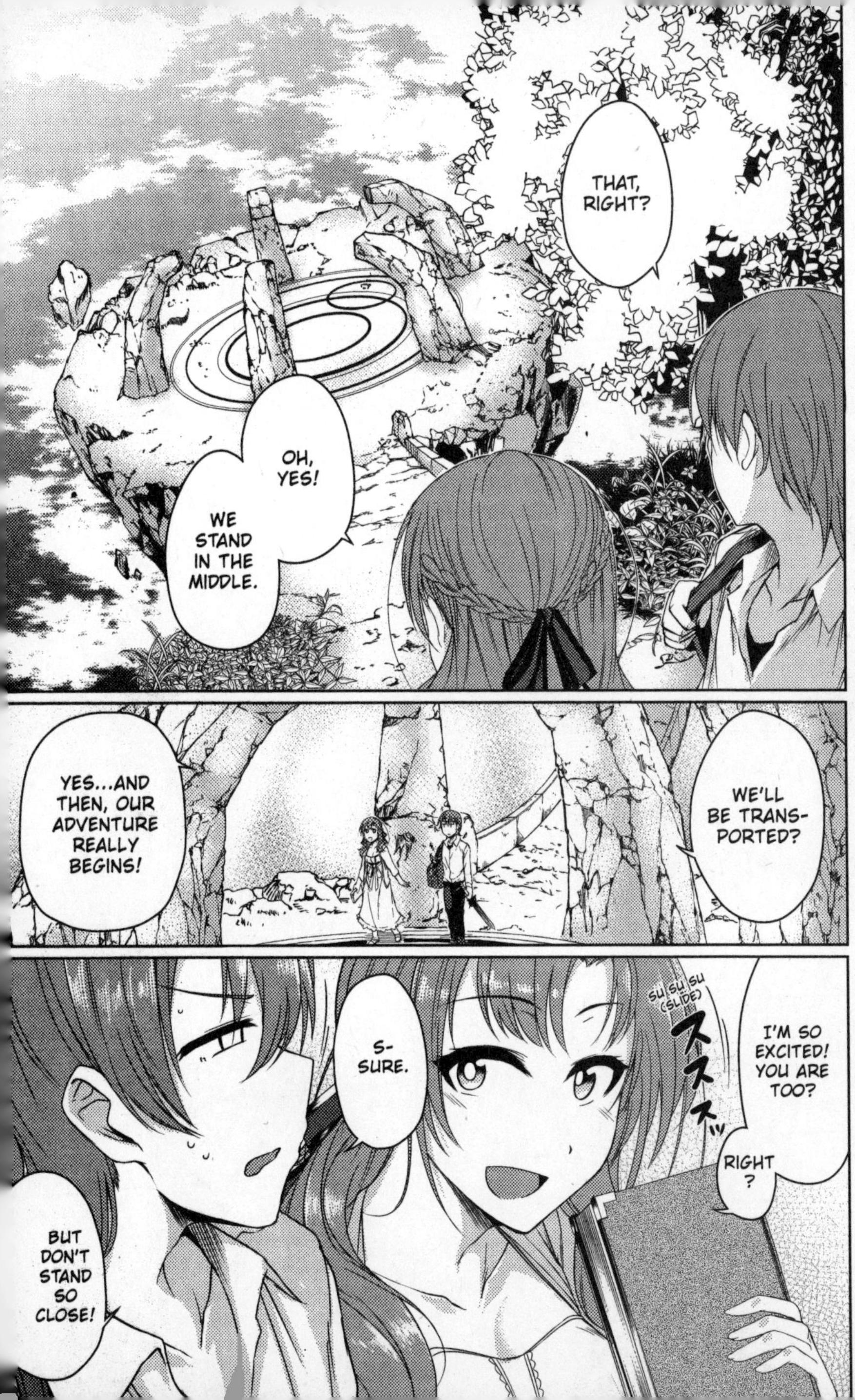
THAT, RIGHT?
OH, YES!
WE STAND IN THE MIDDLE.
WE'LL BE TRANSPORTED?
YES...AND THEN, OUR ADVENTURE REALLY BEGINS!
I'M SO EXCITED! YOU ARE TOO?
RIGHT?
SU SU SU (SLIDE)
スススッ
S-SURE.
BUT DON'T STAND SO CLOSE!

OH!
POWUU (VOOOOM)
HERE WE GO.
THIS BOOK SAYS OUR NEXT STOP IS THE KINGDOM OF CATHARN.
...
REALLY?
THE KINGDOM OF CATHARN...
I WONDER...
PASHUU (VOOOSHH)
...WHAT IT'S LIKE.

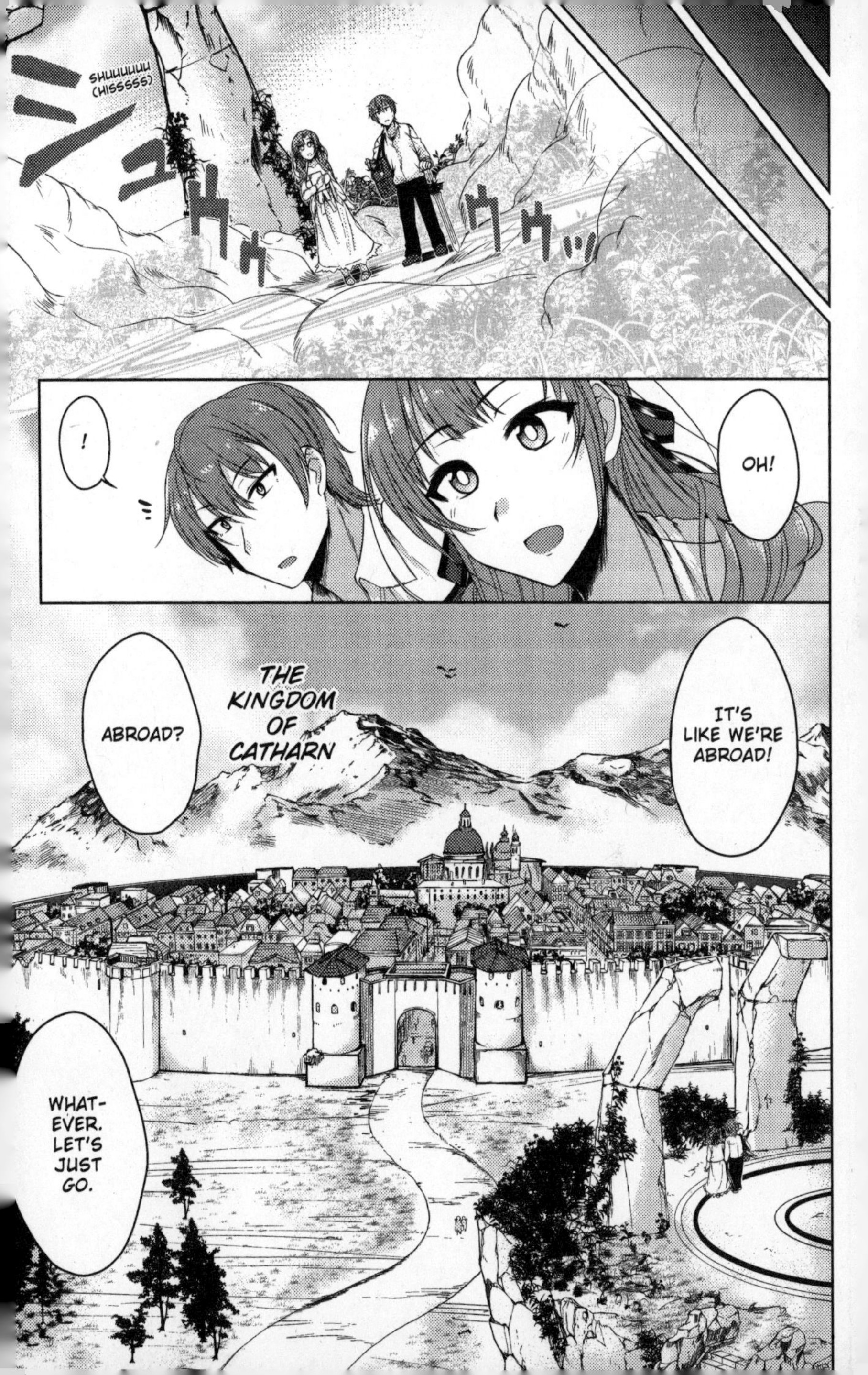
SHUUUUUUU (HISSSSS)
OH!
!
IT'S LIKE WE'RE ABROAD!
THE KINGDOM OF CATHARN
ABROAD?
WHAT-EVER. LET'S JUST GO.

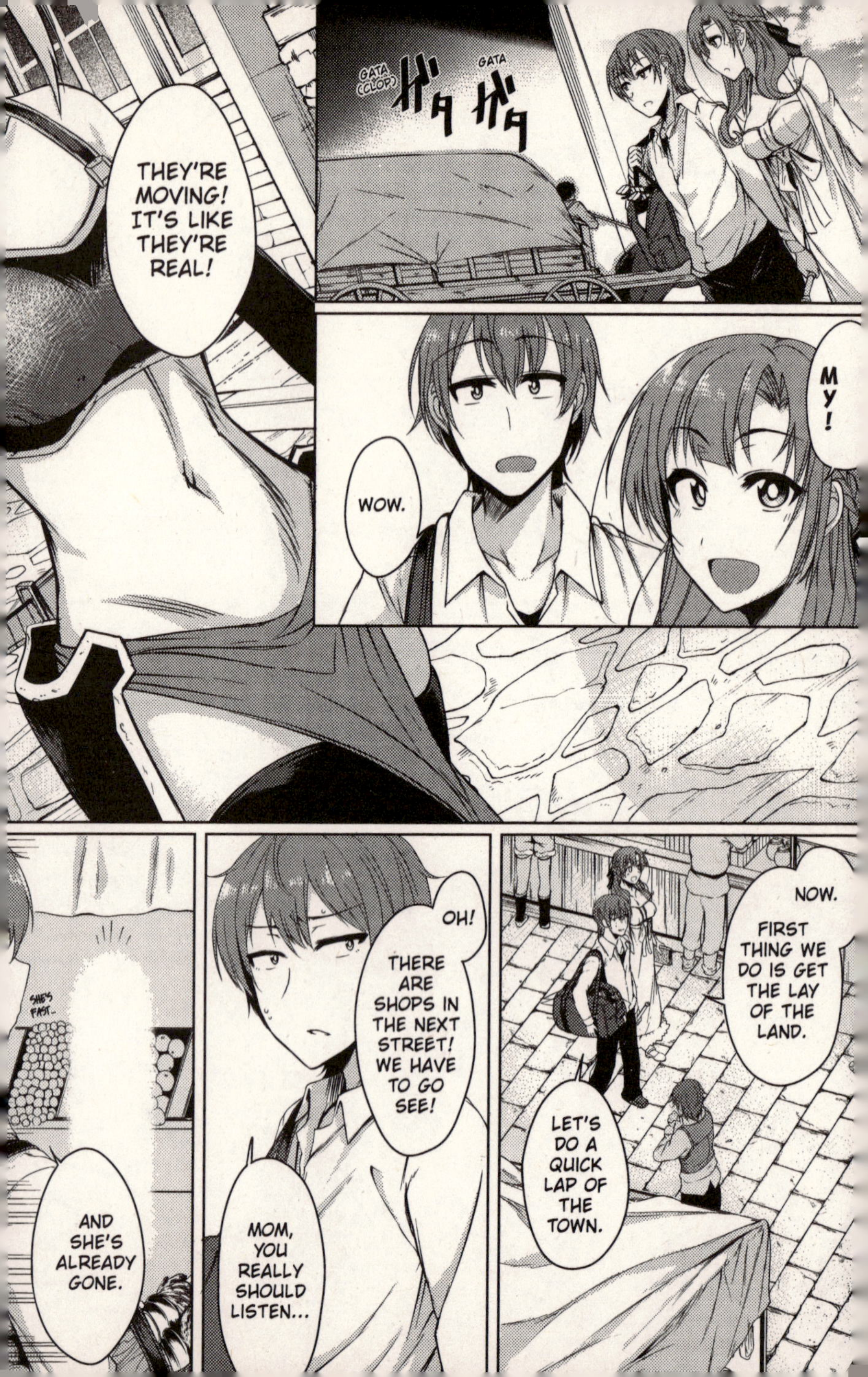

GATA (CLOP)
ガタ
GATA
ガタ
MY!
WOW.
THEY'RE MOVING! IT'S LIKE THEY'RE REAL!
NOW.
FIRST THING WE DO IS GET THE LAY OF THE LAND.
LET'S DO A QUICK LAP OF THE TOWN.
OH!
THERE ARE SHOPS IN THE NEXT STREET! WE HAVE TO GO SEE!
MOM, YOU REALLY SHOULD LISTEN...
SHE'S FAST...
AND SHE'S ALREADY GONE.

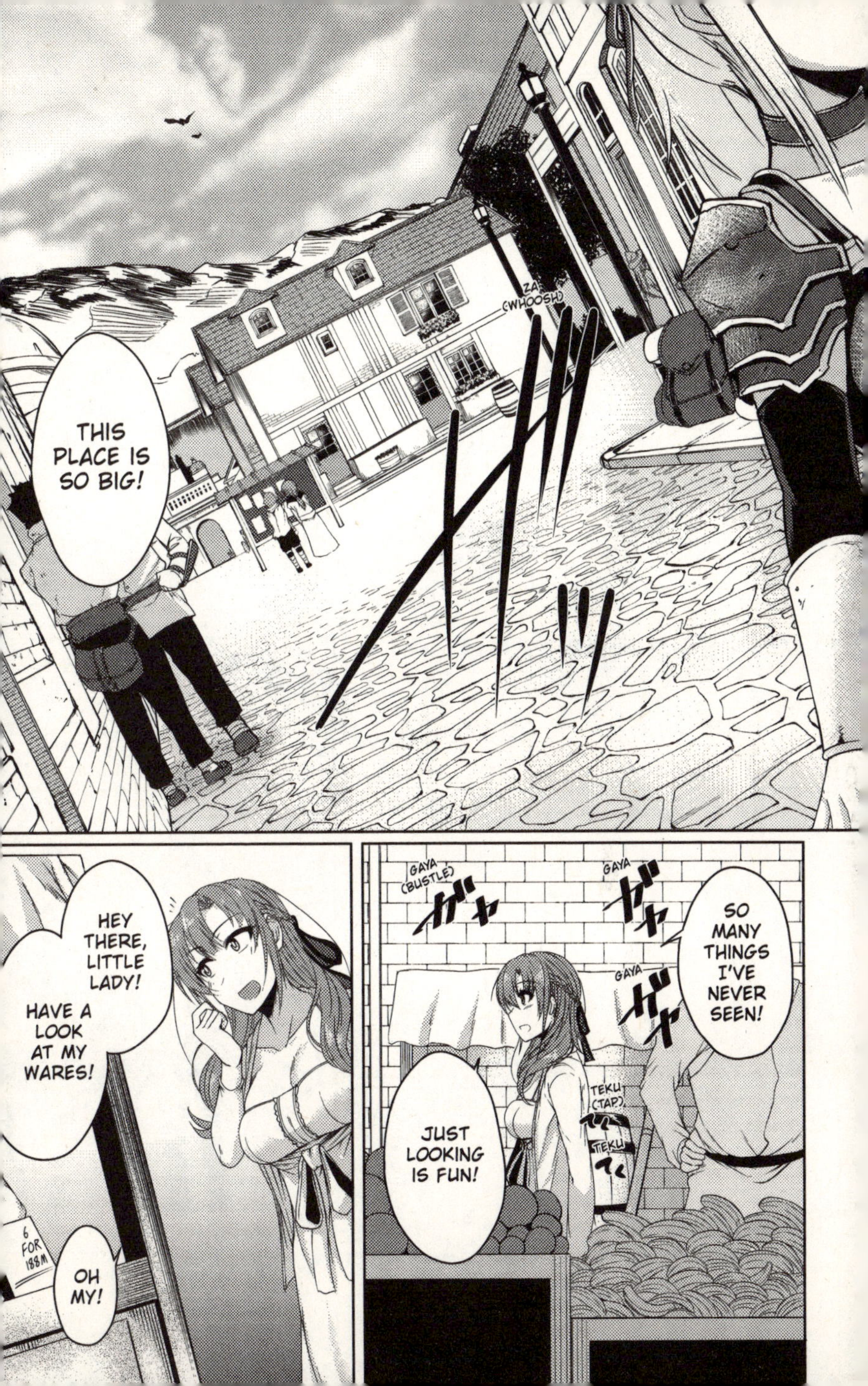
ZA (WHOOSH)
THIS PLACE IS SO BIG!
GAYA
GAYA
SO MANY THINGS I'VE NEVER SEEN!
GAYA (BUSTLE)
TEKU (TAP)
TEKU
JUST LOOKING IS FUN!
HEY THERE, LITTLE LADY!
HAVE A LOOK AT MY WARES!
6 FOR 188M
OH MY!

OH, YOU HAVE NORMAL FOOD FOR SALE TOO!
THEY'RE ALL FRESH!
SIGN: FRESH EGGS
THAT'S SOME UNUSUAL GARB YOU HAVE ON. YOU A TRAVELER?
HA
HA
HA
THERE'S A DISCOUNT FOR BEAUTIFUL LITTLE LADIES LIKE YOU!
OH MY! LITTLE LADY?
I MAY NOT LOOK IT...
...BUT I'VE GOT A SON THIS BIG!
OH, THERE...
...YOU ARE.
HUNH!?
HE'S YOUR SON!?
YOU'RE A MOM!?
YES, AND WE'RE IN A PARTY TOGETHER!
I'VE JOINED MY SON'S PARTY! ISN'T IT LOVELY?
ERRR...
SFX: GO GO GO (RUMBLE)
YOU'RE CONFUSING THE POOR MAN.
OKAY!
GUI (SHOVE)
LET'S GO! FORWARD!
GUI

SORRY! MAYBE NEXT TIME!

COME ON UP!

TAKE A LOOK!

YEAH.

NOW THAT I LOOK...

...THIS IS DEFINITELY A FANTASY RPG.

ARMOR AND WEAPONS ON SALE EVERY-WHERE.

HEY, MA-KUN!

I-I WASN'T!

THAT ISN'T WHY...!

NOW NOW

DON'T STARE AT GIRLS' BACKSIDES! THEY'LL THINK YOU'RE A CREEP!

DOKI (BABUMP)
DOKI!

OH, THAT GIRL MUST BE A MAGE! MY KIND OF FANTASY!

I'M REALLY INSIDE A GAME!

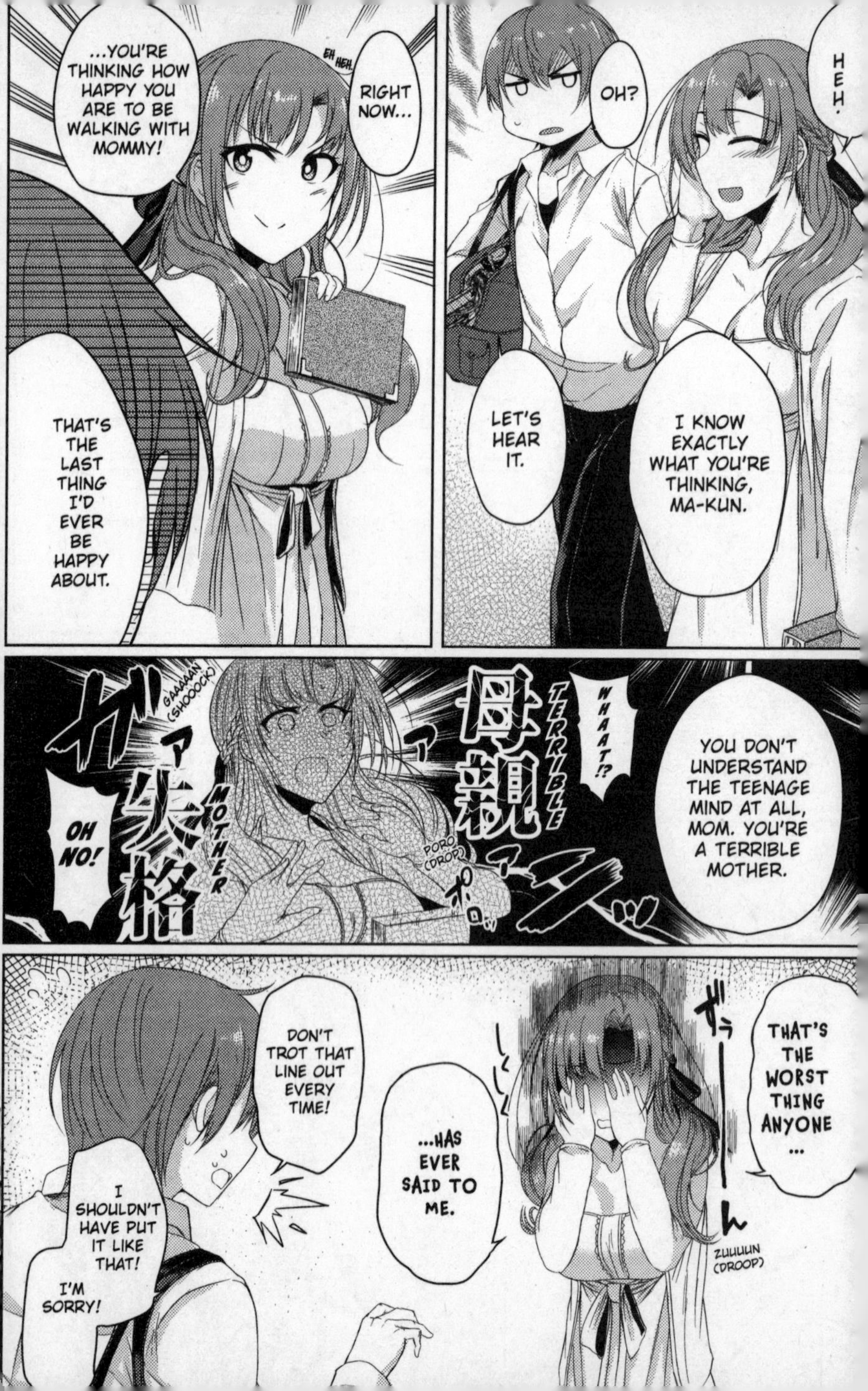
HEH.
I KNOW EXACTLY WHAT YOU'RE THINKING, MA-KUN.
OH?
LET'S HEAR IT.
RIGHT NOW...
EH HEH.
...YOU'RE THINKING HOW HAPPY YOU ARE TO BE WALKING WITH MOMMY!
THAT'S THE LAST THING I'D EVER BE HAPPY ABOUT.
YOU DON'T UNDERSTAND THE TEENAGE MIND AT ALL, MOM. YOU'RE A TERRIBLE MOTHER.
WHAAT!?
母親
TERRIBLE
失格
MOTHER
PORO (DROP)
GAAAAAN (SHOOOCK)
OH NO!
THAT'S THE WORST THING ANYONE ...
ZUUUUN (DROOP)
...HAS EVER SAID TO ME.
DON'T TROT THAT LINE OUT EVERY TIME!
I SHOULDN'T HAVE PUT IT LIKE THAT!
I'M SORRY!

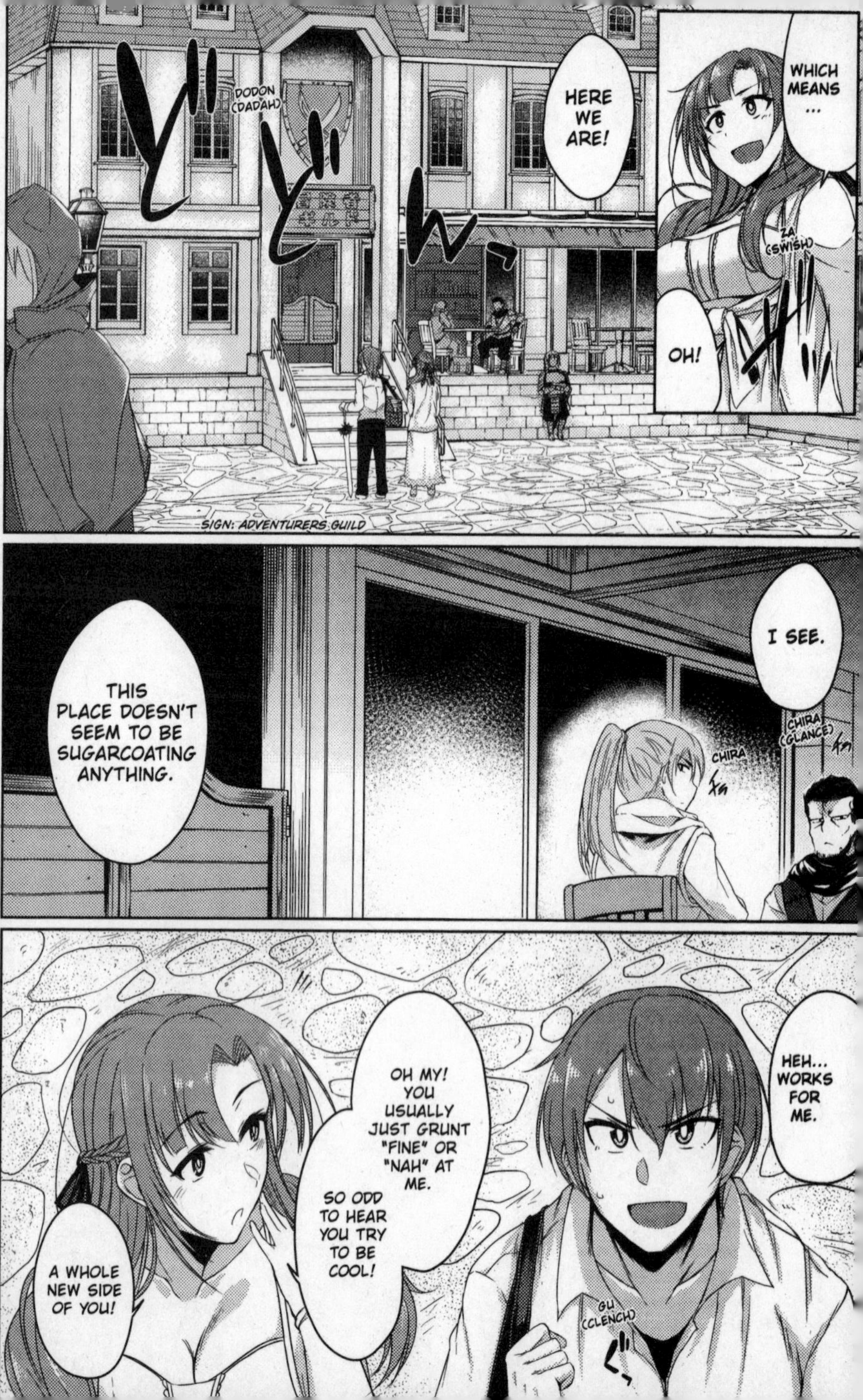
WHICH MEANS ...
ZA (SWISH)
OH!
HERE WE ARE!
DODON (DADAH)
SIGN: ADVENTURERS GUILD
I SEE.
CHIRA (GLANCE)
CHIRA
THIS PLACE DOESN'T SEEM TO BE SUGARCOATING ANYTHING.
HEH... WORKS FOR ME.
OH MY! YOU USUALLY JUST GRUNT "FINE" OR "NAH" AT ME.
SO ODD TO HEAR YOU TRY TO BE COOL!
A WHOLE NEW SIDE OF YOU!
GU (CLENCH)

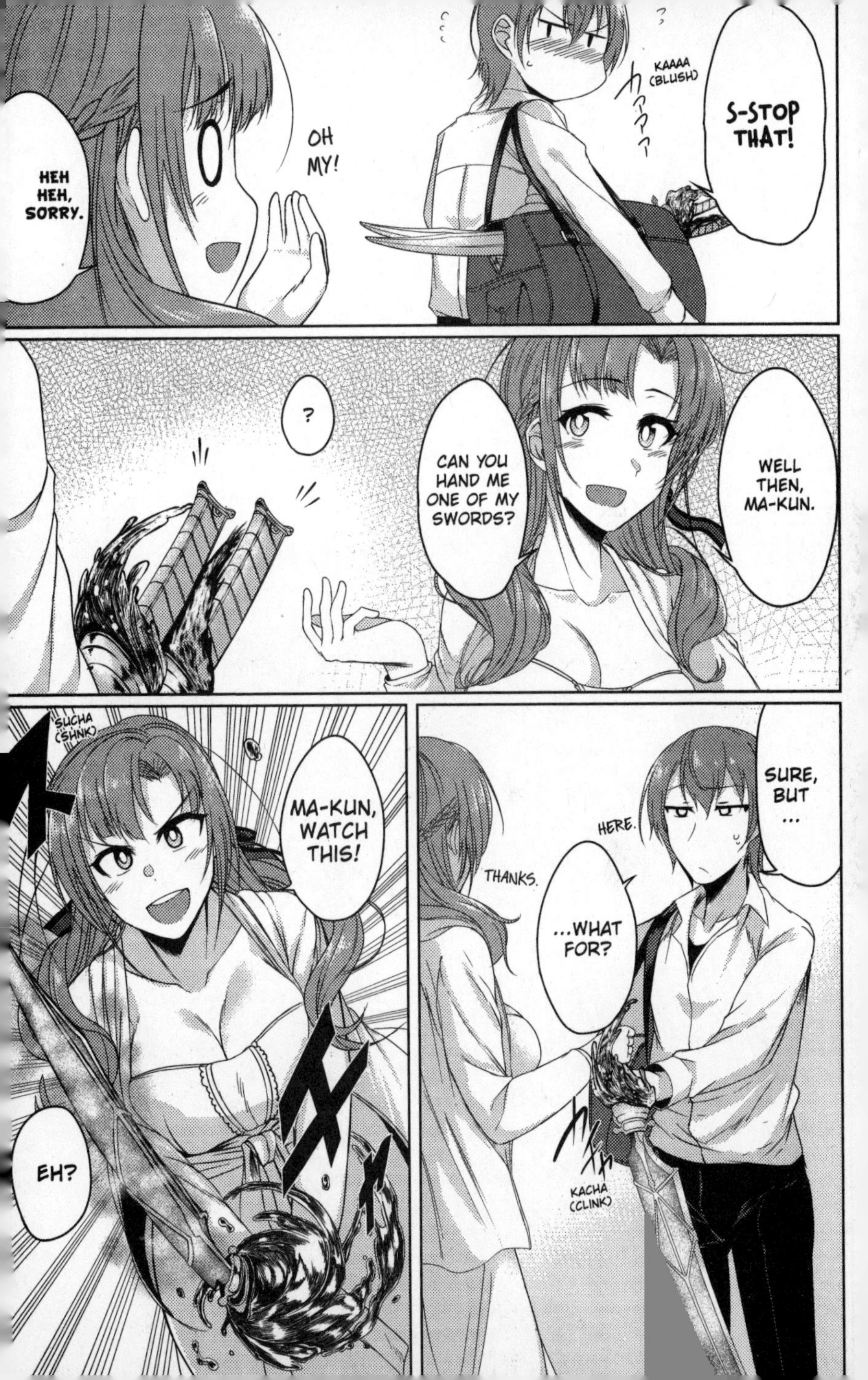
S-STOP THAT!
KAAAA (BLUSH)
OH MY!
HEH HEH, SORRY.
WELL THEN, MA-KUN.
CAN YOU HAND ME ONE OF MY SWORDS?
?
SURE, BUT ...
HERE.
...WHAT FOR?
THANKS.
KACHA (CLINK)
SUCHA (SHNK)
MA-KUN, WATCH THIS!
EH?

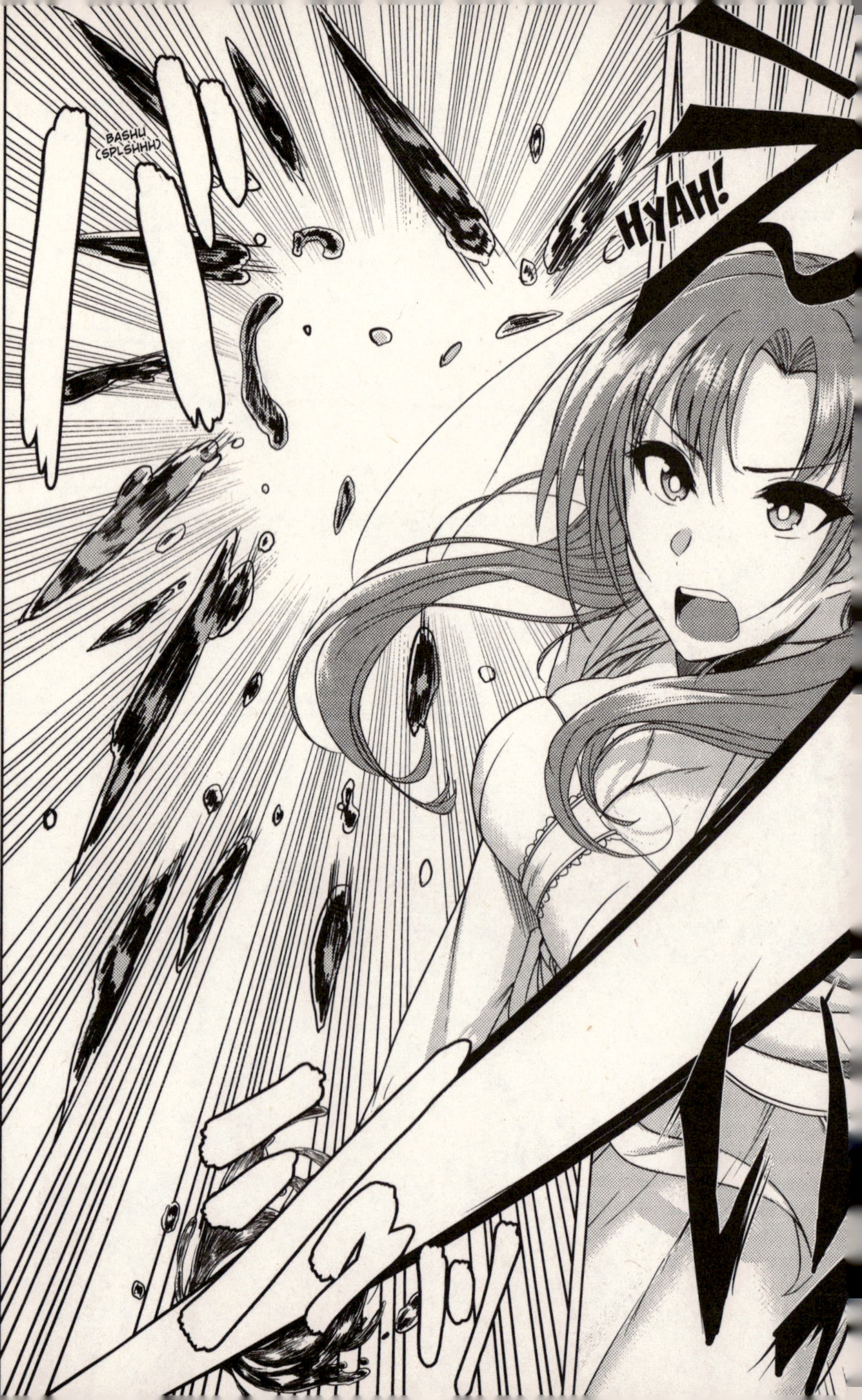
HYAH!
BASHU
(SPLSHHH)

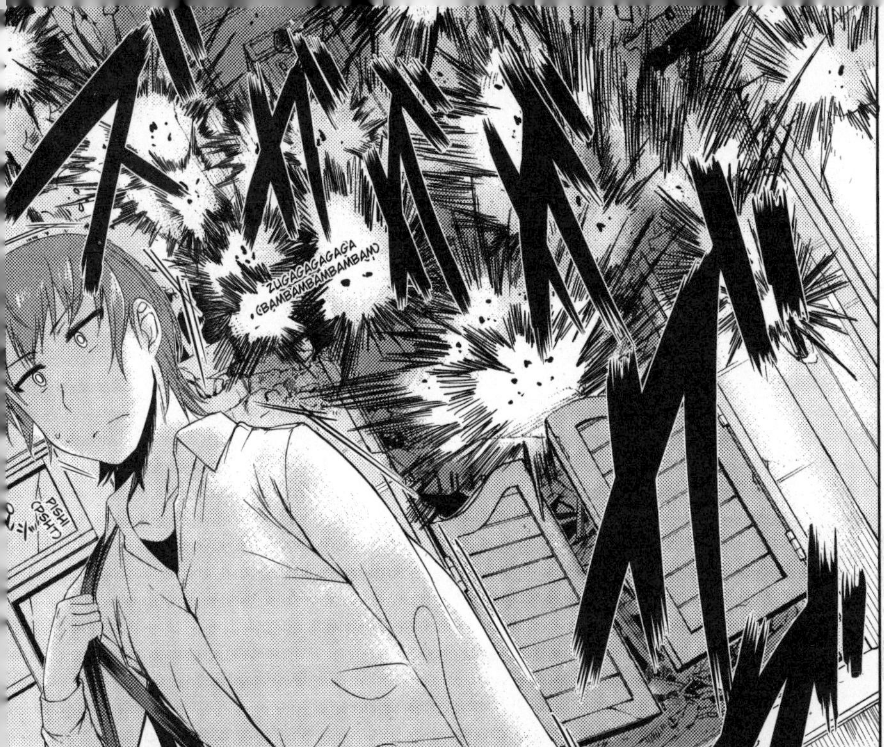
ZUGAGAGAGAGA (BAMBAMBAMBAM)
PISHI (PSHT)
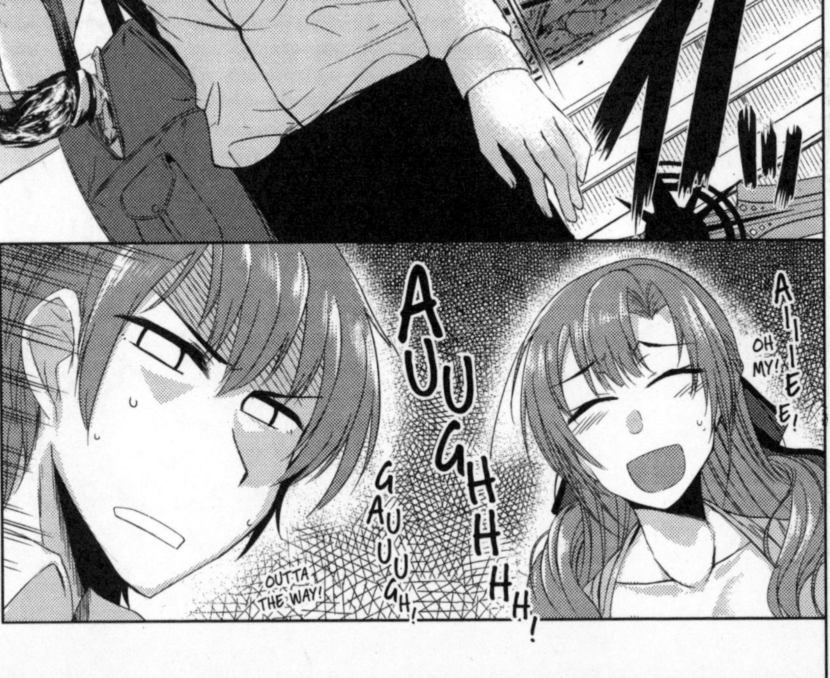
AIIIEE!
OH MY!
AUUGHHHH!
GAUUUGH!
OUTTA THE WAY!

ZUGA (BAN)
GA
GA
GA
GA
PISHI (PSHT)
AIIIEE!
OH MY!
AUUGHHHH!
GAUUUGH!
OUTTA THE WAY!

MA-KUN!

DID YOU SEE THAT!!?

WE CAN'T LET THEM LOOK DOWN ON US! THE GUIDEBOOK SAID TO START BY SHOWING OFF!

THAT'S NOT WHAT "SHOWING OFF" MEANS!

UH, MOM, WHY DID YOU...?

THIS IS SIMPLY PART OF THE PRESEN-TATION.
DOKU
DOKU (DRIP)
TRAVELERS, WELCOME TO THE ADVENTURERS GUILD.
I FEEL LIKE I SHOULD BE CONCERNED ABOUT YOU.
PATSU (BRUSH)
I CAN INFORFORM YOU THAT I AM THE RECEPTIONIST, SHIRARASE.
SHIRASE-SAN, YOU'RE BLEEDING A LOT—
POTA (PLOD)
POTA
SHIRARASE. NOT A PROBLEM. THIS WAY.
UH... OKAY...
END

YOU DON'T UNDERSTAND THE TEENAGE MIND AT ALL, MOM. YOU'RE A TERRIBLE MOTHER.
WHAAAT!?
PORO (DROP)
TERRIBLE MOTHER
OH NO!
GAAAAAN (SHOOOCK)

Do You Love Your Mom?

Chapter 2:

IT'S JUST A COINCIDENCE THEY'RE ALL GIRLS, GOT THAT? WIPE THAT SMIRK OFF YOUR FACE. ②

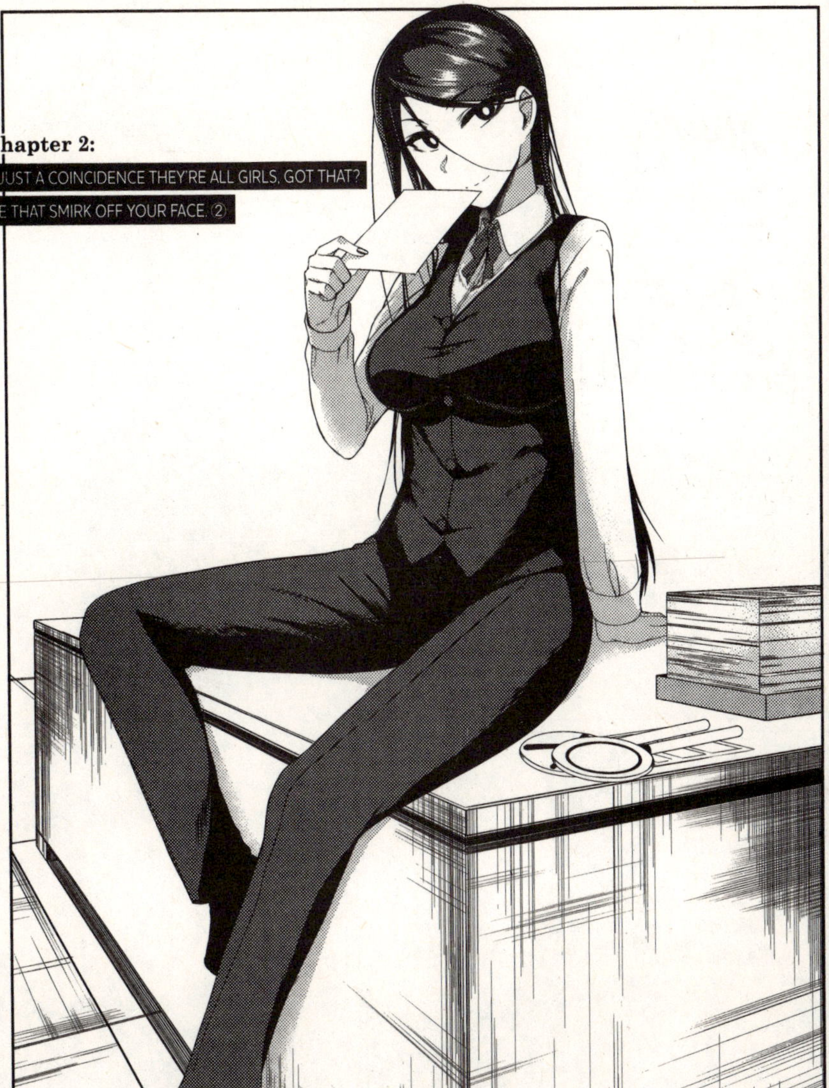

"WELCOME TO THE ADVENTURER GUILD."

"ONCE AGAIN."

SIGN: RECEPTION

"UH, SHI-RASE-SAN..."

SHIRARASE!

"I AM THE RECEPTIONIST, SHIRARASE. I HAVE INFORMED YOU OF THIS ALREADY."

"I AM FULLY CAPABLE OF PULLING UP A SELECTION OF ITEMS NO SON WOULD EVER WANT THEIR MOTHER KNOWING."

"'SHIRARASE' IT IS! WE'VE NEVER MET! WHAT A PLEASURE!"

PARA (CRUMBLE)
PARA
SO, UM...ARE YOU OKAY? YOU'VE BEEN BLEEDING THIS WHOLE TIME.
I'M FINE. PART OF THE PRESENTATION.
AND I AM CLASSIFIED AS AN OBJECT.
SO NO PK PENALTIES WILL BE APPLIED.
THE ABILITY TO DESTROY BUILDING OBJECTS IS ACTUALLY A BUG.
SO REST EASY.
I-I SEE. THAT'S A RELIEF!
WHEW!
ISN'T IT, MOM?
ER...
YES.
SO THERE WAS A GAME OF OBJECT? AND THE NEC'S PC WON THE PK PENALTY KICK?
GOAAAAAL
IT REALLY DOESN'T MATTER, SO LET'S GO WITH THAT!
I AM TO UNDERSTAND YOU ARE HERE SEARCHING FOR NEW PARTY MEMBERS?
UH, YEAH. THAT'S RIGHT.
GOSHI (RUB)
GOSHI

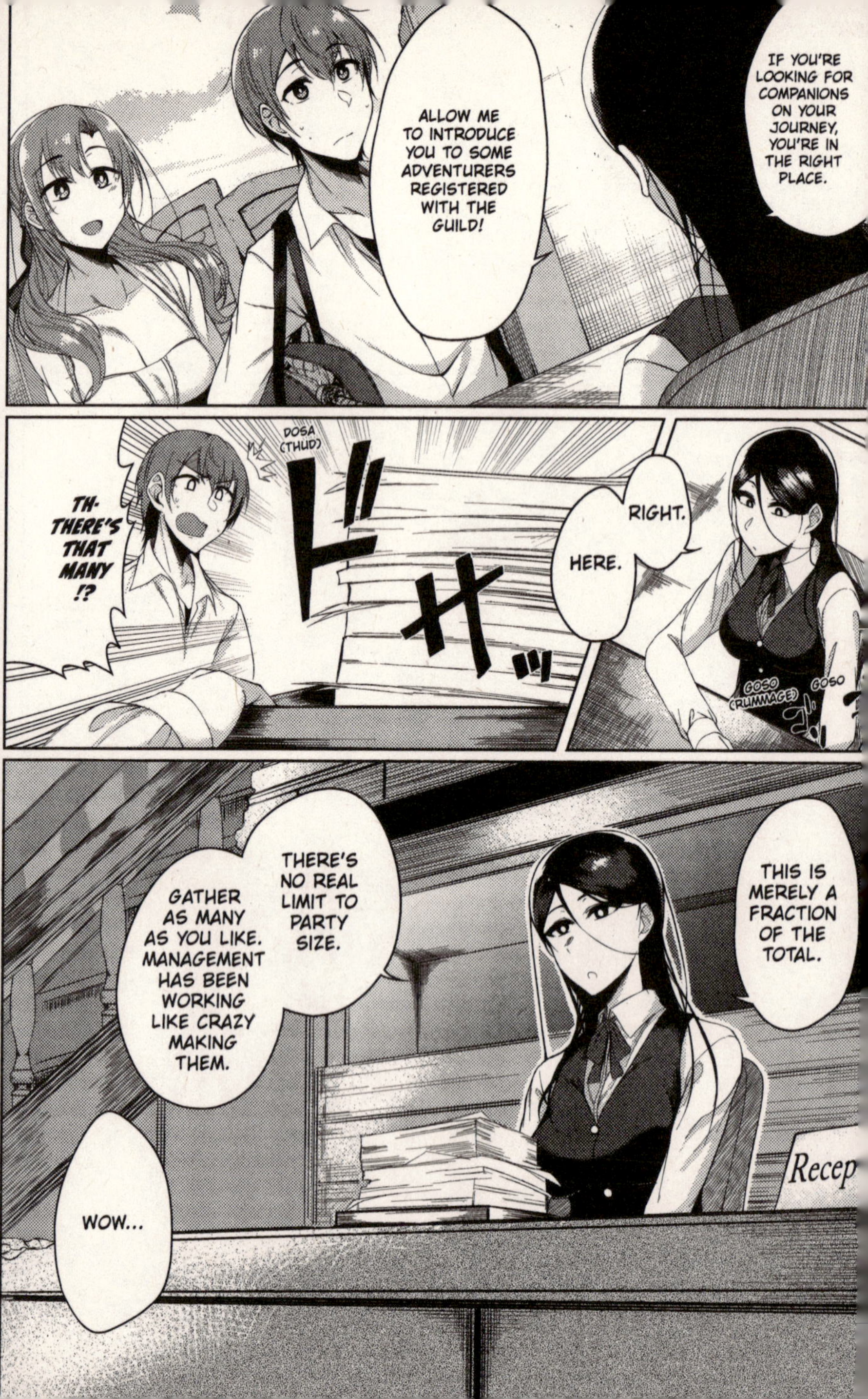
IF YOU'RE LOOKING FOR COMPANIONS ON YOUR JOURNEY, YOU'RE IN THE RIGHT PLACE.
ALLOW ME TO INTRODUCE YOU TO SOME ADVENTURERS REGISTERED WITH THE GUILD!
RIGHT.
HERE.
GOSO (RUMMAGE) GOSO
DOSA (THUD)
TH-THERE'S THAT MANY!?
THIS IS MERELY A FRACTION OF THE TOTAL.
THERE'S NO REAL LIMIT TO PARTY SIZE.
GATHER AS MANY AS YOU LIKE. MANAGEMENT HAS BEEN WORKING LIKE CRAZY MAKING THEM.
Recep
WOW...

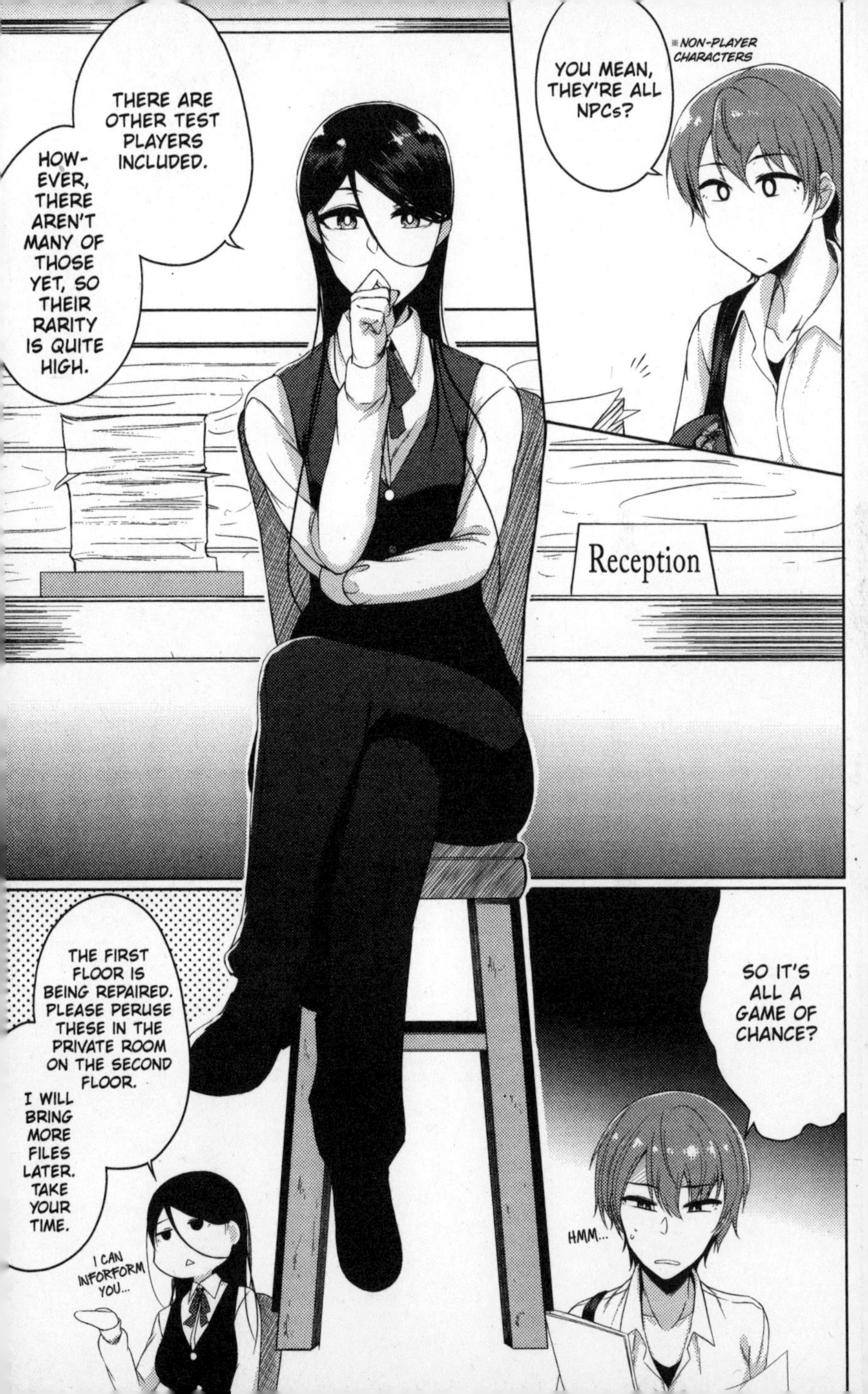

※NON-PLAYER CHARACTERS
YOU MEAN, THEY'RE ALL NPCs?
THERE ARE OTHER TEST PLAYERS INCLUDED.
HOW-EVER, THERE AREN'T MANY OF THOSE YET, SO THEIR RARITY IS QUITE HIGH.
Reception
SO IT'S ALL A GAME OF CHANCE?
HMM...
THE FIRST FLOOR IS BEING REPAIRED. PLEASE PERUSE THESE IN THE PRIVATE ROOM ON THE SECOND FLOOR.
I WILL BRING MORE FILES LATER. TAKE YOUR TIME.
I CAN INFORFORM YOU...

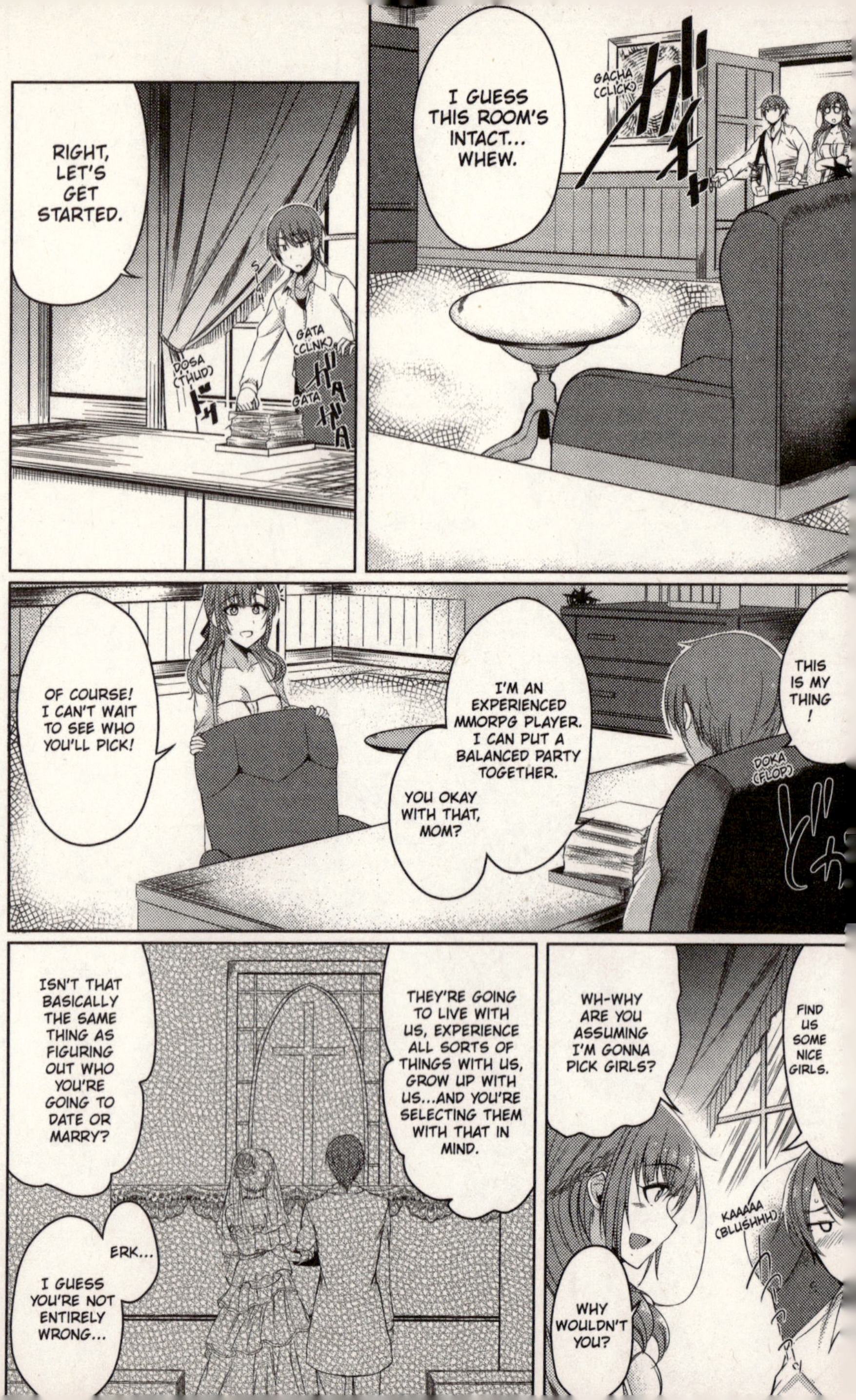
GACHA (CLICK)
I GUESS THIS ROOM'S INTACT... WHEW.
RIGHT, LET'S GET STARTED.
GATA (CLNK)
GATA
DOSA (THUD)
THIS IS MY THING!
DOKA (FLOP)
I'M AN EXPERIENCED MMORPG PLAYER. I CAN PUT A BALANCED PARTY TOGETHER.
YOU OKAY WITH THAT, MOM?
OF COURSE! I CAN'T WAIT TO SEE WHO YOU'LL PICK!
FIND US SOME NICE GIRLS.
WH-WHY ARE YOU ASSUMING I'M GONNA PICK GIRLS?
KAAAAA (BLUSHHH)
WHY WOULDN'T YOU?
THEY'RE GOING TO LIVE WITH US, EXPERIENCE ALL SORTS OF THINGS WITH US, GROW UP WITH US...AND YOU'RE SELECTING THEM WITH THAT IN MIND.
ISN'T THAT BASICALLY THE SAME THING AS FIGURING OUT WHO YOU'RE GOING TO DATE OR MARRY?
ERK...
I GUESS YOU'RE NOT ENTIRELY WRONG...

BUT THIS IS JUST A PARTY! PLAIN AND SIMPLE.

OUR MAIN CRITERIA HAS TO BE COMBAT BALANCE. WE'VE GOT TWO PHYSICAL DPS UNITS SO...

FIRST, A TANK.

I'LL PROTECT YOU!

KAKIN (CLANG)

OH!

I'D LIKE A HEALER, MAGICAL DPS, AND SUPPORT...

I'LL HANDLE SUPPORT!

ALSO CRAFTING JOBS! NEED AT LEAST ONE WHO CAN MAKE ITEMS.

I'LL MAKE MY—

VERY USEFUL

SHOULD WE GO FOR A TEAM OF SEVEN?

HMM.

OH! HERE'S A GOOD START.

KASA (RUSTLE)

CANDIDATE 1: LUCERA (16). JOB: HEAVY KNIGHT.

TANK SPECIALIZING IN DRAWING ENEMY ATTACKS.

HAS A SKILL THAT ADDS DAMAGE RECEIVED TO HER ATTACK, SO CAN PUT OUT DECENT DPS TOO!

CANDIDATE 2: SALITE (19). JOB: PRIEST.

RECOVERY MAGIC EXPERT. CAN PURIFY THE UNDEAD... AND AN ELF! (AGE GIVEN IN HUMAN YEARS.)

CANDIDATE 3: TORINO (14), CLASS: THIEF.

SUPPORT SKILL BOOSTS THE PARTY'S FIRST ATTACK AND SPEED.

ALSO PICKS LOCKS....

RIGHT! WE'LL START WITH THESE THREE.

SU (SLIIIDE)

GOSH, SUCH ADORABLE GIRLS!

THEY'RE ALL YOUR TYPE, MA-KUN?

THAT'S NOT THE GOAL HERE!

THEY JUST HAPPEN TO LOOK LIKE THIS!

TOTAL COINCIDENCE!

AUGH!

SU SU SU

EH-HEH-HEH, IF YOU INSIST.

NEXT, I'LL HAVE TO INTERVIEW THEM!

...HUNH?

THESE AREN'T POTENTIAL GIRLFRIENDS! JUST OUR PARTY!

WAIT!

ASE (FLUSTER)

YOU DON'T THINK ADVENTURING WITH THEM COULD LEAD TO FALLING IN LOVE?

UH...

HNGG

I-I MEAN...

88

THAT'S NOT THE GOAL HERE!
NO REASON WHY THEY HAVE TO PASS THE MOM TEST!
GACHA (CLICK)
I'VE HEARD EVERYTHING!
I CAN INFORFORM YOU THAT THE MOM TEST...
...HAS MY SEAL OF APPROVAL.
NU (LOOM)
ARGH!
I CAME PREPARED.
NU
I CAN INFORFORM YOU THAT SHIRARASE HAS EVERYTHING COVERED.
UH... FINE.

DON (DAH)

SIGN: FIRST ROUND MOM INTERVIEWS

DODON (DADAH)

SFX: DOKI (BABUMP) DOKI

OH! SHE'S HERE.

KON (KNOCK) KON

C-COME IN!

THIS IS MOMMY'S INTERVIEW, SO I'LL BE ASKING ALL THE QUESTIONS.

R-RIGHT.

DO YOUR WORST, THEN.

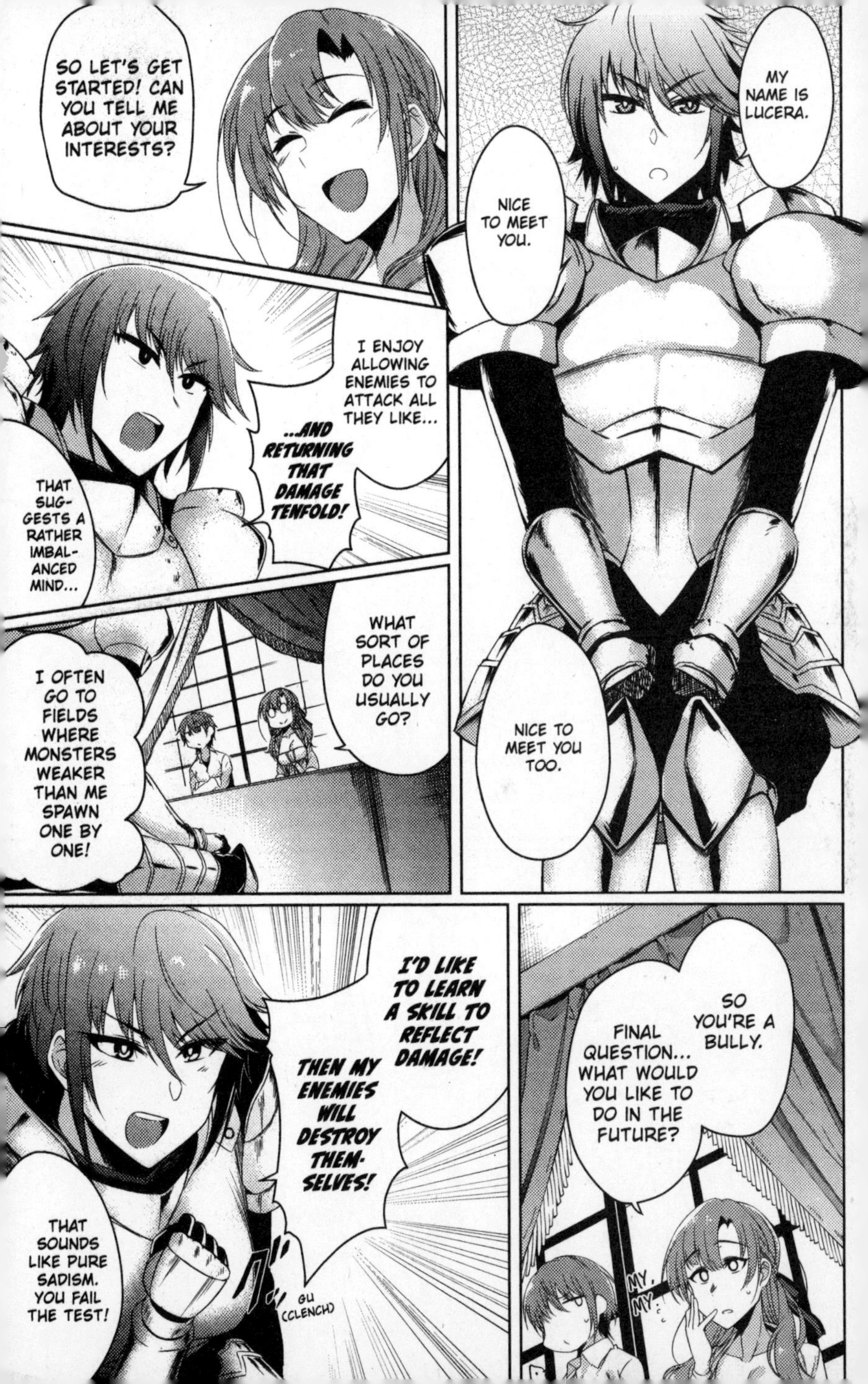

MY NAME IS LUCERA.
NICE TO MEET YOU.
NICE TO MEET YOU TOO.
SO LET'S GET STARTED! CAN YOU TELL ME ABOUT YOUR INTERESTS?
I ENJOY ALLOWING ENEMIES TO ATTACK ALL THEY LIKE...
...AND RETURNING THAT DAMAGE TENFOLD!
THAT SUGGESTS A RATHER IMBALANCED MIND...
WHAT SORT OF PLACES DO YOU USUALLY GO?
I OFTEN GO TO FIELDS WHERE MONSTERS WEAKER THAN ME SPAWN ONE BY ONE!
SO YOU'RE A BULLY.
FINAL QUESTION... WHAT WOULD YOU LIKE TO DO IN THE FUTURE?
MY, MY
I'D LIKE TO LEARN A SKILL TO REFLECT DAMAGE!
THEN MY ENEMIES WILL DESTROY THEMSELVES!
GU (CLENCH)
THAT SOUNDS LIKE PURE SADISM. YOU FAIL THE TEST!

MY NAME IS SALITE.
NICE TO MEET YOU.
SHAN (SHIMMER)
NICE TO MEET YOU TOO.
SO WHAT DO YOU DO WITH YOUR SPARE TIME?
I OFFER UP DAILY PRAYERS TO MY GOD.
300 TIMES A DAY.
ASSUMING SIX HOURS OF SLEEP...
...THEN YOU'D HAVE TO PRAY ONCE EVERY FOUR MINUTES!
WELL, WHERE DO YOU LIKE TO GO?
I VISIT CHURCHES IN FORESTS AROUND THE WORLD, OFFERING UP PRAYERS.
I TRY TO VISIT AT LEAST TWELVE A DAY.
THAT LEAVES LITTLE TIME FOR ANYTHING ELSE.
HMM.
THEN WHAT ARE YOUR DREAMS FOR THE FUTURE?
I PRAY THAT ALL PEOPLE WILL RETURN TO THE SERVICE OF GOD ALMIGHTY.
SOUNDS LIKE PRAYER IS ALL YOU HAVE...
THANKS FOR COMING! YOU FAIL THE TEST.

SNATCHIN' STUFF! PUNCH 'EM ONCE, STEAL AN ITEM!	YOUR INTERESTS ARE...? SUPER-FUN!	HEY, I'M TORINO! 'SUP?
FEES ARE HIGH, BUT HE'LL BUY WHATEVER! MY FENCE!	YOU OFTEN GO TO...	N-NICE TO MEET YOU.
SO... NO. BUUU (BZZZT) SA (SHH)	ANY THIEF'S DREAM! MWA HA!	I'D LOVE TO CLEAN OUT THE PALACE TREASURE ROOM! IN THE FUTURE, YOU'D...

HEY! WAIT A SEC, MOM!
BA (WAVE)
WHY DID YOU FAIL THEM ALL?
AT LEAST ONE OF THEM SHOULD HAVE BEEN FINE!
FIRST, LUCERA. THERE WAS JUST SOMETHING WRONG WITH HER.
THAT WAS ALL TOTALLY NORMAL TANK STUFF!?
NEXT, SALITE...
I'M ALL FOR FREEDOM OF RELIGION, BUT...
...IF SHE WERE IN OUR PARTY, SHE'D KEEP ASKING US TO VISIT DUBIOUS PLACES.
I'M NOT GOOD AT TURNING THOSE THINGS DOWN!
SIGN: INTERVIEW
AND TORINO!
ERP... I KINDA HAVE TO AGREE WITH YOU ON THAT POINT...
MM? WHAT, WHAT?
YOU'RE COMING WITH ME.
PON (PAT)
TO THE POLICE.
GU (YANK)
WHAAA!?
GU
HOW ARE YOU SO STRONG!?
GU
WAIT, MOM!? CALM DOWN! THIEVES ARE OKAY! IT'S A NORMAL JOB IN A GAME WORLD!!!
END

GOSH, SUCH ADORABLE GIRLS!
THEY'RE ALL YOUR TYPE, MA-KUN?
AUGH!
THAT'S NOT THE GOAL HERE!
THEY JUST HAPPEN TO LOOK LIKE THIS!
TOTAL COINCI-DENCE!
SU (SLIIIDE)
SU
SU SU SU

Do You Love Your Mom and Her Two-Hit Multi-Target Attacks?

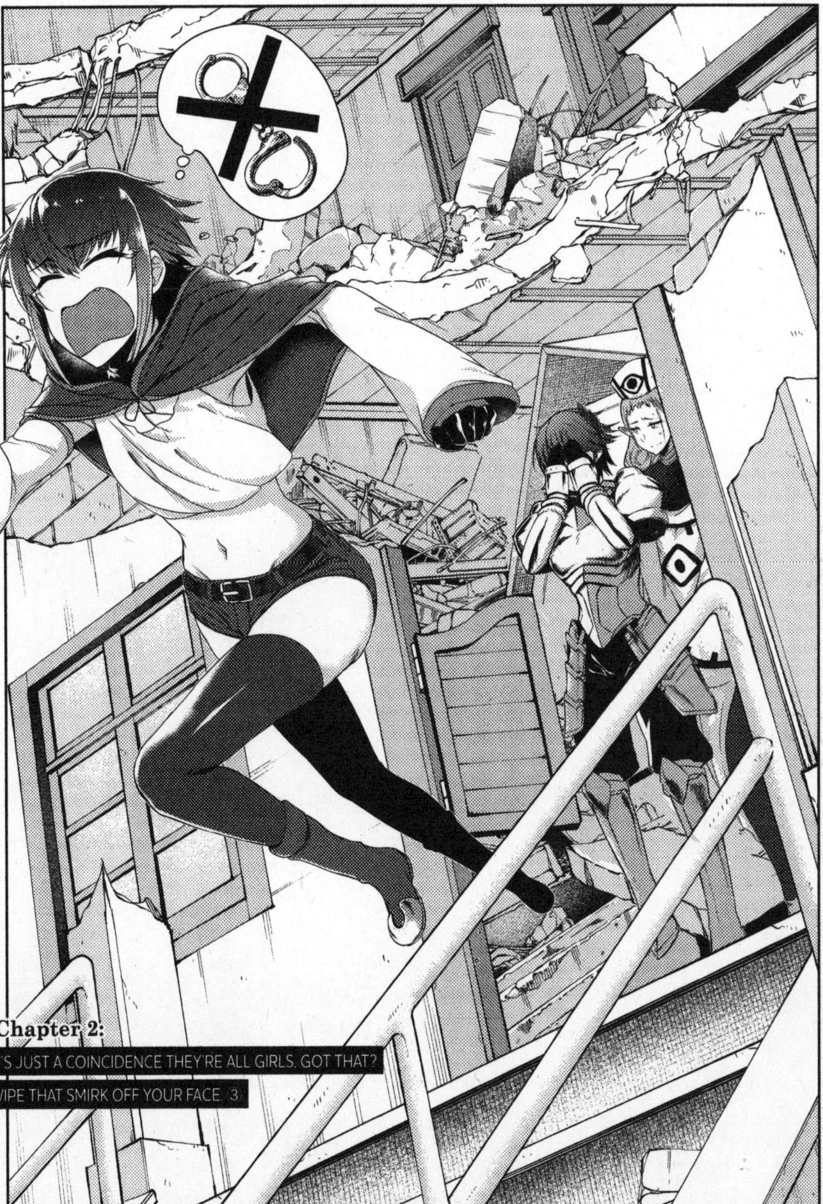

Chapter 2:
IT'S JUST A COINCIDENCE THEY'RE ALL GIRLS. GOT THAT? WIPE THAT SMIRK OFF YOUR FACE. (3)

"HOW ABOUT MORE RELIABLE OCCUPATIONS? LIKE... A POLICE OFFICER?"

"CAN'T BELIEVE THEY ALL FAILED."

"ACK."

"AH... THEY ALL LEFT..."

"SIGH..."

THEY DON'T HAVE THOSE IN FANTASY RPGS!

"SHIRARASE BROUGHT SOME MORE, SO LEMME LOOK..."

BASA (FOOMP)

Kasha
Intro
Aura
EXTRA FILES SHIRARASE

"UGHHH... OKAY, FINE!"

GASA (RUSTLE)

"I DUNNO IF ANYONE WILL MEET MOM'S STANDARDS, THOUGH..."

"MM? HANG ON..."

WISE, HUH? SHE'S A SAGE... WOW.
ATTACK AND RECOVERY MAGIC... PRETTY IMPRES-SIVE.
SU (SHH)
MY! THAT IS NICE!
MOMMY ALWAYS WANTED TO BE A MAGICAL GIRL!
OH?
SO MAGES ARE COOL WITH YOU.
BUT NOT THIS ONE.
WHY NOT? SHE'S CUTE AND CAN USE TWO TYPES OF MAGIC!
OH?
HMPH
BUT LOOK AT THIS NOTE!
Notes
IF YOU DON'T PICK ME, I'LL CHAIN CAST DEATH SPELLS ON YOU.
BI (BZZT)
IT PROVES SHE'S AN IDIOT.
AND LOOK AT THOSE EYES!
DEFI-NITELY THE HAUGHTY TYPE WHO LIKES TO BOSS EVERYONE AROUND.
BUT IF YOU GET TO KNOW HER, MAYBE YOU'LL FIND MORE TO LIKE!
I PROMISE THAT'LL NEVER HAPPEN. BYE, WISE!
SCRUNCH
POI (TOSS)
OW!
POKO (DONK)
TRASH
POTE (THNK)
...? DID YOU HEAR THAT?
WHAT?
MUST HAVE IMAG-INED IT.

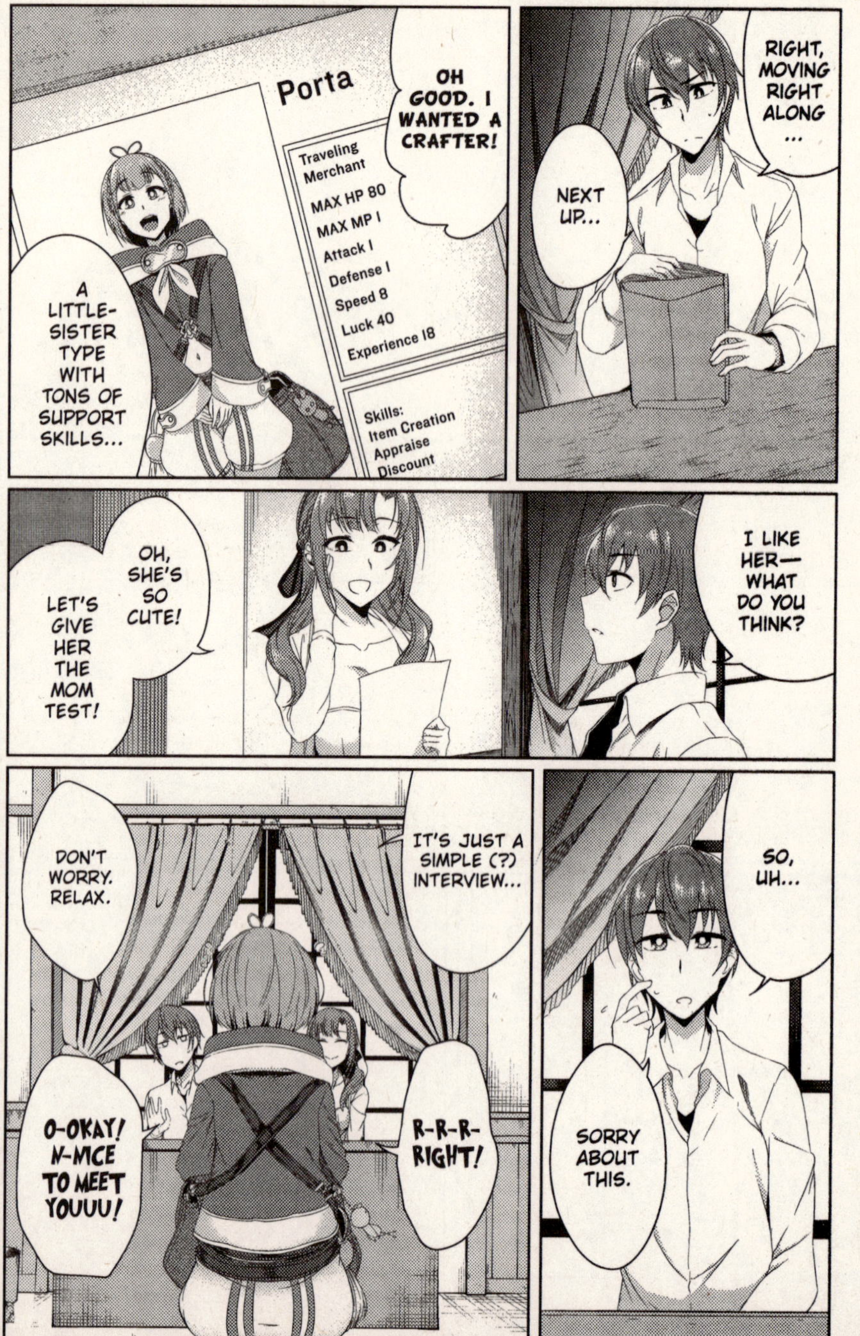
RIGHT, MOVING RIGHT ALONG ...
NEXT UP...
OH GOOD. I WANTED A CRAFTER!
Porta
Traveling Merchant
MAX HP 80
MAX MP 1
Attack 1
Defense 1
Speed 8
Luck 40
Experience 18
Skills:
Item Creation
Appraise
Discount
A LITTLE-SISTER TYPE WITH TONS OF SUPPORT SKILLS...
I LIKE HER—WHAT DO YOU THINK?
OH, SHE'S SO CUTE!
LET'S GIVE HER THE MOM TEST!
SO, UH...
SORRY ABOUT THIS.
IT'S JUST A SIMPLE (?) INTERVIEW...
DON'T WORRY. RELAX.
R-R-R-RIGHT!
O-OKAY! N-NICE TO MEET YOUUU!

OF COURSE!
LOVELY TO MEET YOU.
NO NEED TO BE SO NERVOUS.
CAN YOU INTRODUCE YOURSELF?
RIGHT!
I'M PORTA!
I'M A TEST PLAYER!

- SO WHERE IS YOUR MOTHER?
- A TEST PLAYER! WE GOT A RARE ONE, HERE!
- YES!
- OH, YOU ARE TOO!?
- M-MY MOTHER?

- THAT'S WEIRD... BUT IF THE ADMINS APPROVE, WHATEVER.
- SHE'S TAKING A BREAK FROM THE GAME FOR WORK.
- IT'S ALL BEEN APPROVED BY THE ADMINS, DON'T WORRY!
- I SEE, YOUR MOTHER MUST BE SO BUSY!

- I'VE GOT A QUESTION.
- YOU READY?
- OKAY!

- MOM! MAYBE A DIFFERENT PHRASING...?
- ISN'T THAT LOVELY!? YOU'RE LIKE A WALKING COUPON, PORTA!
- UUUUM... I CAN GET US DISCOUNTS AT INNS AND SHOPS!
- CAN YOU TELL US HOW YOU'D HELP OUR PARTY?
- YOU'RE A MERCHANT, SO I ASSUME YOU'RE GOOD AT TRADING?

SIGNS: INNS / ITEMS / WEAPONS

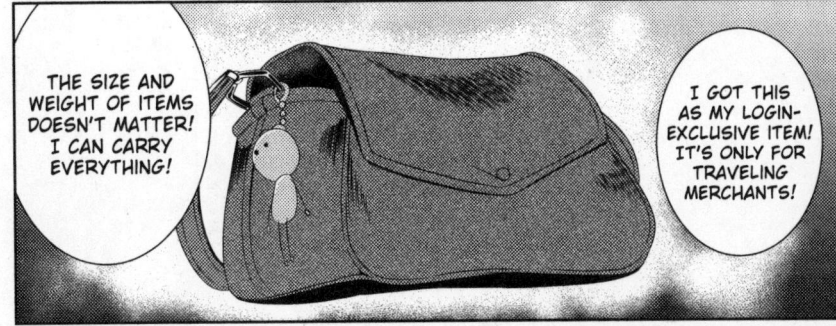

"I'M GUESSING THAT BAG?"

"YOU MEAN, YOU'D CARRY EVERYTHING?"

HOW?

"I CAN ALSO MANAGE ALL THE PARTY'S ITEMS."

"WE CAN CARRY FAR MORE THAN USUAL!"

"THE SIZE AND WEIGHT OF ITEMS DOESN'T MATTER! I CAN CARRY EVERYTHING!"

"I GOT THIS AS MY LOGIN-EXCLUSIVE ITEM! IT'S ONLY FOR TRAVELING MERCHANTS!"

AHEM.

"I CAN TELL WE'D WANT A TRAVELING MERCHANT IN THE PARTY."

"THAT'S NOT ALL, THOUGH, IS IT?"

"THE ONES YOU PUT THE COMFORTERS IN EVERY SUMMER?"

"I WORK UP SUCH A SWEAT! AND YOU NEVER HELP..."

"SORRY...I WILL NEXT TIME..."

"SEE? THIS BAG CAN STORE UP TO THREE HUNDRED ITEMS!"

"WHAT A USEFUL TOOL!"

"AND HERE I WAS IMPRESSED BY VACUUM STORAGE BAGS."

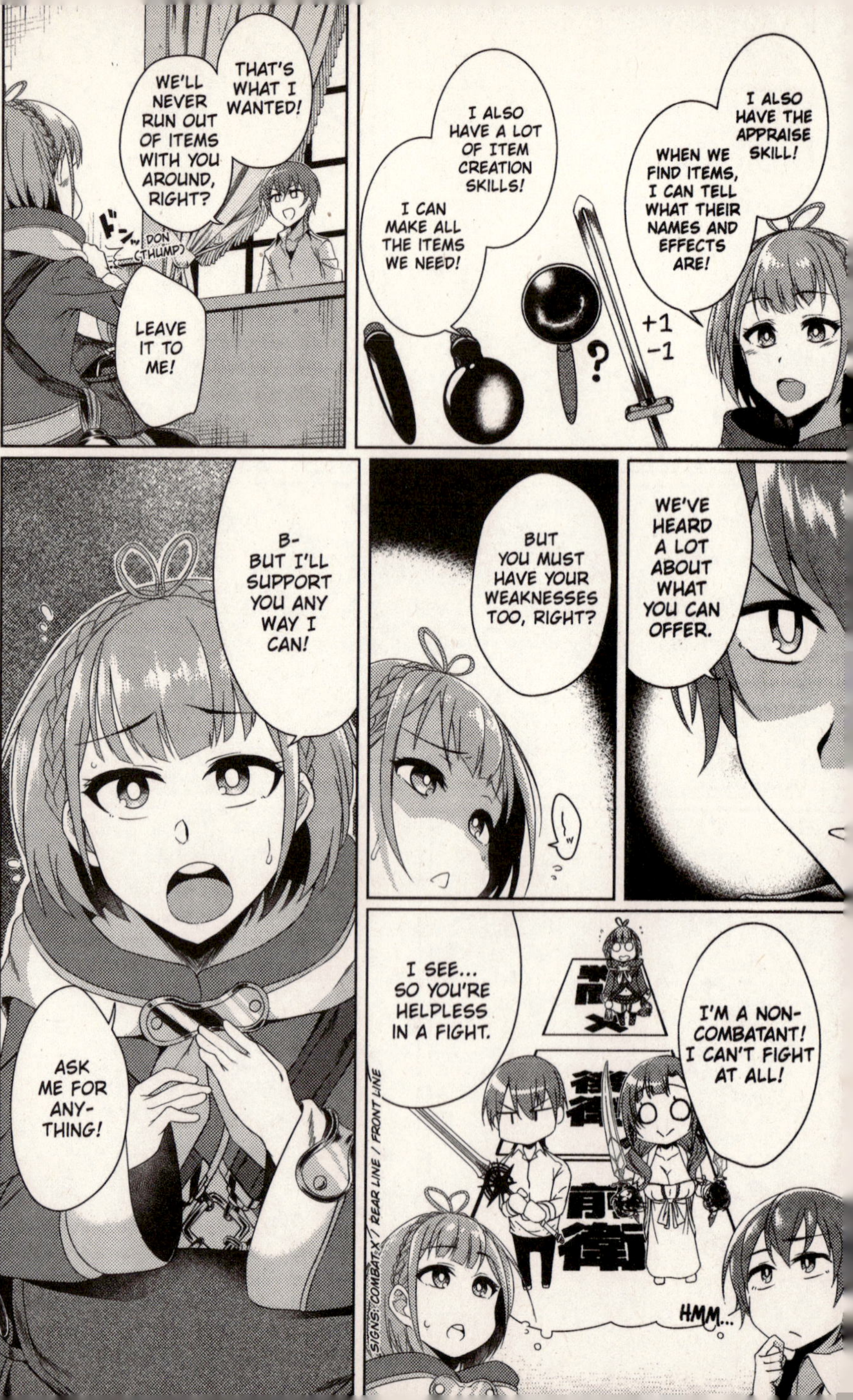
I ALSO HAVE THE APPRAISE SKILL!
WHEN WE FIND ITEMS, I CAN TELL WHAT THEIR NAMES AND EFFECTS ARE!
+1
-1
?
I ALSO HAVE A LOT OF ITEM CREATION SKILLS!
I CAN MAKE ALL THE ITEMS WE NEED!
THAT'S WHAT I WANTED!
WE'LL NEVER RUN OUT OF ITEMS WITH YOU AROUND, RIGHT?
DON (THUMP)
LEAVE IT TO ME!
WE'VE HEARD A LOT ABOUT WHAT YOU CAN OFFER.
BUT YOU MUST HAVE YOUR WEAKNESSES TOO, RIGHT?
I'M A NON-COMBATANT! I CAN'T FIGHT AT ALL!
I SEE... SO YOU'RE HELPLESS IN A FIGHT.
HMM...
SIGNS: COMBAT-X / REAR LINE / FRONT LINE
B-BUT I'LL SUPPORT YOU ANY WAY I CAN!
ASK ME FOR ANYTHING!

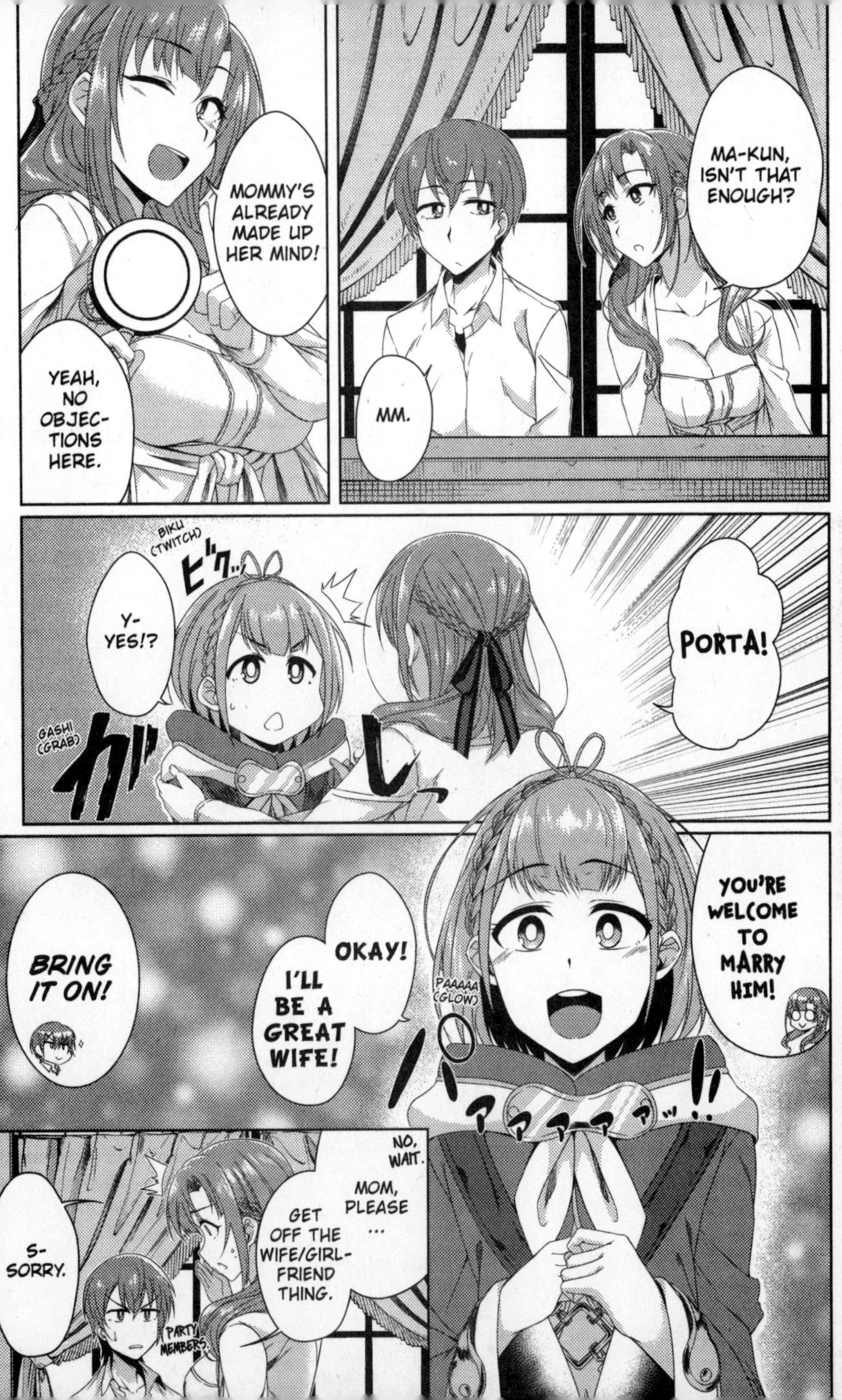
MA-KUN, ISN'T THAT ENOUGH?
MM.
MOMMY'S ALREADY MADE UP HER MIND!
YEAH, NO OBJECTIONS HERE.
PORTA!
BIKU (TWITCH)
Y-YES!?
GASHI (GRAB)
YOU'RE WELCOME TO MARRY HIM!
PAAAAA (GLOW)
OKAY! I'LL BE A GREAT WIFE!
BRING IT ON!
NO, WAIT.
MOM, PLEASE ...
GET OFF THE WIFE/GIRL-FRIEND THING.
S-SORRY.
PARTY MEMBERS.

MOMMY'S ALREADY MADE UP HER MIND!

YEAH, NO OBJECTIONS HERE.

MA-KUN, ISN'T THAT ENOUGH?

MM.

Y-YES!?

BIKU (TWITCH)

GASHI (GRAB)

PORTA!

BRING IT ON!

OKAY! I'LL BE A GREAT WIFE!

PAAAA (GLOW)

YOU'RE WELCOME TO MARRY HIM!

S-SORRY.

NO, WAIT. MOM, PLEASE... GET OFF THE WIFE/GIRLFRIEND THING.

PARTY MEMBERS.

THEN...
MASATO AND MAMA!
WILL THAT BE FINE?
GATA (CLATTER)
COOL. HOPEFULLY, YOU'LL BE A LITTLE MORE RELAXED IN TIME...
...BUT THAT SHOULD HAPPEN NATURALLY AS WE TRAVEL.
YES!
I'LL DO MY BEST!
WHAT AN ADOR-ABLE CREA-TURE.
EEK! THAT TICKLES!
MUNI (YOINK)
YOU KNOW YOU LIKE IT!
HA (GASP)
YOU KNOW...
MA-KUN!?
S-STOP THAT!
WHY DO YOUR EYES LOOK SO SAD!?

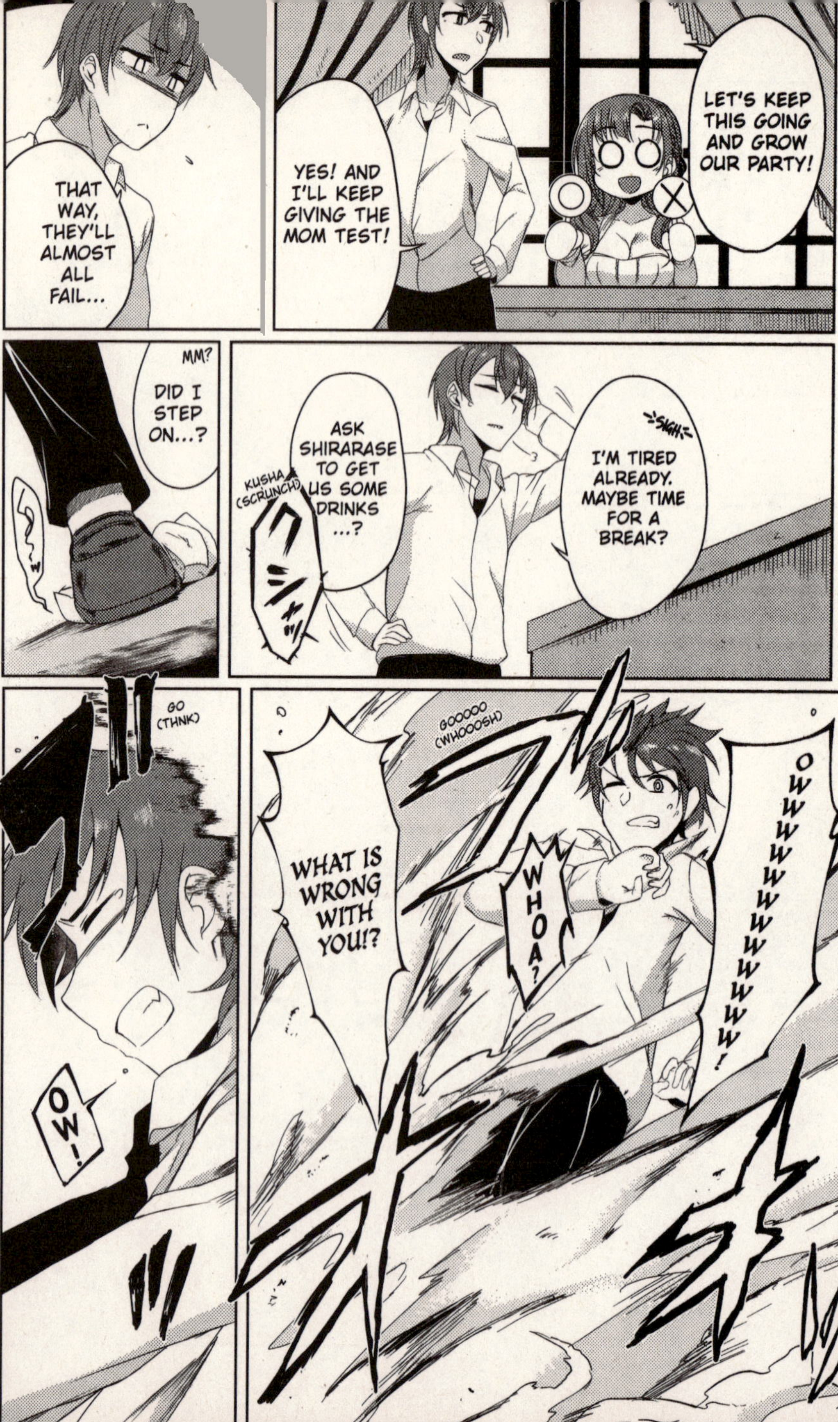
LET'S KEEP THIS GOING AND GROW OUR PARTY!
YES! AND I'LL KEEP GIVING THE MOM TEST!
THAT WAY, THEY'LL ALMOST ALL FAIL...
SIGH
I'M TIRED ALREADY. MAYBE TIME FOR A BREAK?
ASK SHIRARASE TO GET US SOME DRINKS ...?
KUSHA (SCRUNCH)
MM?
DID I STEP ON...?
GOOOOO (WHOOOSH)
OWWWWWWWWWWWWW!
WHOA?
WHAT IS WRONG WITH YOU!?
GO (THNK)
OW!

OW!
WH-WHAT THE?
GORO (ROLL)
GORO
YOU THERE!
WHAT IS YOUR PROB-LEM!?
ZA (SWSH)
SO MUCH FOR BEHAVING MYSELF!
MAYBE I REALLY WILL CHAIN CAST DEATH SPELLS ON YOU!
DON (FOOM)
YOU WANT A DOZEN FUNER-ALS!?
KII (RAGE)
A DOZEN... LIKE, ACTUALLY TWELVE?
I CAN CHAIN CAST, SO I MIGHT AS WELL GO FOR TWENTY-FOUR!
GULP!

HOW COME YOU'RE SO CALM!?
HNGGG...
UGH! THAT DOES IT!
YOU TREAT ME...
HNGGG!
...LIKE CRAP!
GOSHI (RUB)
GOSHI
I'LL PAY IT BACK IN KIND!
BI (JAB)
...
BRING THAT UGLY MUG OVER HERE!
SPARA LA MAGIA PER MIRARE...
BUN (VVP)
WAIT, WHAT?
PAAAA (FOOSH)
TRANS-PORTARE!
EEP!
OH MY!

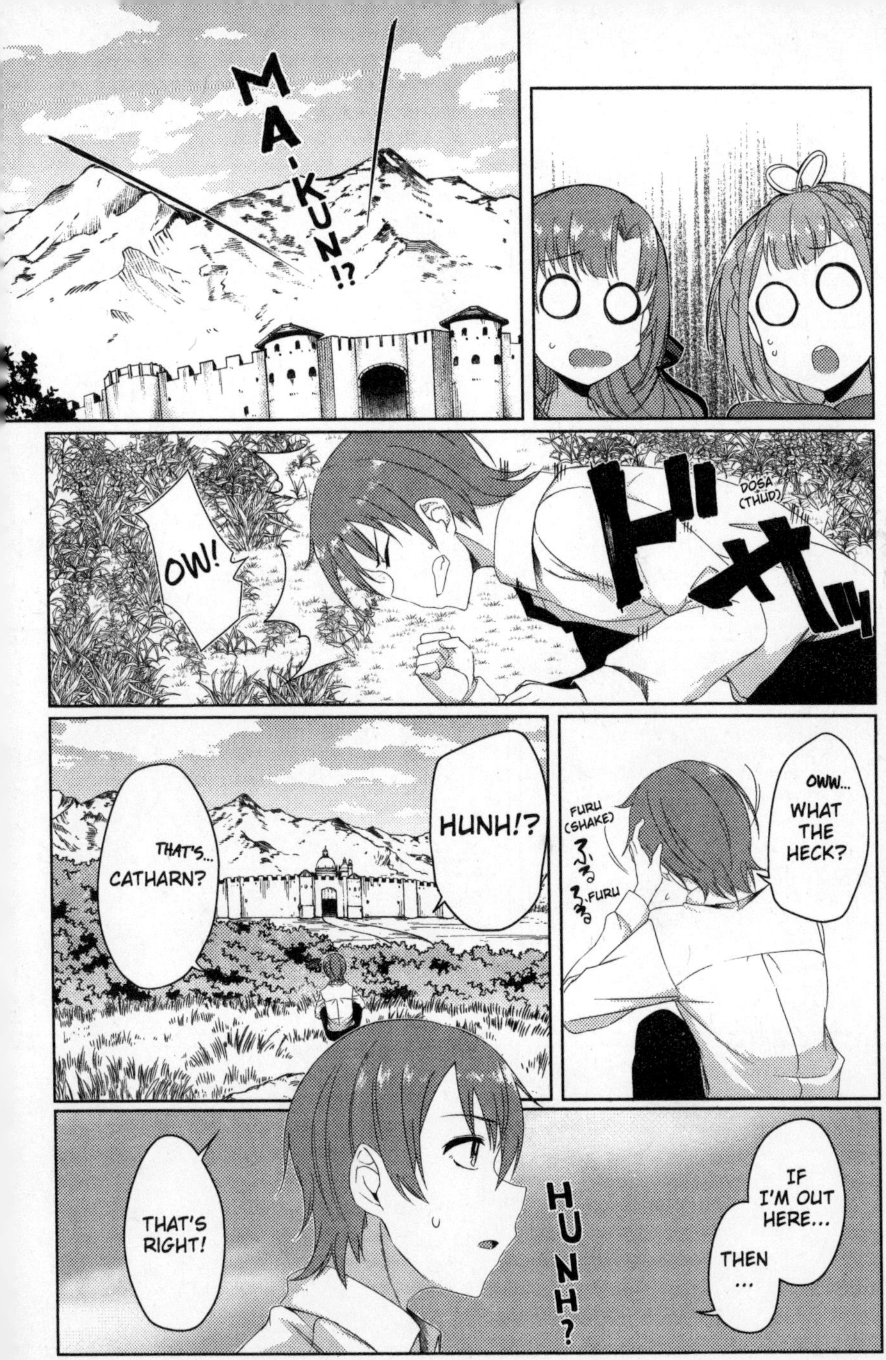
MA-KUN!?
DOSA (THUD)
OW!
OWW... WHAT THE HECK?
FURU (SHAKE)
FURU
HUNH!?
THAT'S... CATHARN?
IF I'M OUT HERE...
THEN ...
HUNH?
THAT'S RIGHT!

I KNEW IT.

GOO (WHOOSH)

OH.

SHE'S EXACTLY WHO I THOUGHT SHE WAS.

I SEE.

BA (SWISH)

REVENGE, RIGHT?

SHE TRANSFORMED HERSELF INTO PAPER TO SURPRISE US AND SELL US ON HER POWER.

START — HMPH!
GOAL — SHOW POWER, JOIN PARTY!
DOCUMENT NOISE
YIKES!
WAIT CHANCE TO SURPRISE

AND I TOTALLY RUINED THAT PLAN.

MUNII (SQUISH)

I TOTALLY...

...CALLED THIS ONE.

WHEW. THAT BREEZE FEELS AMAZING.

SUKKIRI (REFRESHED)

I'LL TELL YOU ONE THING.

AND THAT IS?

THIS IS MY FAVORITE PLACE.

ZAAAAA (SHHHHAAA)

I DON'T CARE.

YEAH, FINE. WE'RE EVEN.

SO... YOU SATISFIED? WE EVEN NOW?

HMPH. YOU JUST LET ME STOMP YOU, HUH?

HYUUUUUU (WHOOOSH)

I'LL GIVE YOU CREDIT FOR THAT, AT LEAST.

SO? YOU BROUGHT ME OUT HERE... FOR WHAT?

THANKS.

YOU'RE FLASHING ME.

FOR THE LOVE OF...

WORKING ON IT.

HMPH!

FUKI (WIPE) FUKI

OH, SHUT UP!

I THOUGHT YOU'D FIGHT ME WHEN I TRIED TO STOMP YOU BACK THERE...

...SO I BROUGHT US SOMEWHERE I COULD FLING MAGIC AROUND WITHOUT BOTHERING ANYONE ELSE.

GOOD PLAN.

BUT YOU JUST LET ME DO IT!

RUINED THE WHOLE THING.

...

SIGH... THE WIND FEELS SO GOOD... I REALLY LOVE THIS PLACE.

MMM!

WHATEVER. I'M JUST GONNA GO BACK TO MY ORIGINAL PLAN.

HMPH.

I REALLY DON'T CARE.

LIKE I SAID.

GRR... WELL, IF YOU BOIL IT DOWN...

JUST THE TWO OF US... IN A PLACE I LOVE! PERFECT SETUP FOR AN IMPORTANT CONVERSATION!

WHAAA?

WELL, YOU SHOULD! THINK ABOUT IT!

YOU WANT TO JOIN OUR PARTY, RIGHT? YOU'VE GOT SOME REASON WHY YOU HAVE TO?

IF YOU'VE GOT SOMETHING TO SAY... JUST SAY IT.

THEN SIT DOWN. I'LL HEAR YOU OUT.

FINE, THEN.

PON (PAT)
PON

UH...

NO BUGS, RIGHT?

Y-YOU SAID TO SIT HERE!

GASP!

A LITTLE CLOSE, AREN'T YOU?

YEAH, YEAH.

A LITTLE FARTHER.

MAKING ADJUSTMENTS

I'M WISE. I'M A SAGE.

MY LOGIN EXCLUSIVE WAS A MAGIC TOME WITH A PASSIVE THAT BOOSTS MAGIC POWER.

I CAN HANDLE ANYTHING FROM OFFENSIVE TO SUPPORT SPELLS.

THANKS, I GUESS.

UM... SO YOU ALREADY READ MY PROFILE...

I MIGHT AS WELL INTRODUCE MYSELF.

YEP, A FIFTEEN-YEAR-OLD HIGH SCHOOL GIRL TEST PLAYER. WANNA SEE MY ID?

IF YOU'VE GOT A LOGIN BONUS, THEN YOU'RE A TEST PLAYER?

HERO? THAT'S HILARIOUS.

I'M MASATO. MY JOB IS...A WARRIOR TYPE.

THEY'RE CALLING IT HERO.

SU SU SU (SLIIIDE)

PFFT. HEE HEE.

OH, RIGHT. GOOD POINT.

CAREFUL WITH THE PERSONAL INFO.

WASN'T MY IDEA! DON'T BLAME ME.

PLEASE.

116

BUT MY POINT IS...
...HOW MUCH DO YOU KNOW ABOUT WHAT'S GOING ON HERE?
YOU MEAN ABOUT US BEING INSIDE THIS GAME?
I'VE GOT A LOT OF QUESTIONS ABOUT WHY MY MOM'S HERE TOO.
YOUR MOM'S HERE...
THEN...
...I CAN ANSWER THAT.
IN OTHER WORDS...
...BECAUSE THIS GAME...
...IS AN MMMMMM-ORPG...

...MAKING-UP-WITH-OFFSPRING ROLE-PLAYING GAME.

MOM'S MASSIVELY MATERNAL MULTI-PLAYER...

YOU HAVE GOT TO BE KIDDING ME.

I WISH I WAS!

BLAME THE IDIOTS WHO CAME UP WITH THIS CRAP! I'M JUST TELLING YOU THE TRUTH, SO YOU'D BETTER LISTEN!

AS LONG AS THE LAST SPELL LEAVES ME ALIVE, I THINK I'M GOOD.

SIGH...

YOU'LL DIE AND COME BACK UNTIL I RUN OUT OF MAGIC! OR I'LL ALTERNATE DEATH AND REVIVAL SPELLS!

"So we're paired up. Told we have to stay together. The point of this game is for parents and children to adventure together, improving their relationships."

"But I promised I'd hear you out, and I will."

"But there is one thing I know for sure."

"What?"

"I have no idea how they made this game... I don't know any more than you do there."

"If you don't meet the victory condition... ...you can't go back to the real world."

"Wait, seriously?"

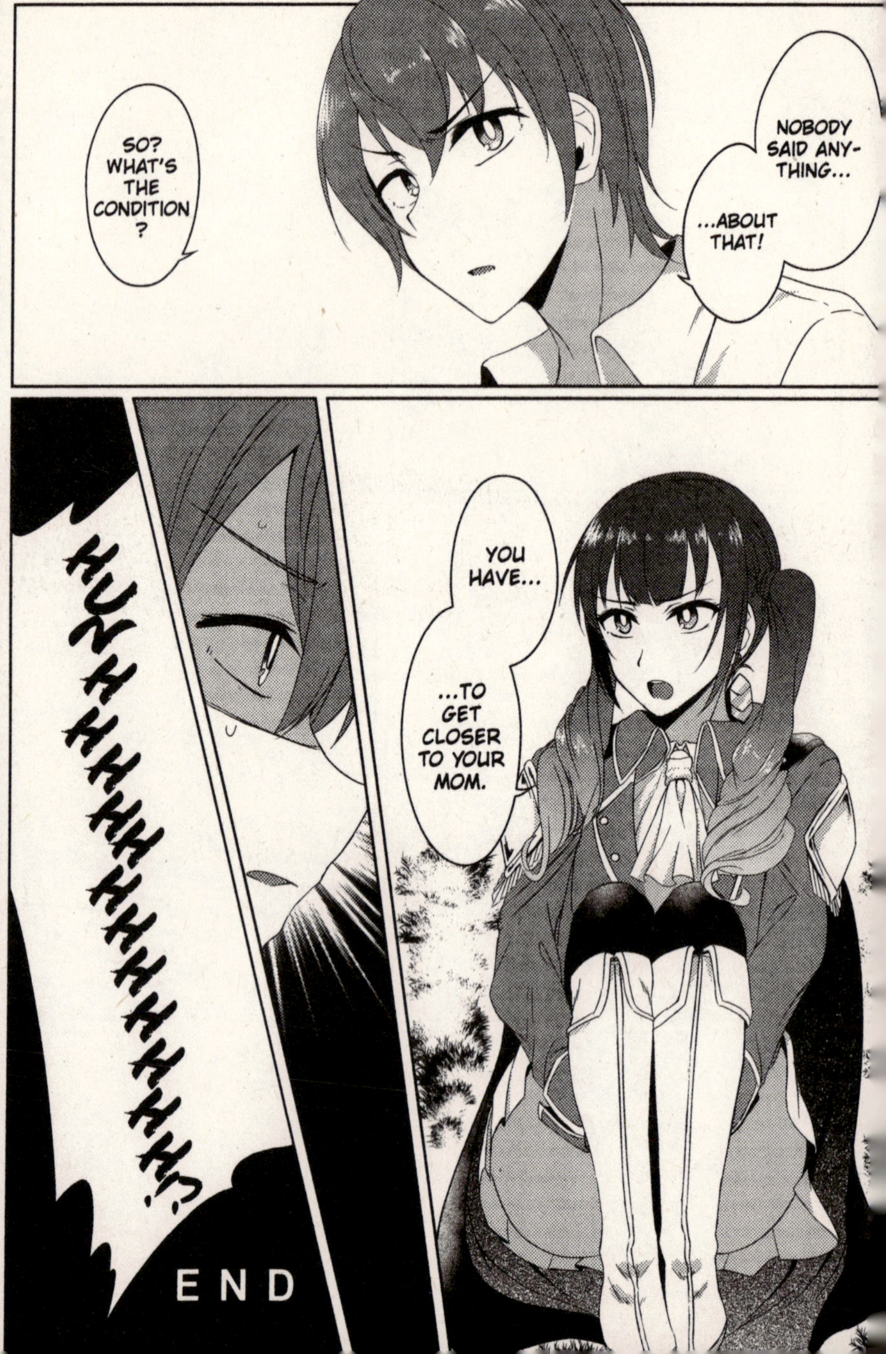
NOBODY SAID ANY-THING...
...ABOUT THAT!
SO? WHAT'S THE CONDITION?
YOU HAVE...
...TO GET CLOSER TO YOUR MOM.
HUNHHHHHHHHHHHHHHHH!?
END

Do You Love Your Mom and Her Two-Hit, Multi-Target Attacks?

Do
You Love
Your Mom
and Her
Two-Hit,
Multi-
Target
Attacks?

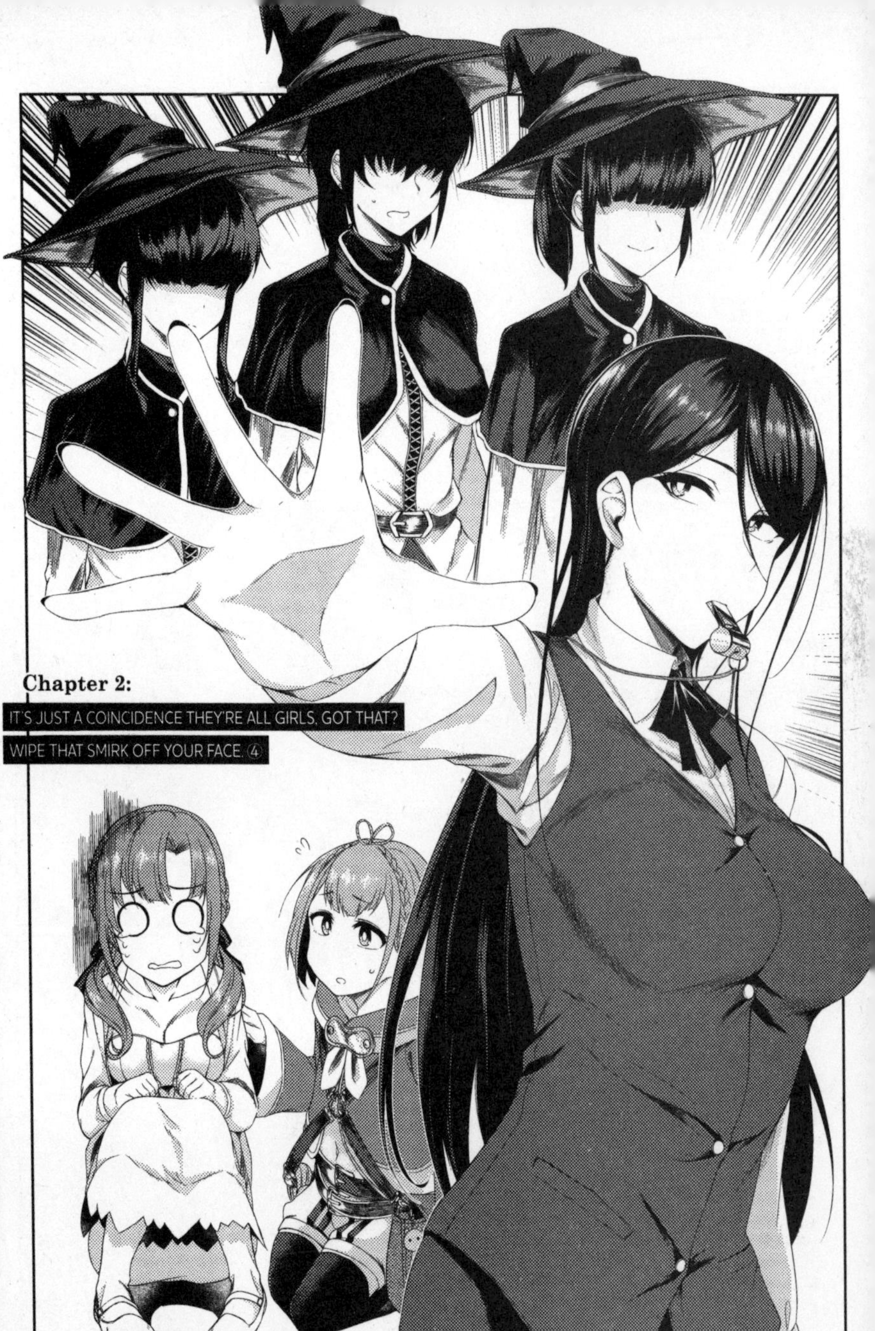
Chapter 2:
IT'S JUST A COINCIDENCE THEY'RE ALL GIRLS. GOT THAT?
WIPE THAT SMIRK OFF YOUR FACE. ④

"GET CLOSER TO YOUR MOM!?"

...WHEN SHE TOLD ME.

MINE JUST YANKED ME IN HERE...

I KNOW!

WHAT KIND OF VICTORY CONDITION IS THAT!?

THAT MAKES NO SENSE!

I WIPED IT OFF LATER!

R-RIGHT.

TRY TO CONTROL YOURSELF.

THERE WAS SNOT EVERY- WHERE!

DAMN, GIRL.

I WAS SO SHOCKED, I STRAIGHT UP PASSED OUT.

HEH.

DON'T LOOK AT ME.

BUT IT OUGHTA BE EASY FOR A BOY...

...WITH AN OEDIPAL COMPLEX.

I DUNNO HOW CLOSE YOU HAVE TO GET TO MEET THIS CONDITION.

JILL (GLARE)

I HAVE NO IDEA WHAT YOU'RE TALKING ABOUT.

...SIGH...
BUT IF YOU REALLY CAN'T STAND YOUR MOM, YOU'RE STUCK HERE.
LIKE... A CERTAIN SAGE WE KNOW?
HMPH.
I STARTED OUT TRAVELING WITH MY MOM. THEN WE HAD A BIG FIGHT AND SPLIT UP.
PLAYING A GAME WITH YOUR PARENTS IS IMPOSSIBLE TO BEGIN WITH.
SIGH...
YEAH... I'D SURE RATHER NOT.
BUT THAT MEANS I'M TRAPPED IN THIS WORLD!
JUST A POOR LITTLE PRIN-CESS.
NO ONE WOULD EVER MISTAKE YOU FOR THAT.
HEH HEH. PRINCESS.
MM.
YOU REALLY PISS ME OFF!
SO? WHY JOIN MY PARTY?

"YOU WANT US TO CLEAR IT SO YOU CAN PIGGYBACK HOME? THAT IT?"

"OH, WAIT."

NII (SMIRK)

"SHE MAY BE EVIL...!"

YIKES!

"...CLEAR THIS DUMB CONDITION, AND GET HOME."

"SO I'M GONNA MAKE IT SO SHE'S MY MOM TOO..."

"YOUR MOM SEEMS LIKE THE NICEST LADY EVER!"

"ER..."

"THAT'S THE PLAN ANYWAY."

HEH HEH.

KARAN KARAN (DING-DONG)
カラーン
ウララーン
OH GOD!
WE GOT MARRIED!
PIRORIN (DING-A-LING
ピロリン♪
BUT IF YOU'RE MY MOM'S KID, YOU'D BE HER DAUGHTER-IN-LAW...
WAIT, THAT MEANS ...
WHAT? THERE A PROBLEM WITH...
PYA (SHUDDER)
ぴゃっ
D—
HYUN (VVP)
DON'T BE STUPID!
GOKYAN (CRACK)
BWEEEP
WHYYY?

ADOPTION EXISTS!
THAT WAY, WE'D BE...
...BROTHER AND SISTER!
R-RIGHT, GOOD POINT.
PIKON (FLASH) PIKON
HP
HAFF
I DON'T NEED A MAGIC WIFE WITH...
...HEAVY BLUNT FORCE ATTACKS ANYWAY.
AND I DON'T NEED A BOY WITH AN OEDIPAL COMPLEX.
I SWEAR I DON'T HAVE ONE.
ANYWAY, I UNDERSTAND YOUR PLAN.
OOF.
THEN ADD ME TO YOUR PARTY!
I'LL DO WHATEVER IT TAKES TO WIN YOUR MOTHER OVER!

EH HEH...
MOOOM...
BWA HA HA!
I'LL FAKE BEING CUTE...
...AND TOTALLY MAKE HER WANT ME AS A DAUGHTER!
YET, WITH ME, YOU REVEAL YOUR DARK SIDE.
CAN I ASK ONE THING?
KEEP IT SNAPPY.
I SUPPOSE. BUT JUST ONE!
THEN I'LL GET RIGHT TO THE POINT.
PIKU (TWITCH)
CAN'T YOU JUST... MAKE UP WITH YOUR MOM?
GYU (CLENCH)
I CAN'T. OBVIOUSLY.
THERE'S NO WAY MY MOM AND I WILL EVER GET ALONG.
IT'S NONE OF YOUR BUSINESS.
DON'T STICK YOUR HEAD IN OTHER FAMILIES' AFFAIRS!

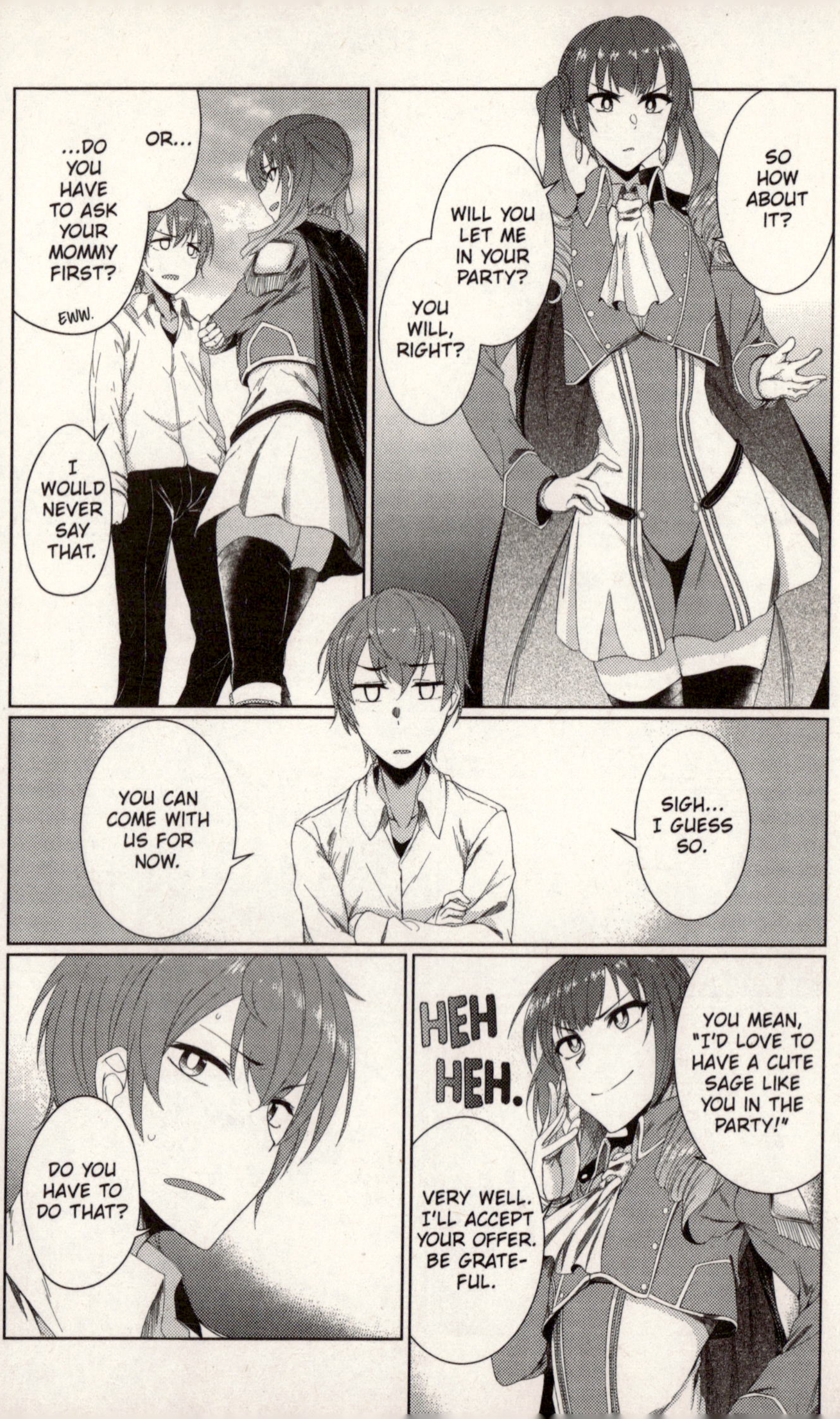
SO HOW ABOUT IT?
WILL YOU LET ME IN YOUR PARTY?
YOU WILL, RIGHT?
OR...
...DO YOU HAVE TO ASK YOUR MOMMY FIRST?
EWW.
I WOULD NEVER SAY THAT.
SIGH... I GUESS SO.
YOU CAN COME WITH US FOR NOW.
HEH HEH.
YOU MEAN, "I'D LOVE TO HAVE A CUTE SAGE LIKE YOU IN THE PARTY!"
VERY WELL. I'LL ACCEPT YOUR OFFER. BE GRATE-FUL.
DO YOU HAVE TO DO THAT?

WELL, MY PLAN WAS TO POP OUT AND SURPRISE YOU WHEN YOU WERE PICKING A PARTY.
BUT IF YOU LET ME IN, THAT'S GOOD ENOUGH.
I DUNNO WHY YOU'RE SO HUNG UP ON THAT PLAN.
BUT IN THAT CASE...
SU (SHF)
Y-YEAH...
BIKI (CRACK)
GO (RUMBLE) GO GO GO GO
EEK.
WH-WHAT THE?
AN EARTHQUAKE?
DOGO (WHUMP)

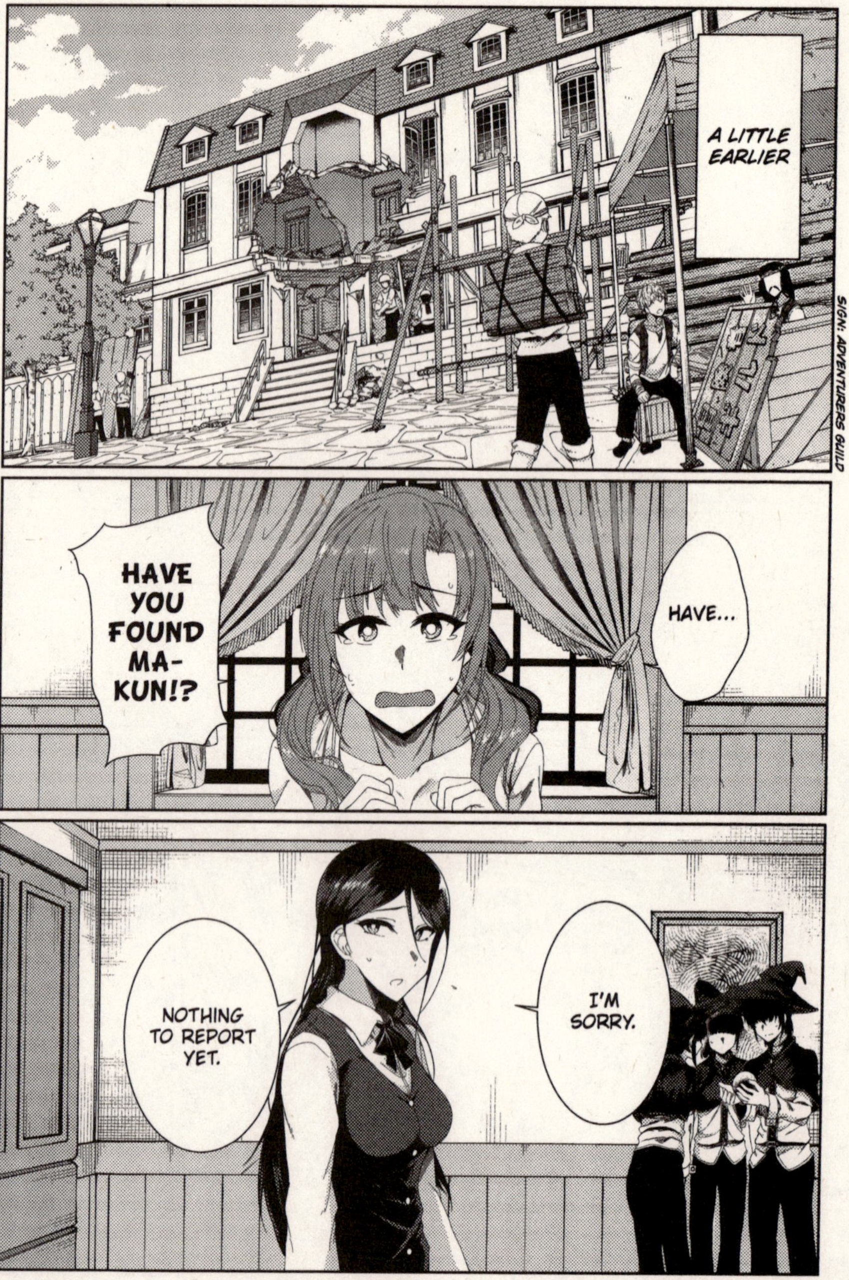
A LITTLE EARLIER
SIGN: ADVENTURERS GUILD
HAVE...
HAVE YOU FOUND MA-KUN!?
I'M SORRY.
NOTHING TO REPORT YET.

PRIVACY REGULATIONS HAVE PREVENTED US...
...FROM IMPLEMENTING A SYSTEM TO TRACK BETA TESTERS.
I SEE...I UNDERSTAND.
SORRY FOR THE TROUBLE.
PLEASE THANK EVERYONE FOR ME.
PEKO (BOW)
LEAVE THIS TO ME.
GOT IT.
IF YOU FIND ANYTHING, LET ME KNOW.
ROGER THAT.
MAMA ...
DON'T WORRY.
MONYUN (SQUEEZE)
WHOA!

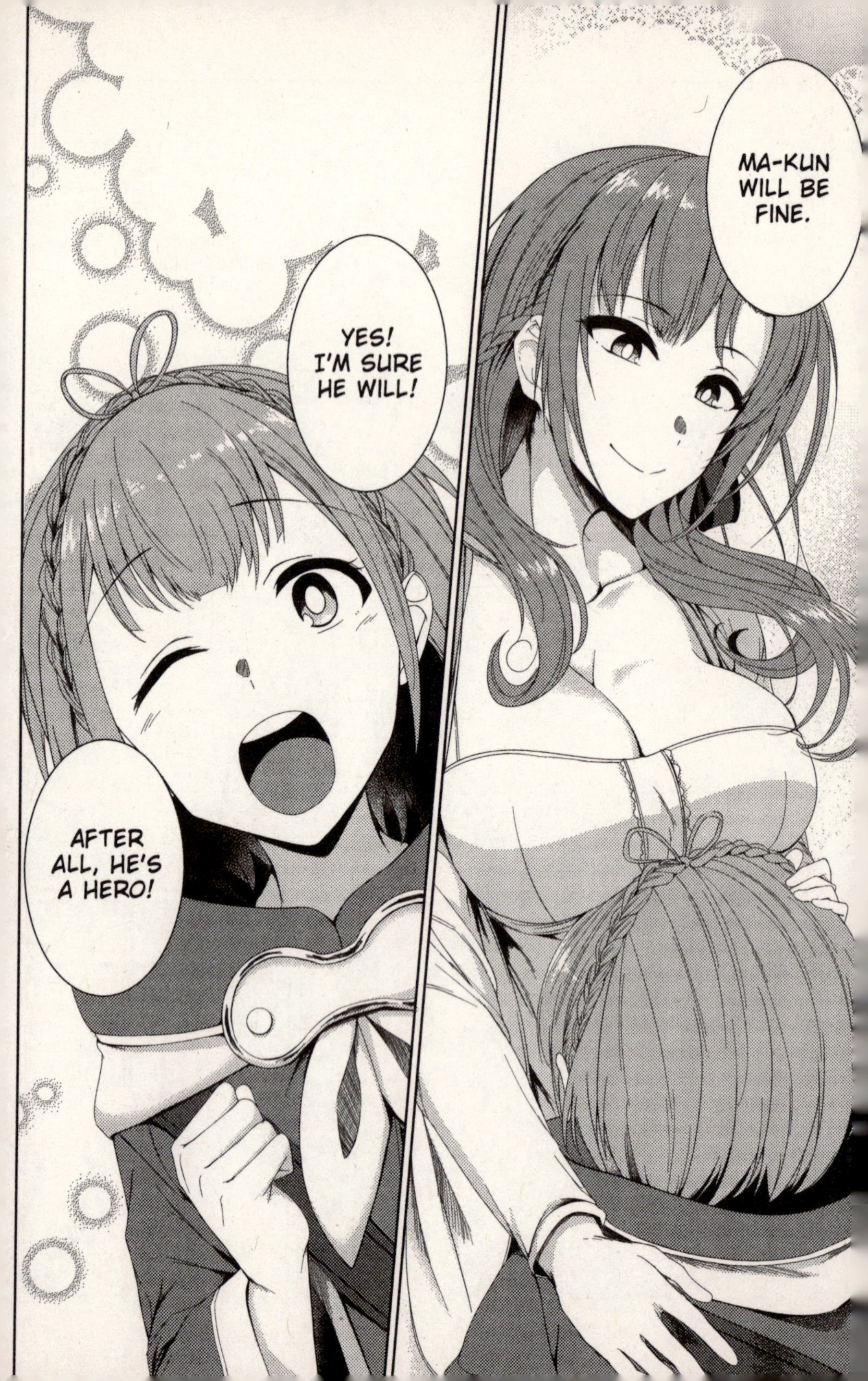
MA-KUN WILL BE FINE.
YES! I'M SURE HE WILL!
AFTER ALL, HE'S A HERO!

YES. UNLIKE ME...
HE MAY ONLY HAVE ONE-HIT, SINGLE-TARGET ATTACKS, BUT...
...HE'LL BE FINE!
GU (CLENCH)
THAT MAKES HIM SOUND LIKE A VERY NORMAL PERSON!
BUT HE'S MASATO!
RIGHT! MY SON!
HE'LL BE FINE!
...
BUT...IT'S JUST...
I DON'T KNOW HOW TO EXPLAIN IT.
I JUST FEEL LIKE...
...SOMETHING BAD IS GOING TO HAPPEN.
HMM.
LIKE...HE MIGHT GET ATTACKED BY MONSTERS!?
MM...
NOT QUITE LIKE THAT.

MORE LIKE...
HMM...
I DUNNO.
SOMETHING THAT WOULD BE BAD FOR ME?
FOR YOU, MAMA?
OH, I KNOW!
GASP!
IF MA-KUN FORGETS ABOUT ME...
...AND GETS CLOSER TO SOMEONE ELSE...
...THAT WOULD BE VERY BAD!
ZU
ZU
ZU
ZU
ZU (DUN)
ER? W-WOULD IT?
MA-KUN'S SUPPOSED TO BE HAVING AN ADVENTURE AND GETTING CLOSER TO ME!
IF HE GOT CLOSER TO SOMEONE ELSE AND ABANDONED ME TO BE WITH THEM...
...I'D BE SO SAD! I'D JUST CRY!
MA-KUN!
WAIT!

UM...
WELL, I THINK YOU CRYING IS A BAD THING...
I CAN'T JUST WAIT HERE!
BA (WHOOSH)
I HAVE TO FIND MA-KUN RIGHT THIS INSTANT!
IT'S A LONG SHOT, BUT THERE IS ONE THING WE COULD TRY.
NU (LOOM)
REALLY!?
PLEASE TELL ME...
NO!
INFORFORM ME!

NEXT— PORTA. HAND MAMAKO THE HOLY SWORD OF MOTHER EARTH.

R-RIGHT! HERE YOU ARE!

SASAT (SHNK)

TRUST THOSE. TRUST THE BOND YOU HAVE WITH MASATO!

BONDS BETWEEN PARENTS AND CHILDREN ARE EVERYTHING IN THIS GAME.

I DO!

I'D BE GLAD TO!

NOW, MAMAKO. HOLD UP THE SWORD AND CALL OUT TO THE EARTH.

TO THE GREAT MOTHER EARTH.

AS A MOTHER HERSELF, SHE MIGHT KNOW HOW YOU FEEL AND ANSWER YOUR CALL.

SHE WILL!?

MOTHER EARTH... IF YOU ARE A MOTHER TOO...

FWOO...

...THEN YOU KNOW HOW I FEEL.

GYU (SQUEEZE)

OKAY! I'LL EVEN BELIEVE A MAYBE!

KOKUN (NOD)

YES... MAYBE!

KIRI (CONFIDENT)

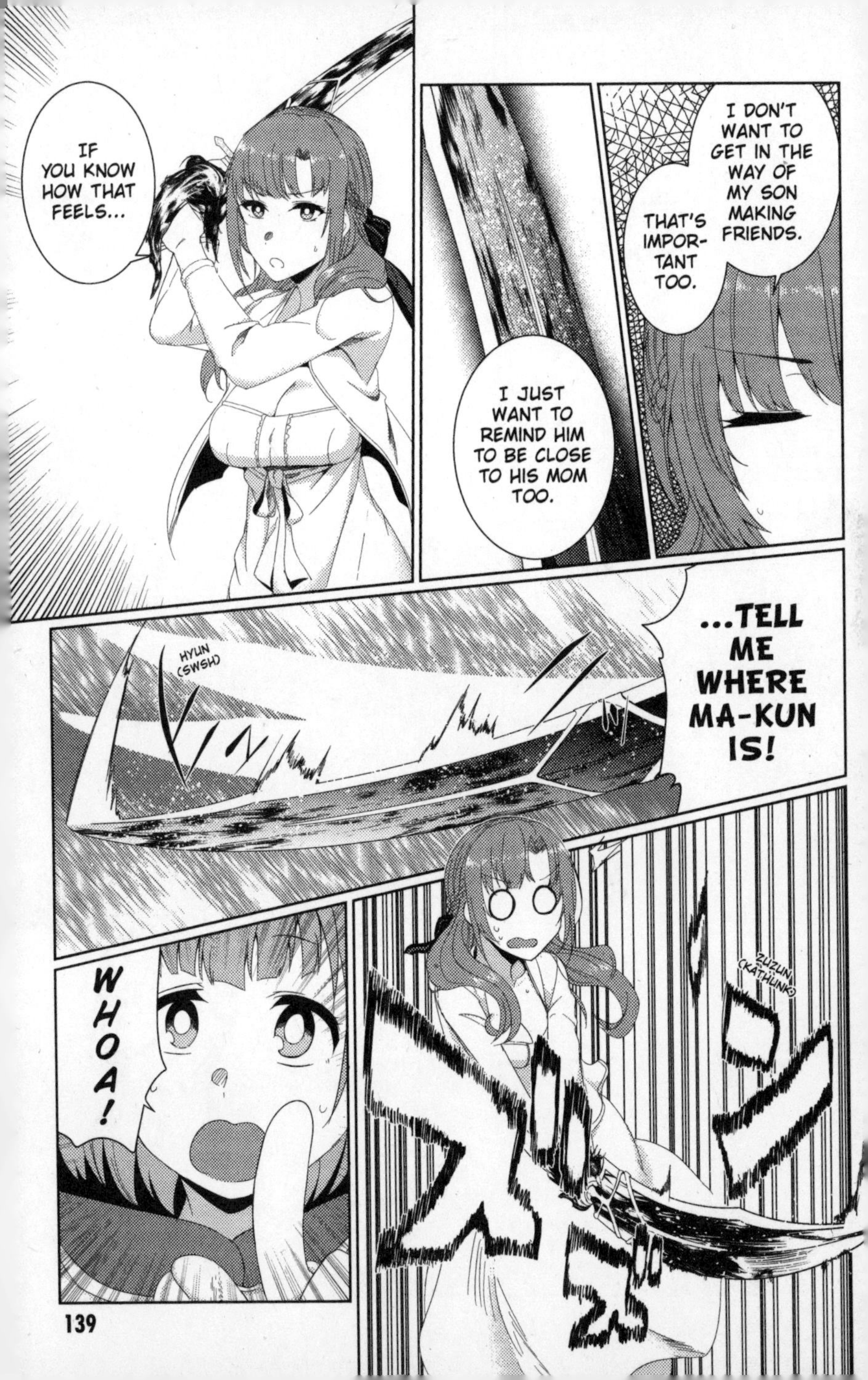
I DON'T WANT TO GET IN THE WAY OF MY SON MAKING FRIENDS.
THAT'S IMPORTANT TOO.
I JUST WANT TO REMIND HIM TO BE CLOSE TO HIS MOM TOO.
IF YOU KNOW HOW THAT FEELS...
...TELL ME WHERE MA-KUN IS!
HYUN (SWSH)
ZUZUN (KATHUNK)
WHOA!

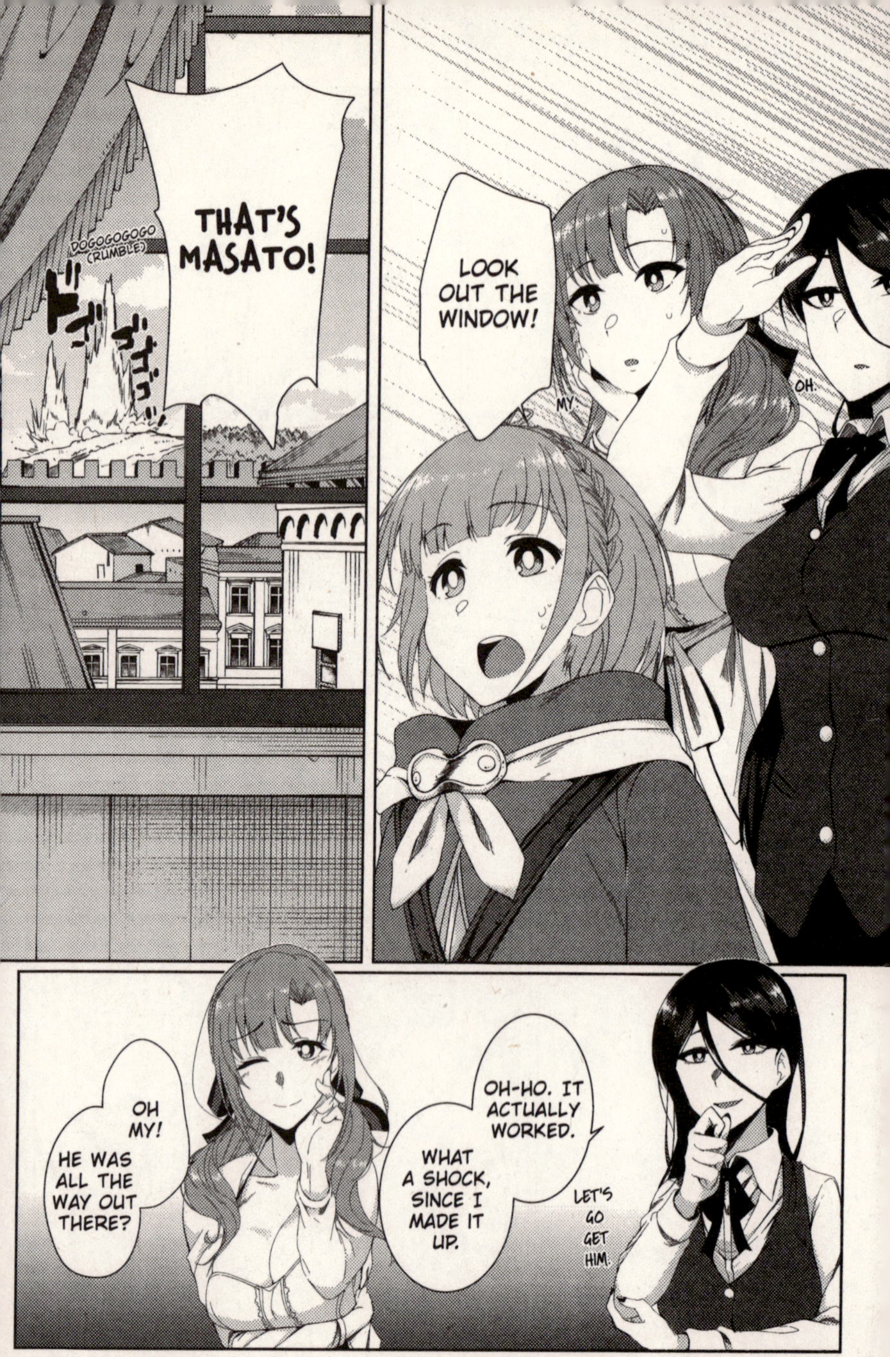
LOOK OUT THE WINDOW!
MY
OH.
THAT'S MASATO!
DOGOGOGOGO (RUMBLE)
ドゴゴゴゴッ
OH-HO. IT ACTUALLY WORKED.
WHAT A SHOCK, SINCE I MADE IT UP.
LET'S GO GET HIM.
OH MY!
HE WAS ALL THE WAY OUT THERE?

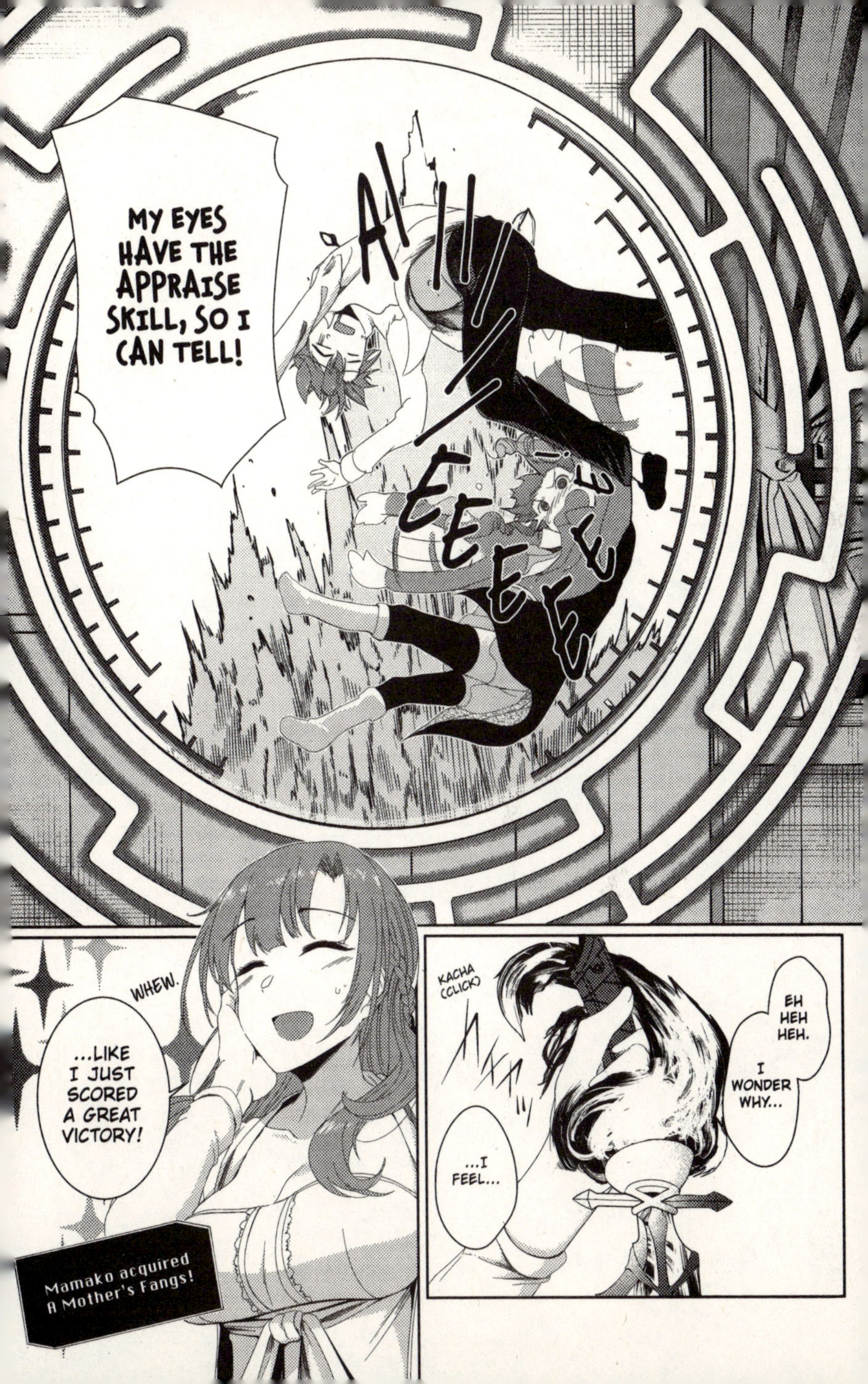
MY EYES HAVE THE APPRAISE SKILL, SO I CAN TELL!
AI!!EEEEEE!
EH HEH HEH.
I WONDER WHY...
KACHA (CLICK)
...I FEEL...
WHEW.
...LIKE I JUST SCORED A GREAT VICTORY!
Mamako acquired A Mother's Fangs!

"If you need anything... just ask!"

"Thank you." "Excuse me!"

"You must be... Wise, the Sage?"

"Yes, Mother. I am a Sage, and my name is Wise. Bound by a prophecy... I am destined to accompany the great hero on his journey. Please allow me the honor of joining your party—"

"I wish only to serve at your side. Nay—of becoming your daughter."

"Hmm."

"Well, Wise. ...there's just one problem."

"Part of me would like to, but..."

"Wh-what problem is that!?"

WAHHH! *GACHA (RATTLE)* *GACHA* WHAT WAS I EVEN ARRESTED FOR!?	IT DOESN'T EVEN MAKE SENSE! I KNOW! YOU'VE BEEN ARRESTED. *GACHAN (CLANG)*

...THAT WISE'S ATTACK REDUCED MASATO'S HP...

...TO CRITICAL LEVELS.

OUR DATA SHOWS...

HUNH!? WHEN!?

WELL, YOU ATTEMPTED A PK AGAINST ME, SO...

YOU MEAN THAT!? *GOKYAN (CRACK)* *GAAN (SHOCK)* OH

EVEN A MAGE'S PHYSICAL ATTACK...

...CAN EASILY PLACE HIM AT DEATH'S DOOR.

MASATO IS STILL LEVEL 1 AND HAS NO ARMOR EQUIPPED.

CAN'T WE JUST, LIKE, STRIKE A PLEA BARGAIN AND GET ME OUT OF HERE?
SURE, I'D LOVE TO DO THAT, BUT...
BUT WE SHOOK HANDS!
YOU WELCOMED ME INTO YOUR PARTY!
ORO (PANIC)
ORO
WISE, HONEY, DO YOU MIND?
WHAT!?
ACK!
I-I-I MEAN, WHAT IS IT, MOTHER MAMAKO?
MA-KUN FILLED ME IN ON YOUR LITTLE PLAN, WISE.
AND I JUST THINK...
...INSTEAD OF THESE CRAZY SCHEMES, YOU AND YOUR MOTHER SHOULD...
GASHA (SHNK)
OUT OF THE QUES-TION!
OH, DON'T SAY THAT.
AT LEAST CONSIDER IT!
I SAID NO! IMPOS-SIBLE!
NEVER!
I COULD NEVER PATCH THINGS UP WITH THAT AWFUL WOMAN!

GOGOGOGOGO (RUMMMBLE)
IF THAT'S MY ONLY OPTION...
...I'D RATHER DESTROY THE WORLD!
YO, HANG ON...
ISN'T "I'D RATHER DIE" THE MORE COMMON SAYING HERE?
THAT WOULD JUST MEAN MOM WON!
TO HELL WITH THAT!
BISHI (POINT)
I'M GONNA OUTLIVE HER!
I'M GONNA MAKE THIS PLAN WORK NO MATTER WHAT IT TAKES!
HEH HEH HEH! MWA HA HA!
WANTING TO LIVE IS CERTAINLY PRAISE-WORTHY.
A FEW BAD THINGS HAPPENING...
...IS NO REASON TO THROW YOUR LIFE AWAY.
I KNOW!
NOT AN ISSUE YOU'LL HAVE WITH ME!
I HAVE THE POWER OF CONVICTION! I CAN STAND UP TO MY MOM!

THAT'S WHY...
...I WANNA BE YOUR DAUGHTER!
PAN (CLAP)
PLEASE! LET ME!
NO. I CAN'T MAKE YOU MY DAUGHTER, WISE.
CAN'T WE JUST ...?
BUT I'D BE HAPPY TO HAVE YOU JOIN OUR PARTY AND ADVENTURE WITH US.
ER... WHAT ...?
WHAT DO YOU MEAN?
WHAT DO I MEAN?
MA-KUN, DO YOU KNOW?
UH.
I CAN IMAGINE.
YOU'RE PLANNING ON TAKING HER WITH US FOR NOW...
...FINDING HER MOM SOMEWHERE, AND THEN BEING A GIANT BUSYBODY, RIGHT?
EXACTLY!
PAAA (GLOW)
LIKE MOTHER, LIKE SON! WE THINK ALIKE!
!?

IF THAT'S WHAT YOU'RE PLOTTING, I'M OUT! I WON'T JOIN YOUR PARTY!
OH? WHAT A SHAME. I GUESS THIS IS GOOD-BYE!
BYE.
ENJOY YOUR ATTEMPTED-PK-ACTIVITY-RESTRICTION PENALTY.
W-WAIT, WHAT!?
THAT'S NOT WHAT I WANT!
THEN... I HAVE NO CHOICE BUT TO DO AS YOU SAY...
HENYA (DEFLATE)
へにゃあっ
SHIRE (DEADPAN)
しれっ
INCIDENTALLY, FOR TEST PURPOSES, THE PENALTIES ARE BASED ON REAL WORLD LAWS.
SO YOU'LL BE IN CUSTODY FOR THE NEXT FIFTEEN YEARS.
GAAAAAAN (SHOCK)
がぁあああん!!
WHAA-AAAAT!? THAT'S WAY TOO LONG!

I'M JUST TRYING TO BE HELPFUL. THAT'S ALL!
I'M NOT GOING TO ORDER YOU AROUND OR FORCE YOU TO MAKE AMENDS.
DO WE HAVE A DEAL?
WELL?
HNGGG.
BUT... IT JUST ISN'T...
LOOK, WISE.
WHAT !?
YOU'VE GOT REALLY AMAZING MAGIC.
IT WOULD REALLY HELP US OUT.
IF YOU THINK OF IT AS DOING US A FAVOR ...
OH, YOU'RE BEGGING ME FOR HELP NOW?
WELL, IF YOU PUT IT THAT WAY!
HA-HAH!
FINE. I'LL JOIN YOUR PARTY!
GET ME OUTTA HERE.
YOU'RE SO EASY...
I'M GLAD THIS WORKED OUT.

YOU MAKE LOTS OF PLANS, BUT YOU SUCK AT EXECUTION!

YOU'RE AN AWFUL SAGE.

ARGHH... HAHH.

THIS IS SO NOT WHAT I HAD IN MIND...

ZA (SCRUNCH)

ZA

YOU DIDN'T EVEN LIFT A FINGER!

SHE'S THE ONE WHO DECIDED I COULD JOIN THE PARTY!

MAMAKO'S GOT MORE FIREPOWER THAN YOU!

GUSA (SHNK) GUSA GUSA

IRA (THROB)

THAT WAS MY MOMENT TO ASSERT MYSELF, AND I TOTALLY DIDN'T...

DON'T POKE ME WHERE IT HURTS...

THAT'S BEEN BUGGING ME THIS WHOLE TIME!

AND YOU'RE A LOUSY HERO WHO CAN'T EVEN MAKE HIS OWN DECISIONS!

SHUT UP!

HNgg

149

I KNEW JUST HOW YOU FELT, MA-KUN!
THAT'S WHY I SPOKE FOR YOU!
MINDS-ONE!
URGHH.
MM?
PITA (STOP)
WHAT'S UP?
I DO APOLOGIZE, BUT I MUST LEAVE YOU NOW.
I HAVE TO FILE A REPORT ON THE PROGRESS OF THE OOSUKI FAMILY.
AND ONES ON PORTA AND WISE AS WELL.
OH?
WORK, THIS LATE? SUCH A DEMANDING JOB.
IT IS, BUT I HAVE A HOUSE-HOLD TO SUPPORT.
WELL, THEN. OH... WISE, PORTA.
LISTEN UP.
THERE'S SOMETHING I NEED TO SAY TO YOU BOTH.
I'VE HAD ENOUGH LECTURES...
Y-YES? WHAT IS IT?

DON'T FORGET THAT.	REMEMBER BEING SELECTED AS A TEST PLAYER... ...AND BEING IN THIS WORLD... IS A PRIVILEGE.

NO, MA'AM. I'LL DO MY BEST.	YEAH, YEAH, I GET IT ALREADY. OKAY! I WON'T!
I DON'T THINK YOU UNDERSTAND AT ALL... ...BUT I HAVE NO INTENTION OF RACKING UP ANYMORE OVERTIME ON YOU. NOW IF YOU'LL EXCUSE ME...	THAT'S EXACTLY WHAT I DON'T WANT! THAT STUPID... DID YOU SAY SOMETHING? ESPECIALLY YOU, WISE. PAY CLOSE ATTENTION TO MASATO AND MAMAKO. USE WHAT YOU LEARN TO REPAIR YOUR OWN RELATIONSHIP.

UGH... THAT LADY...

SHE'S WAY TOO HONEST.

SHE'S DEFINITELY SOMETHING ELSE.

SO... WHAT DO WE DO NEXT?

THAT'S RIGHT. I TOTALLY FORGOT. THEN, UM...

PORTA, CAN I SEE THE GUIDE?

O-OKAY!

IT'S EVENING, SO I REALLY SHOULD START MAKING DINNER.

WE'RE INSIDE A GAME ON AN ADVENTURE... WE DON'T HAVE A HOME.

◇Sleep at inns!
Camping is dangerous!
There are many inns in towns.
Pick the one that's right for you!
Consult your budget.

LET'S STAY AT AN INN!
I HAVEN'T HAD A SLEEP-OVER IN AGES!
PATAMU (SHUT)
NOT SURE ABOUT THAT WORD CHOICE...
...BUT SURE, LET'S FIND A PLACE.
I WONDER WHAT THE INNS ARE LIKE HERE...
I SUPPOSE I COULD BE LAZY ABOUT DINNER, BUT I'D LIKE TO MAKE A PROPER BREAKFAST.
CAN'T WE JUST EAT WHAT THE INN SERVES?
HMM.
NO! I SIMPLY MUST PUT MY FOOT DOWN!
WE MAY BE IN A GAME, BUT IT'S MY JOB TO COOK!
YOU DESERVE THREE HOME-COOKED MEALS A DAY, MA-KUN.
PUN
PUN (FUME)
WE'LL HAVE TO FIND A PLACE THAT'LL LET US USE THEIR KITCHEN.
A CHALLENGE, TO BE SURE. BUT LET THE PARTY HERO SHOW HIS LEADER-
HEH.
I KNOW AN INN LIKE THAT, MAMA!
I'VE BEEN IN THIS TOWN FOR A WHILE!
THERE'S AN INN THAT SERVES A GREAT DINNER AND LETS YOU USE THE KITCHEN FOR BREAK-FAST!
THAT WOULD BE SUCH A HELP!

AND THE GREAT HERO IS USELESS AGAIN. *P.F.F.* *HNGG...*	THANK YOU, PORTA! I KNEW WE COULD RELY ON YOU! NADE (RUB) NADE GYU (SQUEEZE) WHOA!
IT ONLY HAS ROOMS FOR TWO. HOW WOULD WE SPLIT THEM? OH, BUT THE INN I MENTIONED...	BUT I WON'T LET IT GET TO ME! NEXT TIME...I WILL TAKE CHARGE! KIRAN (GLEAM)
YOU'RE TRYING TO KILL ME. NOT HAPPENING. OH-HOH?	IT SEEMS OBVIOUS TO ME. MA-KUN AND MOMMY WILL SHARE?

THEN I'LL STAY IN MAMAKO'S ROOM!
SU SU SU (SLIIDE)
I'LL PLAY THE ROLE OF THE PERFECT DAUGHTER TO THE HILT AND WIN HER OVER!
I MIGHT EVEN USE A CHARM SPELL ON HER!
KEE KEE KEE KEE KEE!
THAT LAUGH MAKES YOU SOUND LIKE A MINI-DEMON.
I CERTAINLY WOULDN'T MIND SHARING WITH YOU, WISE.
BUT THAT WOULD MEAN...
WELL, IT'S A CONCERN.
MA-KUN SEEMS QUITE FOND OF PORTA, AND PORTA, WELL...
I WANT TO BE USEFUL TO MASATO!
ASK ME FOR ANYTHING! I'LL DO WHATEVER YOU WANT!
SHE'S LIKE THIS, WHICH COULD LEAD TO ALL SORTS OF ACCIDENTS.
OH, PLEASE, MOTHER DEAR. YOUR SON IS A PERFECT GENTLEMAN.
HA HA HA.
NIKO (SMILE)
I TRUST YOU, OF COURSE!
I MEAN, YOU JUST DON'T HAVE IT IN YOU TO ASSAULT A CUTE GIRL SLEEPING DEFENSELESSLY RIGHT NEXT TO YOU.
YOU... DON'T HAVE TO TELL ME THAT...

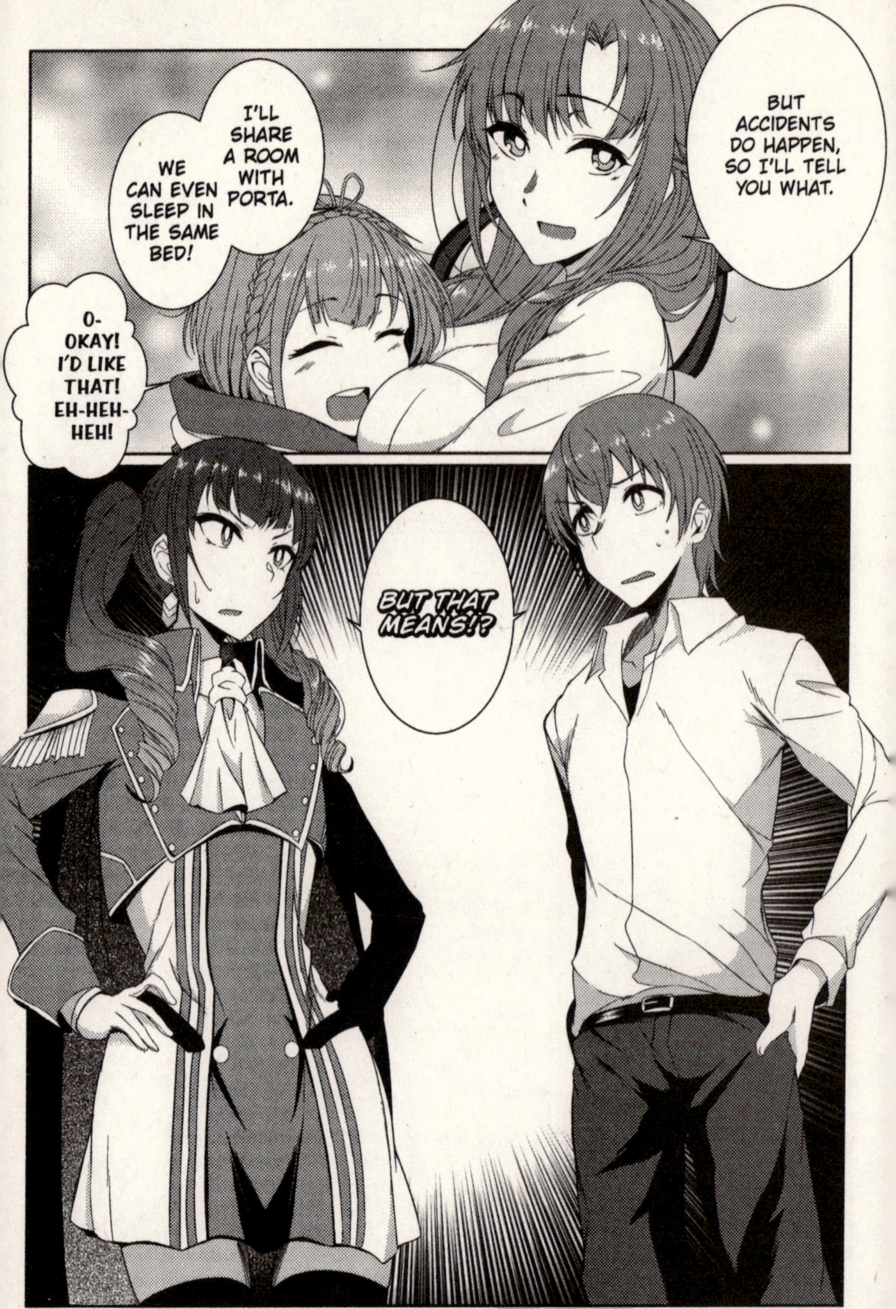

END

CONTINUED IN VOL. 2

HAVE YOU FOUND MA-KUN!?

HAVE...

DO
YOU LOVE
YOUR MOM
AND HER
TWO-HIT,
MULTI-
TARGET
ATTACKS?

Thank you for your time.

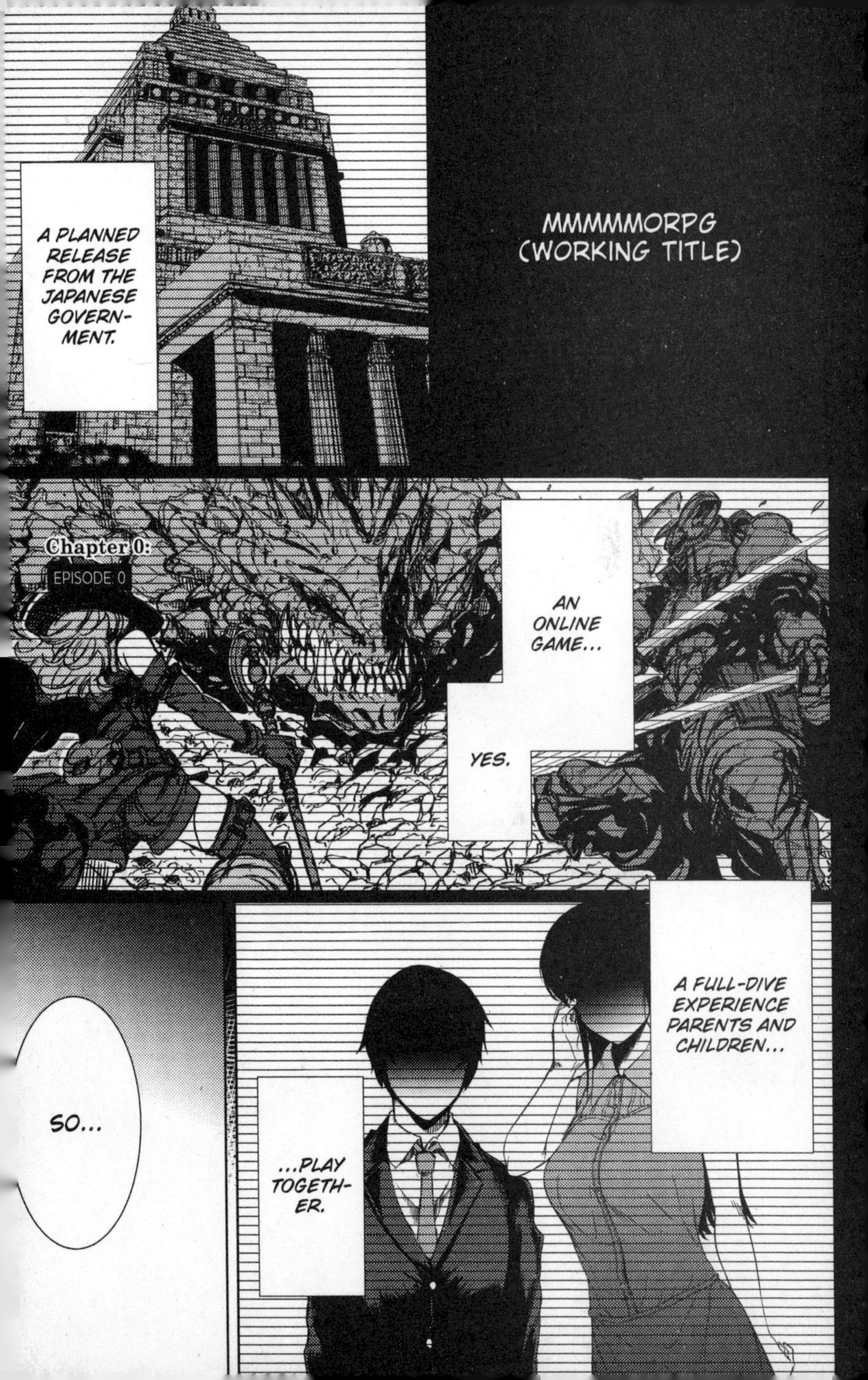
MMMMMORPG (WORKING TITLE)
A PLANNED RELEASE FROM THE JAPANESE GOVERNMENT.
AN ONLINE GAME...
YES.
Chapter 0:
EPISODE 0
A FULL-DIVE EXPERIENCE PARENTS AND CHILDREN...
...PLAY TOGETHER.
SO...

THAT'S THE BASIC GIST OF IT.
Mamako Oosuki
Participation Approval
—SU (SLIDE)
YOU CAN READ ABOUT THE DETAILS HERE.
THIS IS YOUR REGISTRATION PAPER, SO KEEP IT SAFE.
I CAN INFORM YOU...
I BELIEVE THE OOSUKI FAMILY...
...MEETS THE CONDITIONS TO PARTICIPATE IN THE PROGRAM.
!
MY!
THEN...
PAN (CLAP)

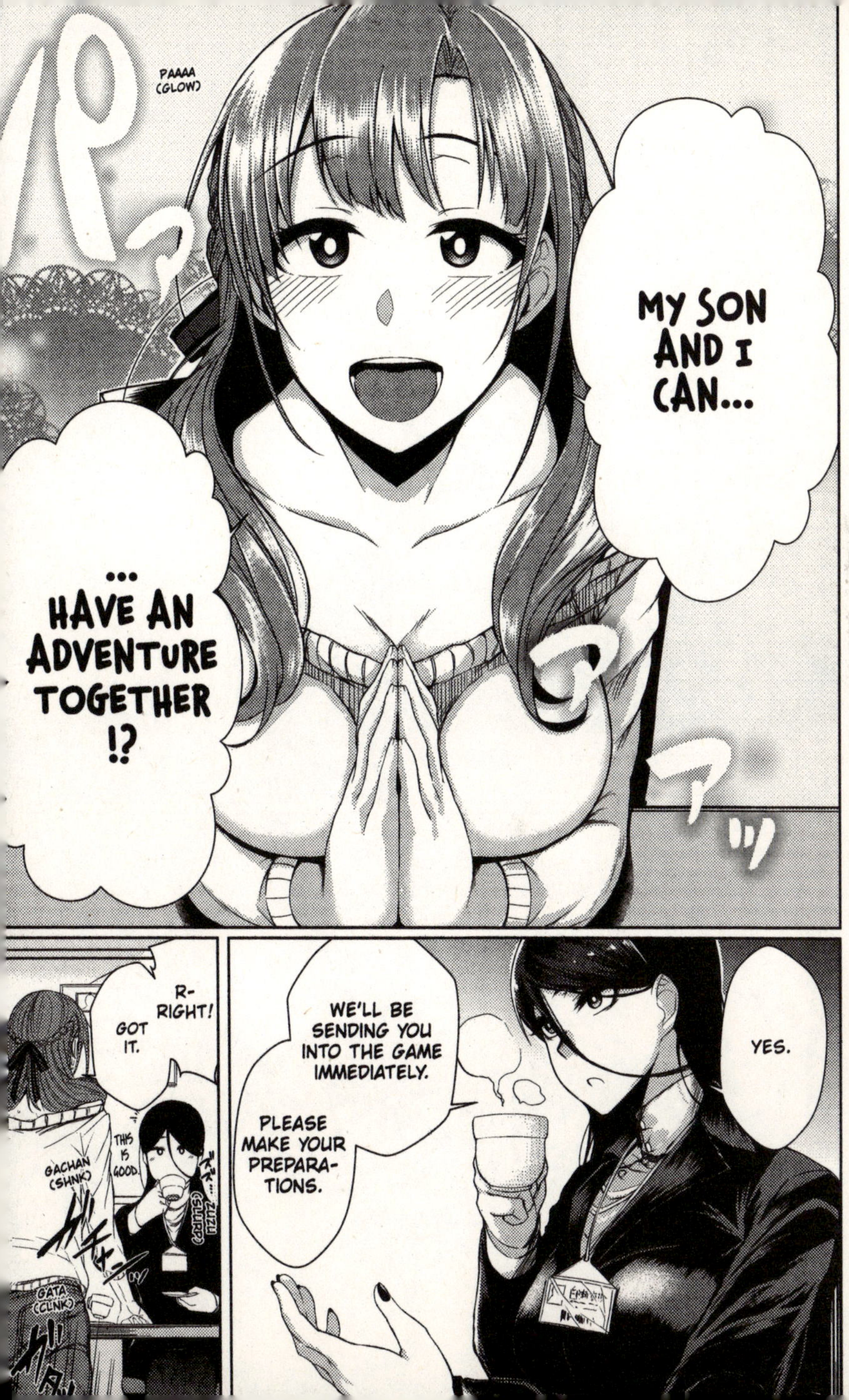

PAAAA (GLOW)
MY SON AND I CAN...
... HAVE AN ADVENTURE TOGETHER !?
YES.
WE'LL BE SENDING YOU INTO THE GAME IMMEDIATELY.
PLEASE MAKE YOUR PREPARATIONS.
R-RIGHT!
GOT IT.
THIS IS GOOD.
ZUZU (SLURP)
GACHAN (SHNK)
GATA (CLINK)

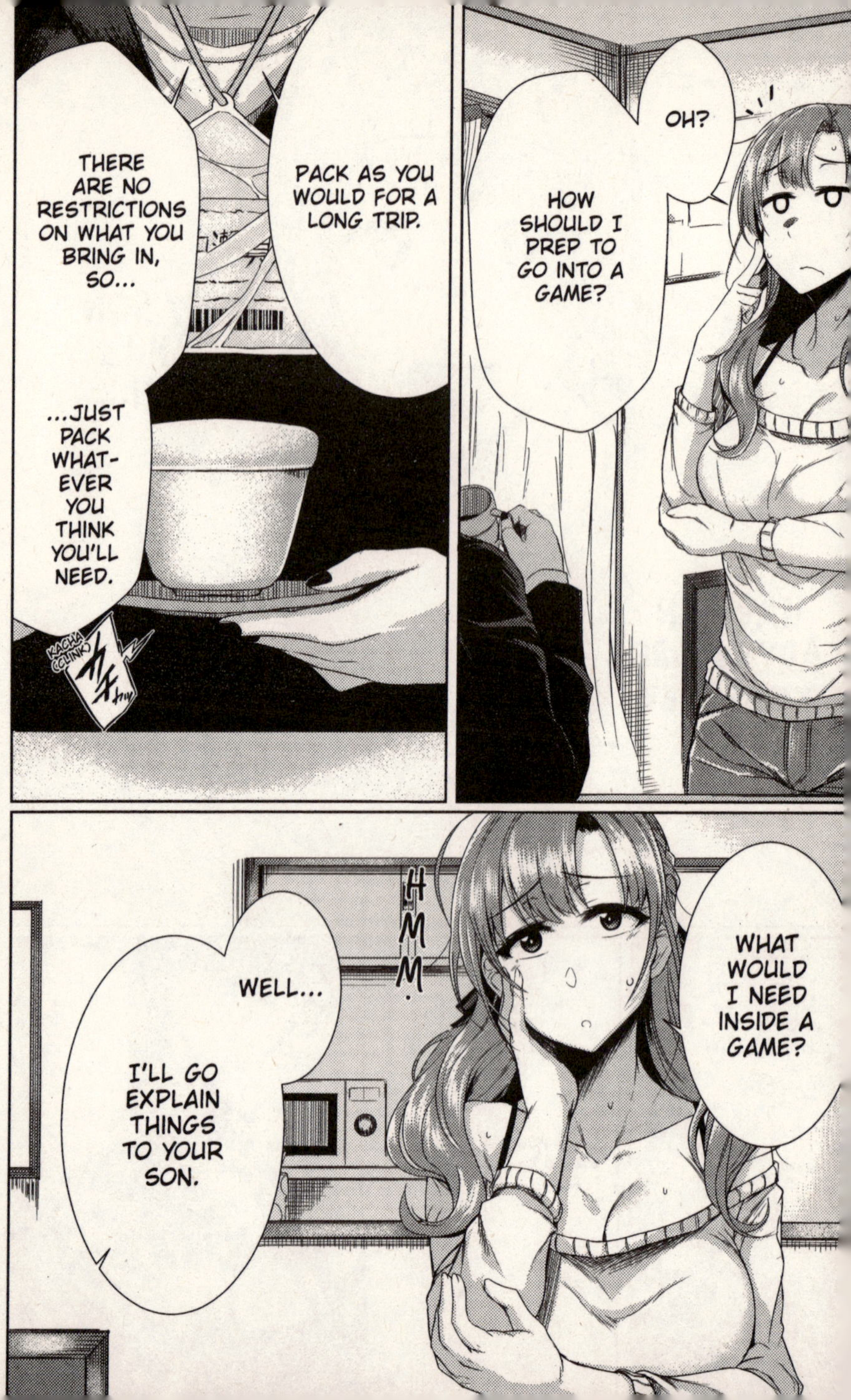
OH?
HOW SHOULD I PREP TO GO INTO A GAME?
PACK AS YOU WOULD FOR A LONG TRIP.
THERE ARE NO RESTRICTIONS ON WHAT YOU BRING IN, SO...
...JUST PACK WHATEVER YOU THINK YOU'LL NEED.
KACHA (CLINK)
WHAT WOULD I NEED INSIDE A GAME?
HMM.
WELL...
I'LL GO EXPLAIN THINGS TO YOUR SON.

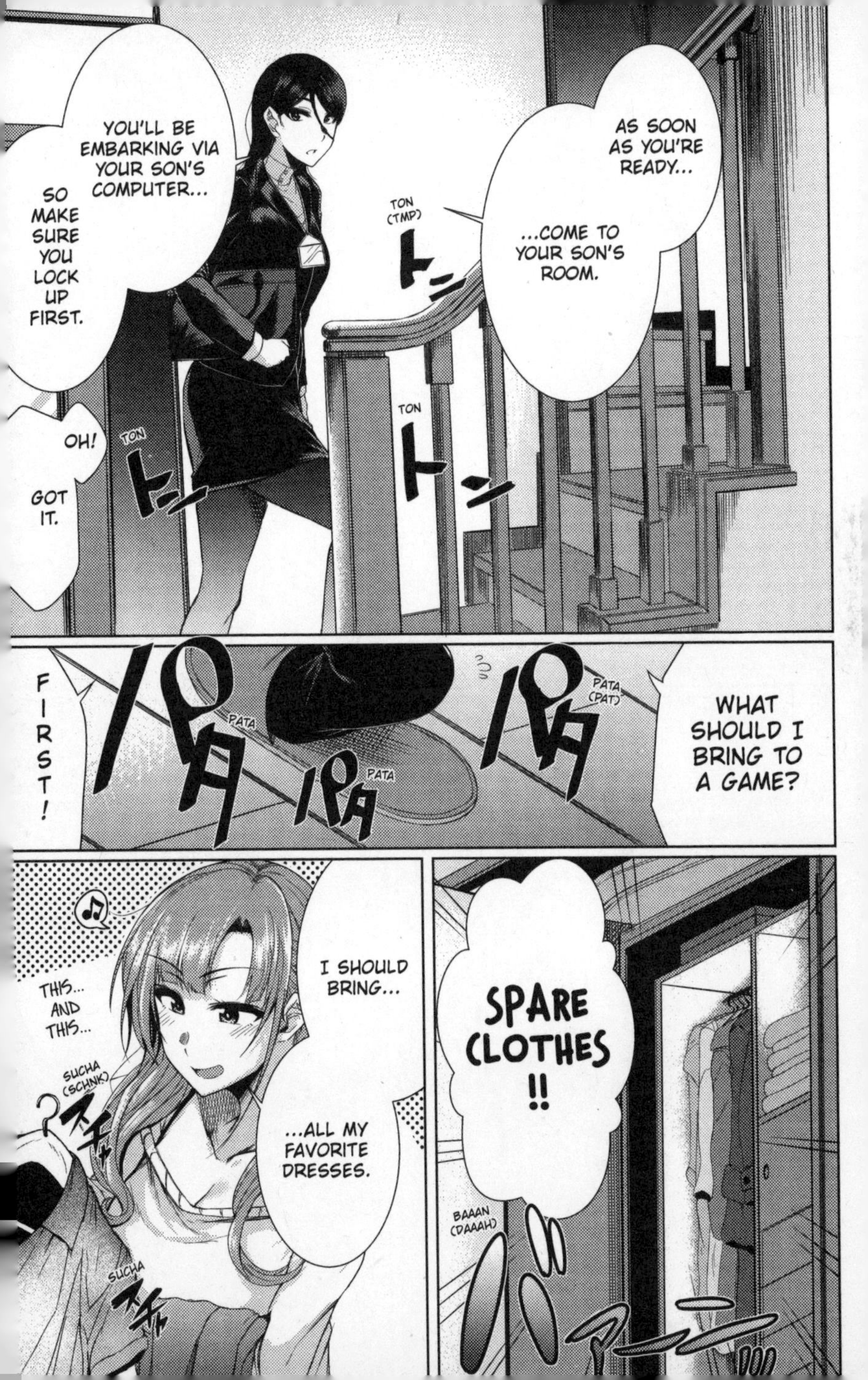
AS SOON AS YOU'RE READY...
...COME TO YOUR SON'S ROOM.
TON (TMP)
TON
YOU'LL BE EMBARKING VIA YOUR SON'S COMPUTER...
SO MAKE SURE YOU LOCK UP FIRST.
TON
OH!
GOT IT.
WHAT SHOULD I BRING TO A GAME?
PATA (PAT)
PATA
PATA
FIRST!
SPARE CLOTHES!!
BAAAN (DAAAH)
I SHOULD BRING...
...ALL MY FAVORITE DRESSES.
THIS... AND THIS...
SUCHA (SCHNK)
SUCHA

"I SHOULD BRING THEM! I HAVEN'T WORN THEM YET."

"...THESE TOO."

GOSO (RUSTLE)

GASA (RUMMAGE)

"OH, AND JUST IN CASE..."

PIRA (STRETCH)

"MY TREASURES... THE ALBUMS SHOWING HOW MA-KUN GREW! THOSE MAY BE USEFUL."

"OH, RIGHT!"

DOSA (WHMP)

Growth Records v3

DOSA

"AND I SHOULD BRING IMPORTANT PAPERS..."

DOSA

"OH— AND!"

"NEXT... OH, MY STAMP AND BANK-BOOK."

"..."

"I WONDER HOW BAD THE ATM FEES INSIDE THE GAME WORLD ARE..."

"WE'LL BE AWAY FOR A WHILE, AFTER ALL."

GYU (STUFF)

GYU

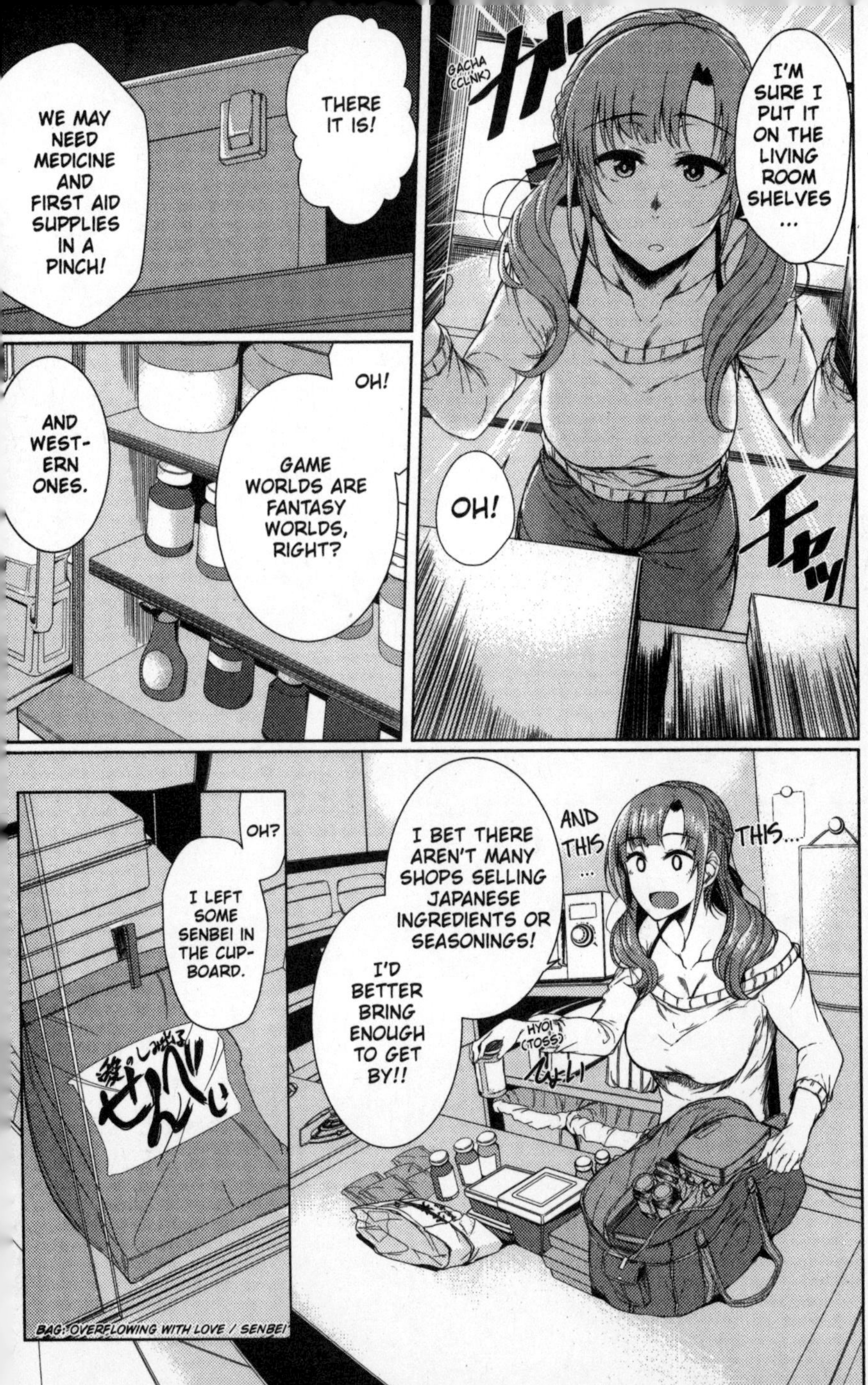
GACHA (CLNK)
I'M SURE I PUT IT ON THE LIVING ROOM SHELVES...
OH!
THERE IT IS!
WE MAY NEED MEDICINE AND FIRST AID SUPPLIES IN A PINCH!
OH!
GAME WORLDS ARE FANTASY WORLDS, RIGHT?
AND WEST-ERN ONES.
THIS...
AND THIS...
I BET THERE AREN'T MANY SHOPS SELLING JAPANESE INGREDIENTS OR SEASONINGS!
HYOI (TOSS)
I'D BETTER BRING ENOUGH TO GET BY!!
OH?
I LEFT SOME SENBEI IN THE CUP-BOARD.
BAG: OVERFLOWING WITH LOVE / SENBEI

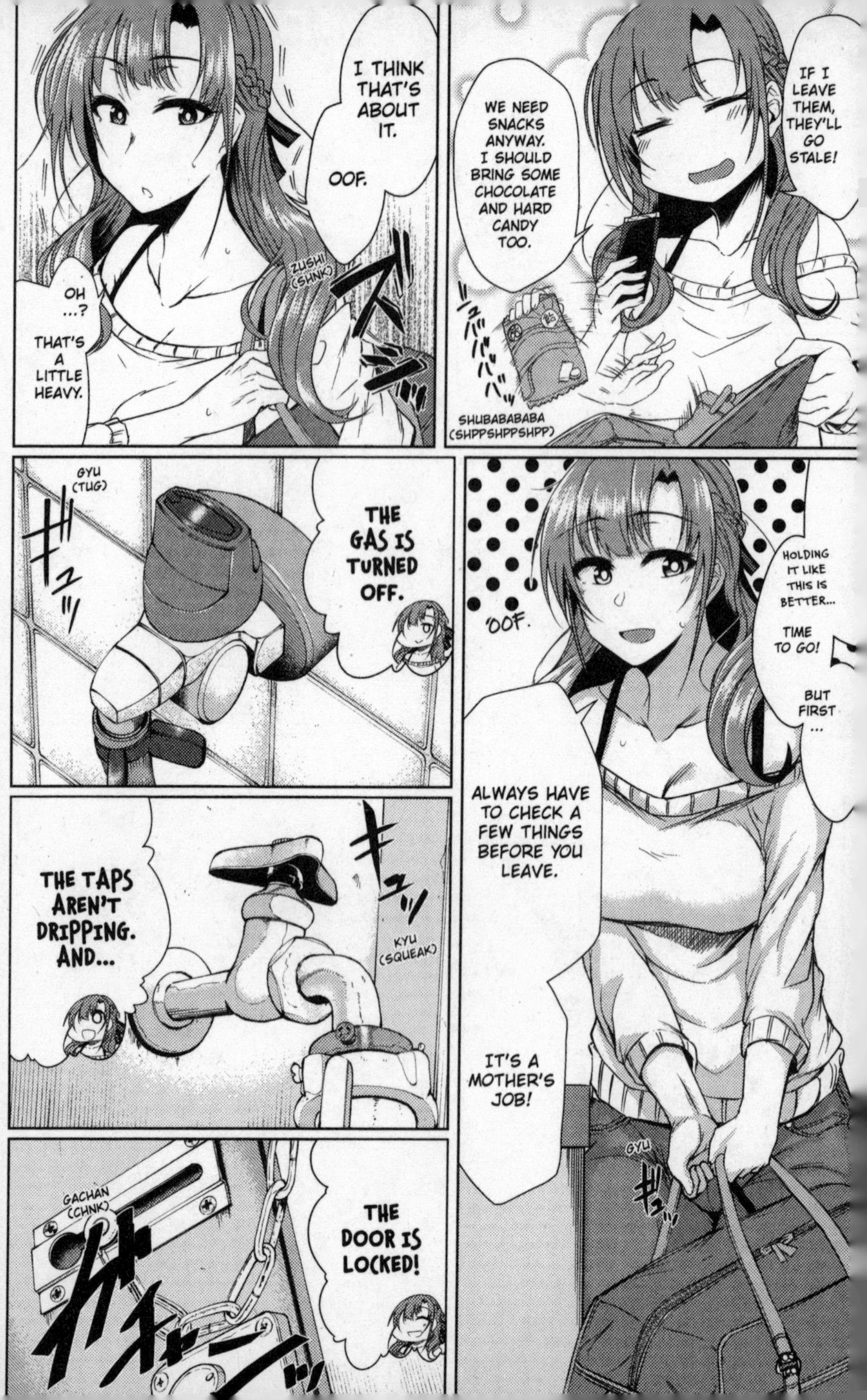
IF I LEAVE THEM, THEY'LL GO STALE!
WE NEED SNACKS ANYWAY. I SHOULD BRING SOME CHOCOLATE AND HARD CANDY TOO.
SHUBABABABA (SHPPSHPPSHPP)
I THINK THAT'S ABOUT IT.
OOF.
ZUSHI (SHNK)
OH ...? THAT'S A LITTLE HEAVY.
HOLDING IT LIKE THIS IS BETTER...
TIME TO GO!
BUT FIRST ...
'OOF.
ALWAYS HAVE TO CHECK A FEW THINGS BEFORE YOU LEAVE.
IT'S A MOTHER'S JOB!
GYU
THE GAS IS TURNED OFF.
GYU (TUG)
KYU (SQUEAK)
THE TAPS AREN'T DRIPPING. AND...
THE DOOR IS LOCKED!
GACHAN (CHNK)

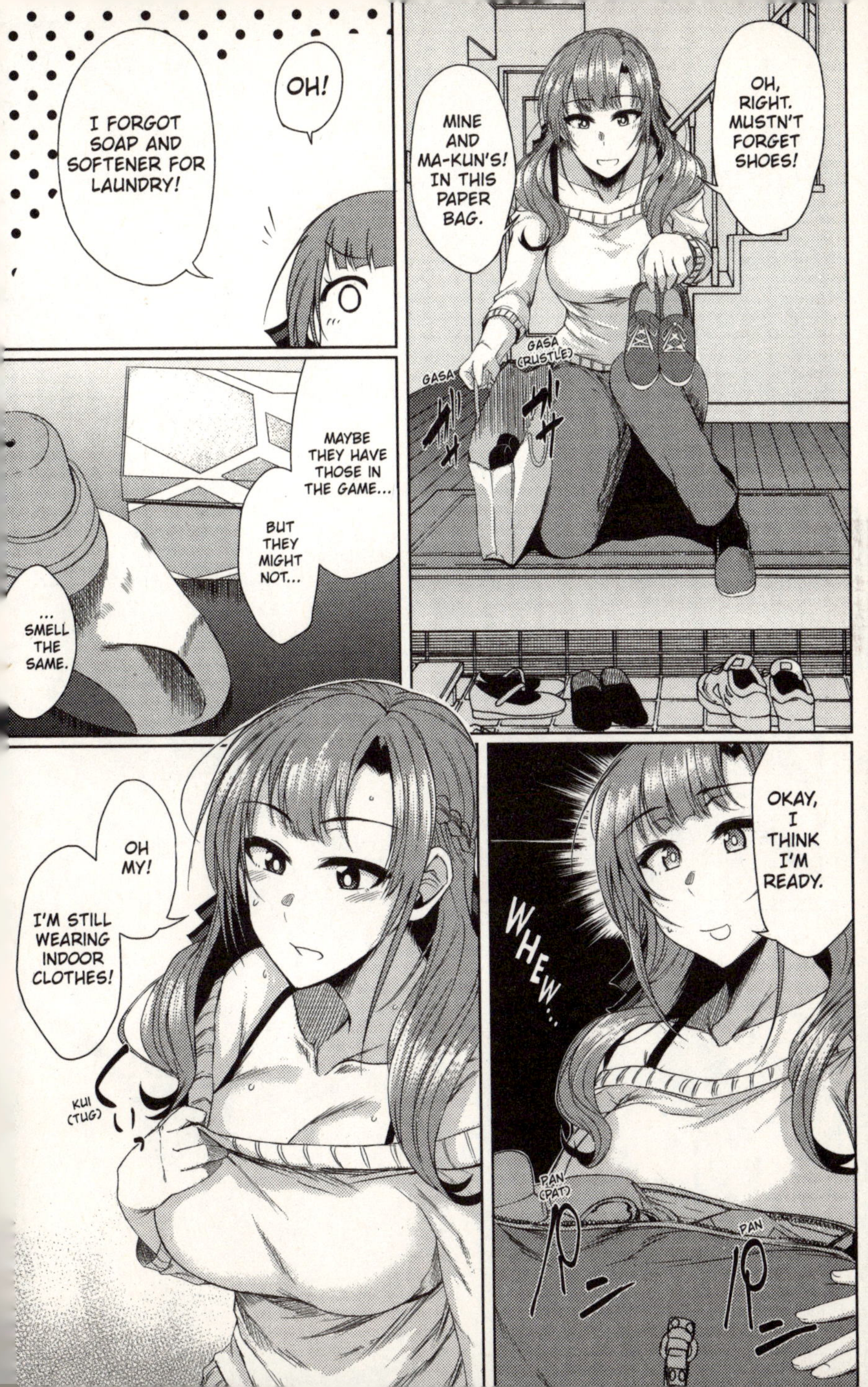
OH, RIGHT. MUSTN'T FORGET SHOES!
MINE AND MA-KUN'S! IN THIS PAPER BAG.
GASA (RUSTLE)
GASA
OH!
I FORGOT SOAP AND SOFTENER FOR LAUNDRY!
MAYBE THEY HAVE THOSE IN THE GAME...
BUT THEY MIGHT NOT...
... SMELL THE SAME.
OKAY, I THINK I'M READY.
WHEW...
PAN (PAT)
PAN
OH MY!
I'M STILL WEARING INDOOR CLOTHES!
KUI (TUG)

HOKAY.
JII (SWSH)
NUGI
HOKAY.
NUGI
NUGI (STRIP)
I EVEN PACKED THE CLOTHES I MEANT TO WEAR...
I'M SUCH A DITZ.
I'M HEEEEEEEEEEEEEEEERE!
EEK!
BIKU (TWITCH)
OH?
WHAAAT?
FUTA
ALREADY!?
ATA (PANIC)

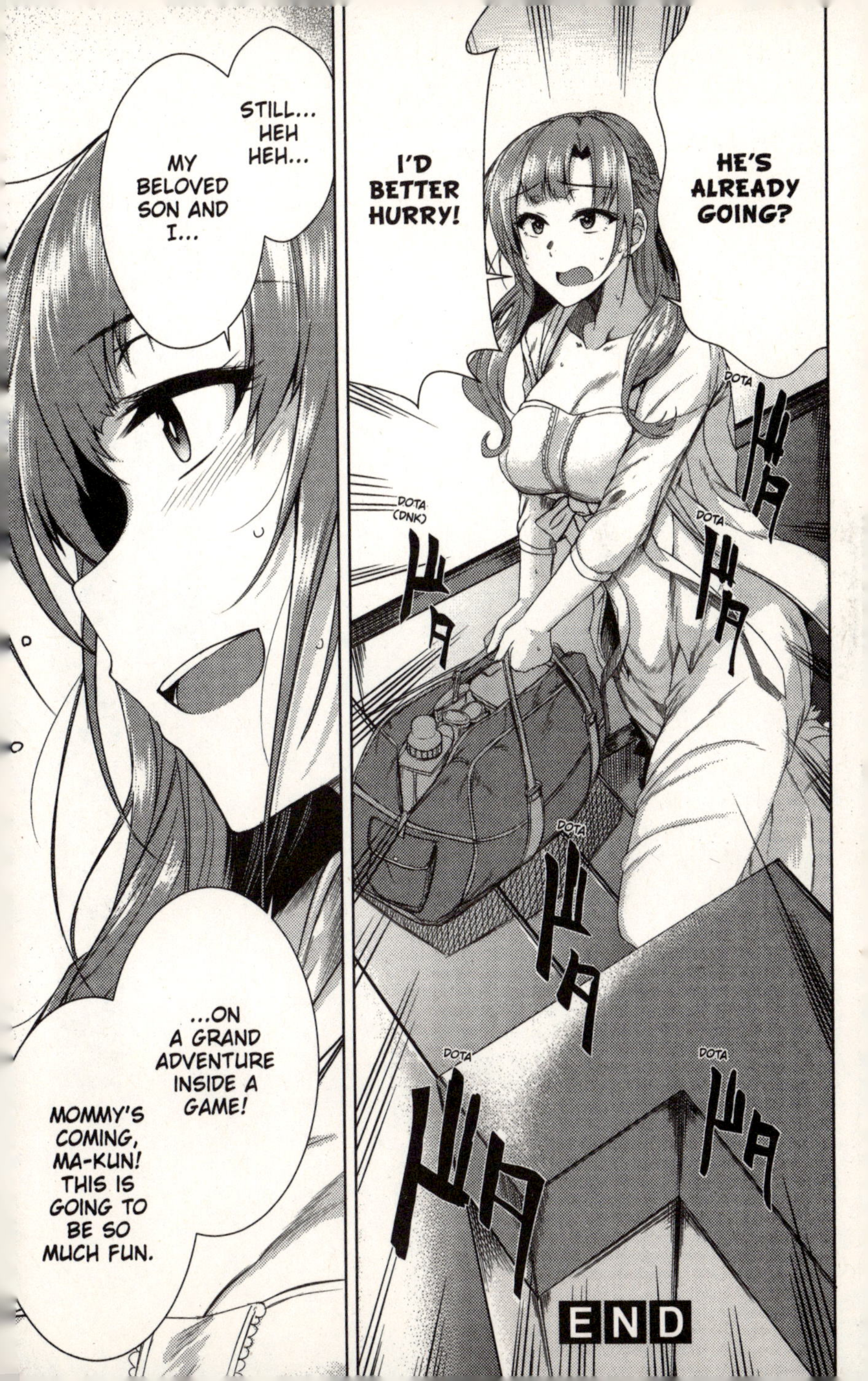
HE'S ALREADY GOING?
I'D BETTER HURRY!
DOTA
DOTA
DOTA (DNK)
DOTA
DOTA
DOTA
END
STILL... HEH HEH...
MY BELOVED SON AND I...
...ON A GRAND ADVENTURE INSIDE A GAME!
MOMMY'S COMING, MA-KUN! THIS IS GOING TO BE SO MUCH FUN.

DO YOU LOVE YOUR MOM AND HER TWO-HIT, MULTI-TARGET ATTACKS?

COMIC: MEICHA
STORY: DACHIMA INAKA, ILLUST: IIDA POCHI.
VOLUME 1

Author: DACHIMA INAKA

Postscript

Thank you. This is Dachima Inaka.
Now that the first volume of the *Mom* manga is on sale,
I'd like to congratulate and thank Meicha, my editor, and
everyone involved in publishing it.
I realize this is a cliché as old as the hills, but drawing manga is
very hard! Unlike novels, you have to draw all necessary
elements again in every panel. I once was seized with the
impulse to draw *Mom* myself and took a stab at it but wasted
half a day getting nowhere, so I have nothing but respect.
And the fruits of all that labor is this *Mom* manga. I hope
you enjoy it as much as the original.
Thank you so much.

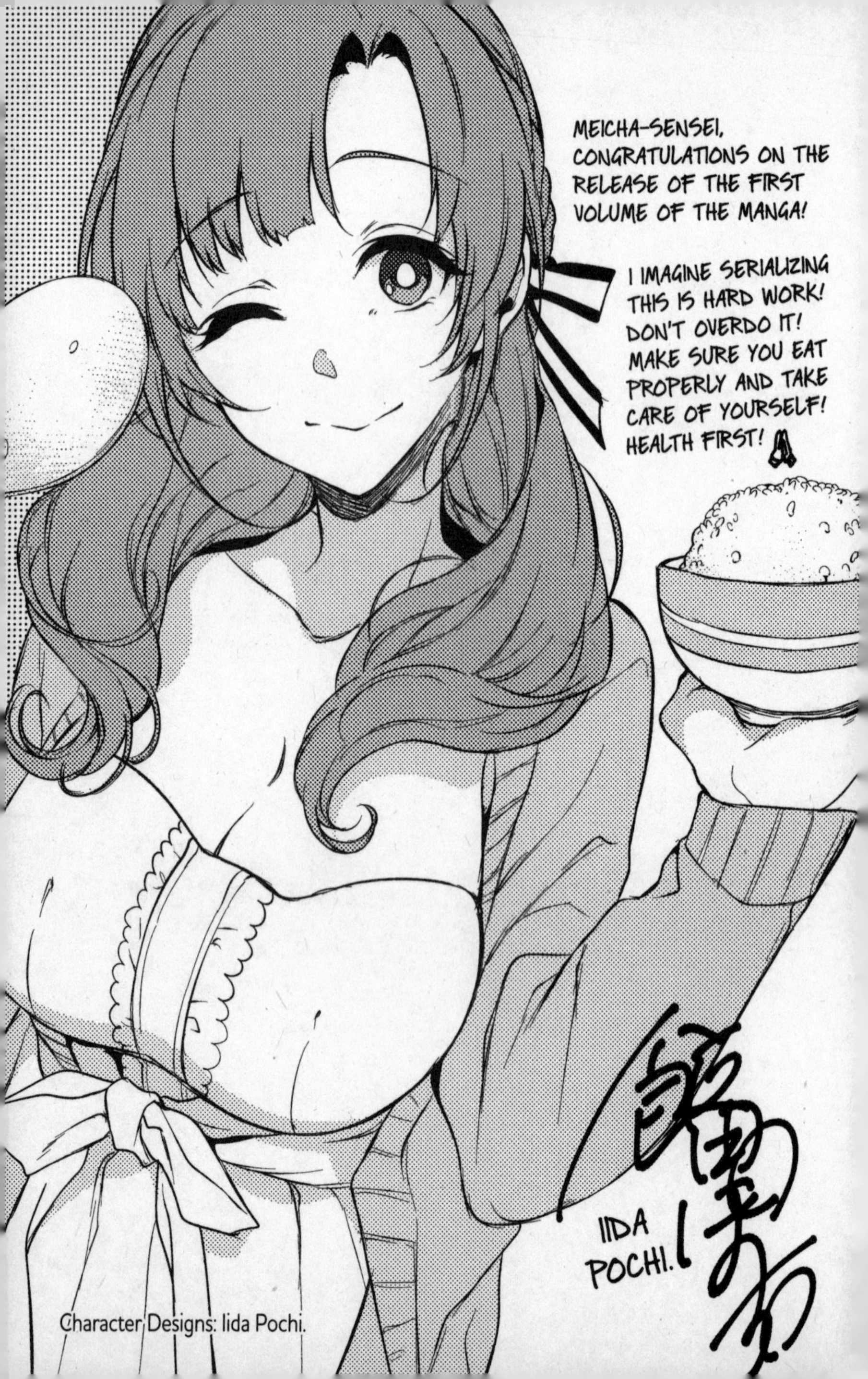
MEICHA-SENSEI, CONGRATULATIONS ON THE RELEASE OF THE FIRST VOLUME OF THE MANGA!
I IMAGINE SERIALIZING THIS IS HARD WORK! DON'T OVERDO IT! MAKE SURE YOU EAT PROPERLY AND TAKE CARE OF YOURSELF! HEALTH FIRST!
IIDA POCHI.
Character Designs: Iida Pochi.

To new readers and old — hi, I'm Meicha. Thanks to any readers who picked this up!

With this manga adaption, I've received a lot of help from Dachima Inaka-sensei and Iida Pochi.-sensei, and I'm really grateful for it. And of course, thank you to anyone reading!

Masato and Mamako's adventure has only just begun! I'm going to work hard to ensure you all enjoy what lies ahead.

Please look forward to it. I hope to see you in the next volume!

Manga: Meicha

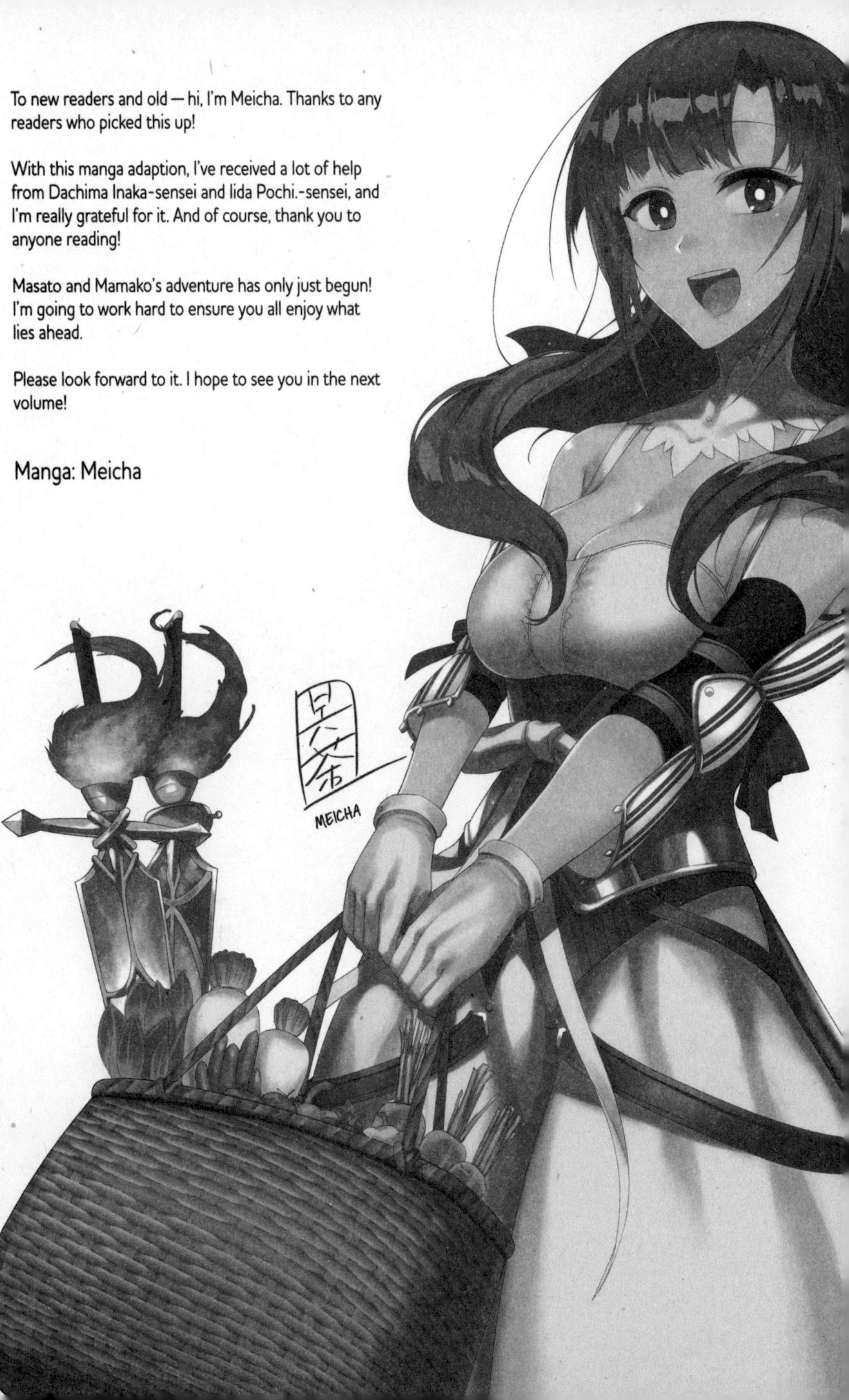
MEICHA

STAFF LIST

The author
Meicha

Assistant
Makoto Fujibayashi
Imizu

Design
Tsuyoshi Kusano Design

Death doesn't stop a video game-loving shut-in from going on adventures and fighting monsters!
KONOSUBA: GOD'S BLESSING ON THIS WONDERFUL WORLD!
IN STORES NOW
Yen Press
MANGA
YEN ON
LIGHT NOVEL
KONOSUBA: GOD'S BLESSING ON THIS WONDERFUL WORLD 1
Oh! My Useless Goddess
Natsume Akatsuki
Kurone Mishima
KONOSUBA: GOD'S BLESSING ON THIS WONDERFUL WORLD! 1
Masahito Watari
Natsume Akatsuki
Kurone Mishima

IN THIS FANTASY WORLD, EVERYTHING'S A GAME—AND THESE SIBLINGS PLAY TO WIN!

A genius but socially inept brother and sister duo is offered the chance to compete in a fantasy world where games decide everything. Sora and Shiro will take on the world and, while they're at it, create a harem of nonhuman companions!

No Game No Life ©Yuu Kamiya 2012 Illustration: Yuu Kamiya
KADOKAWA CORPORATION

LIGHT NOVELS 1-8 AVAILABLE NOW

No Game No Life, Please! © Kazuya Yuizaki 2016 © Yuu Kamiya 2016
KADOKAWA CORPORATION

LIKE THE NOVELS?

Check out the spin-off manga for even more out-of-control adventures with the Werebeast girl, Izuna!

Follow us on

www.yenpress.com

Do You Love Your Mom and Her Two-Hit Multi-Target Attacks?, Vol.1

- Art: Meicha
- Original Story: Dachima Inaka
- Character Design: Iida Pochi.

This book is a work of fiction. Names, characters, places, and incidents are the product of the author's imagination or are used fictitiously. Any resemblance to actual events, locales, or persons, living or dead, is coincidental.

- Translation: Andrew Cunningham
- Lettering: Phil Christie

TSUJYOU KOUGEKI GA ZENTAI KOUGEKI DE NIKAI KOUGEKI NO OKASAN WA SUKI DESUKA? Vol. 1
©Meicha 2018 ©Dachima Inaka 2018 ©Iida Pochi. 2018
First published in Japan in 2018 by KADOKAWA CORPORATION, Tokyo.
English translation rights arranged with KADOKAWA CORPORATION, Tokyo through TUTTLE-MORI AGENCY, INC., Tokyo.

English translation © 2019 by Yen Press, LLC

Yen Press, LLC supports the right to free expression and the value of copyright. The purpose of copyright is to encourage writers and artists to produce the creative works that enrich our culture.

The scanning, uploading, and distribution of this book without permission is a theft of the author's intellectual property. If you would like permission to use material from the book (other than for review purposes), please contact the publisher. Thank you for your support of the author's rights.

First Yen Press Edition: August 2019

Yen Press is an imprint of Yen Press, LLC.
The Yen Press name and logo are trademarks of Yen Press, LLC.

The publisher is not responsible for websites (or their content) that are not owned by the publisher.

- Yen Press
  150 West 30th Street, 19th Floor
  New York, NY 10001

- Visit us at yenpress.com
  facebook.com/yenpress
  twitter.com/yenpress
  yenpress.tumblr.com
  instagram.com/yenpress

Library of Congress Control Number: 2019941096

ISBNs: 978-1-9753-8524-8 (paperback)
978-1-9753-8656-6 (ebook)

10 9 8 7 6 5 4 3 2 1

WOR

Printed in the United States of America